Progay/Antigay

RHETORIC & SOCIETY

edited by Herbert W. Simons
Temple University

EDITORIAL BOARD

This series will publish a broad-based collection of advanced texts and innovative works encompassing rhetoric in the civic arena, in the arts and media, in the academic disciplines, and in everyday cultural practices.

Books in this series:

Control and Consolation in American Culture and Politics: Rhetorics of Therapy
Dana L. Cloud

Communication Criticism: Developing Your Critical Powers
Jodi R. Cohen

Analyzing Everyday Texts: Discourse, Rhetoric, and Social Perspectives
Glenn F. Stillar

Progay/Antigay: The Rhetorical War Over Sexuality
Ralph R. Smith and Russel R. Windes

RALPH R. SMITH
RUSSEL R. WINDES

Progay/Antigay
The Rhetorical War
Over Sexuality

Rhetoric & Society

Sage Publications, Inc.
International Educational and Professional Publisher
Thousand Oaks ▪ London ▪ New Delhi

For information:

Sage Publications, Inc.
2455 Teller Road
Thousand Oaks, California 91320
E-mail: order@sagepub.com

Sage Publications Ltd.
6 Bonhill Street
London EC2A 4PU
United Kingdom

Sage Publications India Pvt. Ltd.
M-32 Market
Greater Kailash I
New Delhi 110 048 India

Printed in the United States of America

Library of Congress Cataloging-in-Publication Data

Smith, Ralph R.
    Progay/antigay: The rhetorical war over sexuality / by Ralph R. Smith, Russel R. Windes.
        p.   cm.—(Rhetoric & society; v. 4)
Includes bibliographical references and index.
    ISBN 0-7619-1646-6 (cloth: alk. paper)—ISBN 0-7619-1647-4 (pbk.: alk. paper)
    1. Homosexuality. 2. Homosexuality—Public opinion. 3. Gay rights.
4. Rhetoric. I. Windes, Russel R. (Russel Rayl), 1930- II. Title.
III. Rhetoric & society (Thousand Oaks, Calif.); v. 4.
    HQ75.15 .S6   2000
    306.76′6—dc21   99-050766

00   01   02   03   04   05   06   7   6   5   4   3   2   1

Acquiring Editor:	Margaret H. Seawell
Editorial Assistant:	Sandra Krumholz
Production Editor:	Astrid Virding
Editorial Assistant:	Victoria Chen
Typesetter:	Marion Warren
Indexer:	Teri Greenberg

Contents

*To a multitude of friends, our "Old Time Throng"
from New York to San Francisco to San Diego,
with whom we shared affinities, adversities, and
achievements, and from whom we learned to cope more
sanely with hostility and more rationally with the
irrational. These loving friendships made our lives together
over forty years a succession of days of wine and roses.*

Foreword

This book brings news of some interesting symmetries between a movement and a countermovement, broadly labeled "progay" and "antigay." In large ways and small, each talks past the other, exhibiting what Barbara Herrnstein Smith has felicitously called the "microdynamics of incommensurabilty." But in a curious way, these antagonists also depend on each other, play off of each other, adapting arguments in light of each other's rhetoric. The prize as usual in conflicts between movements is third party support: news media, legislators, judges, and that amorphous, often fickle entity called "public opinion." But progay and antigay also use rhetoric to shore up support within their ranks. So, different as they are ideologically, each is alike in demonizing the other while masking internal differences as they project myths of unity.

These intricate steps in the dance of progay/antigay are not much different from those found in conflicts between other movements. But movement studies tend to focus on one movement, giving short shrift to the movement's evil twin. And most movement scholars tend to be unschooled in the give and take of argumentation. So this book is valuable, not just as a contribution to gay/lesbian studies, but as a case study in the rhetoric of controversy between movements and countermovements more generally.

Smith and Windes come to the study of progay/antigay as rhetoricians of a certain type. They are Burkeians and they are well up on movement theory by communication scholars and social scientists. The result is an integration of Burkeian rhetorical criticism and movement theory that William Gamson and I could only dream of when I visited with him in Ann Arbor back in 1977. Bill Gamson has done much since then to lay the groundwork for the study of what he calls "issue cultures," textual practices that become relatively fixed in discussions of public controversies. Opposing groups generate "interpretive packages," collections of collectively held ways of seeing and of arguing that, as Smith and Windes put it, are "forged in the crucible of reciprocal antagonism."

"Rhetoric" is an old word, made rich but also ambiguous by a long history of inconsistent usage. Some rhetoricians confine their study to oratory, others to the written word, but Burkeian theory extends the purview of rhetoric to symbol-using (mis-using) of every kind, focusing on reciprocal but "incomplete" antagonism as rhetoric's paradigmatic case. Moreover, in keeping with interpretive social science, Burkeian theory is constructionist, anti-essentialist, focusing not just on what progays and antigays say and believe, but also on the role of rhetoric in the making and molding of identities such as *homosexual* and *heterosexual*.

Arguably, it is impossible to maintain a constructionist stance consistently, for, taken to its logical extreme, such a stance would render issues of truth and non-truth unintelligible, and render activisim of any sort indefensible. Smith and Windes make clear that their constructionism is methodological—a bracketed compartmentalized anti-essentialism that leaves citizens free to act on rights they believe to be inalienable, including the right of all citizens to discover for themselves their sexual orientation, and then to embrace beliefs and behaviors which reflect both that discovery and their inalienable right of choice.

But ironically, their methodological anti-essentialism gives them a certain freedom as scholars to put aside personal predilections and treat progay and antigay rhetorics evenhandedly. Some gay and lesbian scholars/activists will chafe at that. But as Joshua Gamson observed, in a pre-publication review, "the book fills a gap in the literature on political communication surrounding sexuality with sophistication, balance, and thoroughness."

Who, then, is this book for? Josh Gamson concludes that it should have a ready market in university libraries and courses, particularly courses for graduate students and undergraduate students focused on (a) sexuality and sex/gender politics, (b) political communication and rhetoric, (c) social movements and collective identity.

I began the **Rhetoric & Society** series for Sage with a view that a Burkeian approach to rhetoric, a "globalized" rhetoric, as it's been called, was the perfect complement to so much that has been happening in the academy recently under the rubrics of interpretive social science and poststructuralism. Hence the names on the Editorial Board. Hence the books in the series already published.

Yet I believe the Smith/Windes book best exemplifies the promise of a globalized rhetoric. One cannot read it without concluding that the usual distinctions between social science and humanism are untenable.

I say that as an essentialist. I say it also as an anti-essentialist.

Herbert W. Simons
Series Editor

Introduction

Public Policy Debate
About Variant Sexuality

Homosexuality is an increasingly prominent subject of public policy discussion in the United States and other Western nations. In recent years, debates over measures to protect and extend the civil rights and liberties of lesbians and gay men, along with controversies over policies to discourage homosexuality, have increased so dramatically in frequency, number of participants, and prominence in the mass media that the nature of communication about variant sexuality has been fundamentally altered. Legal scholar Janet Halley (1994) correctly concludes:

> The closet no longer reigns in solitary splendor. . . . Its door now opens directly onto the *areopagus,* the forum, the senate hearing room, the court of law—onto scenes of rational debate, public deliberation, and collective decision making, conducted under the aegis of reasonable discourse. (p. 1727)

Symbolic action in these scenes of public policy formation on variant sexuality constitutes our general subject.

Elements of the controversy over the regulation of sexual behavior frequently have been chronicled and assessed. Most of these published works analyze either progay or antigay advocates, or describe one particular controversy. This valuable literature, on which our present study draws, can be usefully supplemented by analysis of how the process of antagonistic confrontation influences the nature of the debate over public policy concerning variant sexuality. Our intent is not definitively to survey this debate, but rather to examine adversarial engagement, a dynamic recurrent in most controversies. The nature and effects of oppositional relationships occurring in public policy struggles over variant sexuality have been previously surveyed, most notably by legal scholar Didi Herman (1994) and by journalists John Gallagher and Christopher Bull (1996). They each investigate the patterns of contention arising from mutual influence that have been significant for public policy discussion of variant sexuality. Our perspective differs from theirs, however, in that we investigate progay/antigay conflict as a process of collision in which multiple symbolic worlds are created and reconstructed when progay and antigay advocates strive in opposition to one another to influence adherents, allies, opponents, bystanders, and government officials. This is a task appropriate for those who examine public persuasion through rhetorical analysis. *Progay/Antigay* traces how competing texts weave around and through each other in an ongoing national town meeting on human sexuality. Specifically, we employ rhetorical analysis to describe: (a) how opposing advocates develop rival symbolic communities; (b) patterns of appeals which are generated by interaction among adversaries; (c) the extraordinary influence which opponents exercise on each other; (d) divisions produced by this influence among advocates allied in general purpose but not assumptions and strategies; (e) the influence of context on the types of appeals produced in deliberating particular issues. With reference to the dynamic of adversarial influence, we conclude with recommendations about how public debate over variant sexuality can be conducted more productively and investigated further.

Rhetorical Analysis of Public Controversy

Our understanding of public controversy over variant sexuality is grounded in the tradition of rhetorical criticism which developed from the seminal writings of Kenneth Burke, "the foremost rhetorician in the 20th century" (Golden, Berquist, & Coleman, 1997, p. 179). We have consistently drawn upon Burke's (1952) insight that the core subject of rhetoric consists of the "possibilities of classification in its *partisan* aspects; it considers the ways in which individuals are at odds with one another, or become identified with groups more or less at odds with one another" (p. 22). We seek to travel what Burke identified as the necessary path of persuasion, into "the Scramble, the Wrangle of the Market Place, the flurries and flare-ups of the Human Barnyard, the Give and Take, the wavering line of pressure and counterpressure" (p. 23). Like Burke, we recognize that the circulation of identification and division around each other "must often carry us far into the lugubrious regions of malice and the lie" (p. 23).

We also accept Burke's methodological insight, cogently described by sociologist Joseph Gusfield (1989a), that understanding rhetorical action demands a "program for analysis of human behavior which is pluralistic and dialectical" (p. 30). In particular, Burke moves us toward the interpretive social sciences, that is, in the direction of "approaches that seek to understand how patterns of consciousness enable us to organize experience" (Gusfield, 1989b, p. 5). We have been particularly impressed by recent social scientific efforts to develop a cultural theory of collective behavior which advances beyond ideology, social strain, and resource mobilization. The "Human Barnyard" cannot be described through theories which solely concern formal belief, social dislocation, or rational actors. By stressing the definitional power of culture, we have sought to bring attention to "how social movement organizations and actors interpret grievances and generate consensus on belief and action . . . create collective identities . . . produce frames of meaning . . . vocabularies of motive, and social dramas necessary to mobilize constituents" (Ellingson, 1997, p. 269). Such a cultural approach recognizes that "social movements tend to become worlds unto themselves that are characterized by distinctive ideologies, collective identities, behavioral routines, and material cultures" (McAdam, 1994, pp. 45-46).

The development of such worlds, and the collisions among them, can be understood in ways which likewise have Burkeian origins. For instance, drawing on Burke's theory of dramatism, sociologists Robert Benford and Scott Hunt (1992) elaborate the principle that "interpreting is a never ending social activity that makes movement scripting, staging and performing possible" (p. 48). They use Burke's method of dramatistic analysis which features "inquiry into cycles or clusters of terms and their functions" (p. 445). Benford and Hunt observe that activists develop lines of action which they believe to be "consistent with their collectively negotiated reality interpretations, idealistic visions and readings of the audiences' interpretations" (p. 48). We agree that social movements are best understood as dramas through which "protagonists and antagonists compete to affect audiences' interpretations of power relations in a variety of domains, including those pertaining to religious, political, economic or lifestyle arrangements" (p. 38).

The terms "identity," "frame," and "movement/countermovement dialectic" further define our perspective. We are centrally concerned with the process of creating identity out of the sociality of collective action. Burke (1959/1937) points out that " 'identification' is hardly other than a name for the *function of sociality*" (p. 266). Rhetorical critic Maurice Charland (1987) extends Burke's point that audience members do not exist prior to communication but come into existence as they "participate in the very discourse by which they would be 'persuaded' " (p. 133). Charland is right that the creation of subject positions is an historically contingent textualizing process. "The subject is a position within a text. To be an embedded subject is to experience and act in a textualized world" (p. 141). We are led by this theory of constitutive rhetoric to accept his conclusion that we ought to be "mindful not only of arguments and ideographs, but of the very nature of the subjects that rhetoric both address and leads to come to be" (p. 148). We have adopted a view which denies a "real" identity existing in advance of communication, believing that every aspect of human interaction—agent, agency, act, scene, and purpose—are problematic because, as Charland states, the "position one embodies as a subject is a rhetorical effect" (p. 148). Specifically, gay people and their opponents—who they are and what they want—do not exist prior to communication, but come into existence through their rhetorical acts.

Our approach which stresses the rhetorical development of identity is supported by recent works describing the construction of the subject within social movement culture. Sociologist Mary Bernstein (1997) notes, for example, that shared collective identity is not only necessary for mobilization, but is a goal of social movement rhetoric as either the construction of an identity or the deconstruction of identity categories, and ultimately is employed in strategies of critique and education (pp. 535, 538). We will explore subsequently how gay/lesbian and traditionalist actors use identity constructs as weapons to achieve dominance. Even the grievances which movements seek to highlight are intimately related to the identities which movements construct and deploy (Johnston, Larana, & Gusfield, 1994, p. 23). Recent interest in identity as rhetorical accomplishment develops out of the poststructuralist trend to question accepted symbolic boundaries: "What appears to be a difference is reinterpreted, discovered to be little more than a distinction rooted in power or a move in a rhetorical game" (Wolfe, 1992, p. 310). Throughout our analysis of the dynamic of antagonistic enjoinment in the variant sexuality controversy, we will be concerned with the rhetorical creation of identity, difference, and boundaries.

Within our approach, identities are rhetorical constructs created through discourse, not simply the products of innate biological and psychological characteristics or the results of dysfunctional social structures. We agree with sociologists Hunt, Benford, and David Snow (1994) that the construction of identity is inherent in social movement framing activities. "Not only do framing processes link individuals and groups ideologically but they proffer, buttress, and embellish identities that range from collaborative to conflictual" (p. 185). Both progay and antigay advocates have created a range of identities in order to accomplish persuasive purposes.

The concept of framing (creating patterns for organizing thought about issues), which is important to our understanding of rhetorical criticism, also has Burkeian origins, specifically in his concept of "terministic screens" (i.e., words which direct our attention into a particular point of view). Burke (1966) observes that "much that we take as observations about 'reality' may be but the spinning out of possibilities implicit in our particular choice of terms" (p. 46). Symbolic framing involves imposing interpretive schemata which simplify and condense experience by "selectively punctuating and encoding objects, situations, events, experiences, and sequences of actions with one's present or past environments" (Snow & Benford, 1992, p. 137). Conceived as modes of articulation and attribution, collective action frames focus attention on situations perceived to be problematic, "making attributions regarding who or what is to blame, and articulate an alternative set of arrangements including what the movement needs to do in order to affect the desired change" (Hunt, Benford, & Snow, 1994, p. 190). In the controversy over variant sexuality, the language which advocates employ creates and limits grievances, casts heroes and villains, projects modes of effective action, and envisions desirable outcomes.

Frames do not exist in isolation, however. They occur as part of a struggle to achieve dominant meaning. Consequently, the agonistic struggle for domination is central to our interpretation of symbolic action. Burke (1952) observed that "individual universes as such do not compete" (p. 22). However, within rhetoric, "their universality becomes transformed into a partisan weapon. For one need not scrutinize the concept of 'identification' very sharply to see, implied in it at every turn, its ironic counter-

part: division" (p. 23). Much of the drama of social controversy lies in division between movements and countermovements, "that a variety of
movement outcomes, from resource mobilization to longevity, depend
upon scripting and sustaining agon" (Benford & Hunt, 1992, p. 51). Put
another way, meaning construction occurs through a "process of contention within a discursive field as speakers jockey to gain legitimacy for their
positions, the support of targeted audiences, and the opportunity to im-
plement their solutions" (Ellingson, 1997, p. 272). Clearly, the struggle to
produce identities and frames is, therefore, undertaken in an atmosphere
charged with conflict, while opposing movements battle "for primacy in
identifying the relevant issues and actors in a given political struggle"
(Meyer & Staggenborg, 1996, p. 1635). In controversies over variant sexuality, struggle against "the enemy" plays an important role in all aspects
of collective behavior.

Our interpretation of the progay/antigay drama has also been influenced by several elements in rhetorical theorist Raymie McKerrow's
(1989) concept of a critical rhetoric which examines "the dimensions of
domination and freedom as these are exercised in a relativized world" (p.
91). We share his interest in a rhetoric which is involved in the process of
"demystifying the conditions of domination" (p. 91) while, at the same
time, recognizing that we have created a partial understanding by patch-
ing together fragments of texts. This is a self-conscious attempt to respond to rhetorician Michael McGee's (1990) challenge to "reconcile traditional modes of analysis with the so-called post-modern condition by
understanding that our first job as professional consumers of discourse is
inventing a text suitable for criticism" (p. 288).

We are working in a relativistic rhetorical tradition which emphasizes
the construction of "truth claims" through symbolic action. Therefore,
we have attempted to discipline our own preferences among these claims
and their political consequences. Our emphasis on the symbolic construction of reality, however, makes us skeptical of claims which are based on
"self-evident" natural facts or faith commitments to a supernatural ordering of the universe. To use philosopher Ian Hacking's (1999) typology of
the varieties of social constructionism, we have taken historicist and
ironic stances toward struggle over the regulation of variant sexuality.
Our purpose does not include proceeding further into the unmasking of
ideas, stripping them of authority in order to serve reformist or revolutionary purposes (pp. 66-67). As politically active individuals who are
committed to voicing many of the ideals and goals which we characterize

as progay, we find such purposes entirely congenial. As activists, we find nothing objectionable to discrediting the worldview and rebutting the truth claims of antigay opponents. But, as rhetorical critics seeking to understand the symbolic acts present in progay/antigay conflict, we strive to limit ourselves to the premises that (a) all constructions of meaning are contingent results of historical circumstances and (b) constructions of reality as they exist are inevitably in the world and cannot rationally be used to refute each other.

Though we are concerned with using rhetorical analysis in a neo-Burkeian mode to understand better progay/antigay debate, we certainly do not limit our interpretation to those propounded by professional rhetoricians, nor do we systematically attempt to improve critical methods. Throughout this discussion, we are frequently drawn to the insights of scholars in a variety of academic fields: anthropology, history, literature, philosophy, political science, and sociology. Without assuming the title of rhetorician, these scholars provide helpful direction for the study of how human beings influence one another through symbols. Nor have we attempted to structure their ideas about symbolic action into an innovative theory. Directly stated, our purpose is to comprehend more completely one aspect of public conversations about sexuality. Our primary concern remains antagonistic enjoinment of progay and antigay discourses, and not centrally the analysis of methods of rhetorical criticism.

Main Arguments of the Analysis

Focus on the mutual influence of adversarial relationships, combined with our concept of rhetorical criticism, pushes us toward a particular program of analysis. This analysis supports the contention that understanding the dynamics through which advocates seek to establish dominance requires appreciation for how rhetorical strategy is influenced by interactions among advocates of rival public policy positions. Rhetorician Celeste Condit Railsback (1984) correctly asserts that critics should not focus "on the advocacy of only one side of a controversy," but instead ought to analyze the "social text created by the advocates of various sides of the controversy, interacting with each other and the public" (pp. 419-420).

Several rhetorical critics have explained how opponents in public controversy constrain one another's strategic choices and persuasive appeals.

Rhetorical critic Jeff Bass (1991) suggests that reactionary rhetoric is often studied in isolation from its opposite, the rhetoric of reform, and that "this kind of analysis tends to deflect our attention away from the manner in which it may interact with and be influenced by reform rhetoric" (p. 427). He concludes that the "strategies employed by one side to persuade an audience influence the other's selection of strategies and appeals far beyond an invitation to engage in a game of rhetorical one-upmanship" (p. 427). Rhetorical critic Charles Taylor (1992) emphasizes the "dialogic" relationship between advocates of creationism and evolution, attempting to explain how each constrains the other (pp. 278-279). These studies, though largely limited to adjustment of argumentative strategy, point toward the uncharted territory in which adversarial supporters of particular public policies are influenced to draw specific appeals from their armamentarium in order to shape one another's identity claims and relational and situational definitions.

The study of communication about public policy toward variant sexuality initially can be organized by recognizing that symmetrical relationships of interdependence and mutual influence developed in recent decades between proponents and opponents of a civic culture which tolerates and even celebrates lesbians and gay men. The symmetry of the contest over sexuality may arise, in part, from the similarities of opponents. With respect to the United States, some analysts have suggested that groups working for and against public policy reforms favorable to gay and lesbian persons resemble one another in their strategies and their location in the political system (Gallagher & Bull, 1996, p. xiv). In this view, each side (a) uses strong emotional appeals to broaden its base of support; (b) functions most effectively when there is an immediate threat to dramatize; (c) achieves power within one political party; (d) must struggle against the skepticism and suspicion of the majority of Americans. Each finds within public struggle a source of empowerment (Hannigan, 1991, p. 325). These claims to similarity, however, must be balanced against recognition that gay/lesbian and traditionalist advocates often seem to be speaking a mutually incomprehensible language, argue from different premises, act within different social milieu, and are, in many other respects, significantly dissimilar. Our central point is that those locked in combat over variant sexuality exercise deep mutual influence over one another. Their oppositional discourses shape presentation of collective identity; they influence definition of controversy, contribute to understanding the relationship between antagonists, and heighten dissent among advocates of any one general position on homosexuality.

The examination of gay/lesbian public policy issues begins in Chapter 1 with a description of the general public policy controversy over variant sexuality and with an overview of the emergence of conditions which produced the current extensive public debate about homosexuality. Significant variations have occurred through time and across cultures in the construction of homosexuality and the degree to which it is accepted. Our own culture's engagement with the public policy implications of homosexuality hinges on the emergence of a particular type of gay/lesbian subject (i.e., a subspecies of humanity). This subject's appearance is the precondition for both the development of a gay/lesbian community and a set of movements which constitute a powerful political force for public policy change. Simultaneously, fundamentalist and other traditionalist movements have gathered strength, in part based on their resistance to homosexual activism. Often working through organizations dedicated to influencing public sentiment, gay/lesbian and traditionalist advocates have become principal voices in our present complex controversy about variant sexuality.

Unraveling the complexity of this controversy requires analysis of the language, collective action, and interactive communication produced within an issue culture. Each kind of analysis provides insight into an aspect of public policy dispute. In our attempt to understand and analyze public policy debate, the production of arguments, ideographs and condensation symbols are important. Equally significant is the mobilization as movements of interpretive communities (i.e., groups which coordinate their personal interpreting behaviors). The concept of issue culture (the textual practices which become relatively fixed in discussion of a public question) allows us to focus on language and social mobilization through the lens of framing processes which occur during the production of interpretive packages (i.e., collections of frames through which advocates seek to impose their point of view about a controversy). These interpretive packages are forged in the crucible of reciprocal antagonism. Chapter 2 elaborates on language, collective action, and interactive communication as means to understand variant sexuality controversies.

Advocates for progay and antigay positions have constructed a variety of elemental appeals which surface in different combinations in most public policy disputes about homosexuality. The generative premise for these appeals is that there is a link between private behavior and public action. Traditionalist discourse consists of appeals which attempt to make homosexuality publicly invisible as well as attacks on public policy programs which encourage homosexuality. In contrast, gay/lesbian discourse consists of efforts to make sexual difference visible in the public sphere, to refute antigay appeals, and to justify public policy favorable to lesbians and gay men. Chapter 3 explains our understanding of this pattern of appeals, stressing that these appeals are not forged through isolated thought, but in the production of discourse intended to achieve symbolic dominance.

Contests of representation provide strategic structure for the variant sexuality issue culture. Through the process of making public claims, traditionalist and progay advocates strategically construct themselves, their relationships to their antagonists, and their legitimate position in the public sphere. Both lay claim to virtue in their struggle against an evil nemesis. The projections generated in contests of representation are creations designed to establish a dominant interpretive package. Chapter 4 traces the interaction between advocates which produces reciprocal influence important to public action concerning variant sexuality.

Both progay and antigay interpretive packages are ambiguous in the sense that they contain not a single position, but a range of alternative claims. Divisions develop among advocates who want their own interpretive versions to be dominant within either the traditionalist or progay positions. These divisions are influenced by concerns with representation in public policy contests. In Chapter 5, we describe the development of such divisions, with major emphasis on disputes within the gay/lesbian political community over competing versions of identity and their strategic consequences for public policy formation.

Different contexts produce different patterns of persuasive interaction because specific public policy disputes filter out particular elements of the traditionalist and progay interpretive packages. The recent Congressional debate on the Defense of Marriage Act is an example of this process. The struggle over gay marriage narrowed the range of gay identity, enhanced themes of gay/lesbian participation in civic life, and raised issues of social stability. The marriage debate will be examined in detail in Chapter 6 as an example of reciprocal influence within an institutional context.

Antagonistic enjoinment in the debate over variant sexuality has significant implications for the study and criticism of public communication. Chapter 7 describes several of these implications, concluding with suggestions for research which might profitably be conducted to advance our understanding of reciprocal influence in a variety of issue cultures. We will suggest that rhetorical critics can contribute to improving the discussion of gay/lesbian public policy questions if they encouraged reduction of opportunistic and shallow argument, the formulation of more substantive appeals, a rethinking of identity claims, and a deeper appreciation of the fundamental challenges which attempts at moral persuasion make to beliefs about how society ought to be constituted.

Analytic Limitations and Difficulties of Terminology

Discussion of the politics of variant sexuality must necessarily recognize that political discourses on homosexuality are nested within a larger culture. Though traditional political theory separates politics and culture, in practice they are closely connected (Bronski, 1998, p. 248). Law professor Robert Cover (1983) provides an important description of the relationship which holds between law and policy on the one hand and the environing moral culture on the other. He writes that "we inhabit a *nomos*—a normative universe." The legal system, principles of justice, formal institutions, and social conventions are "but a small part of the normative universe that ought to claim our attention" (p. 4). As a consequence, Cover asserts, public policy must be understood as part of the complex narrative myths which underlie culture. He argues that these myths establish a "repertoire of moves—a lexicon of normative action—that may be combined into meaningful patterns culled from the meaningful patterns of the past" (p. 9). Variant sexuality is not a separate subject to be explored in isolation from other elements of culture because, as social scientist Jeffrey Weeks (1977) asserts, "attitudes to homosexuality are inextricably linked to wider questions: of the function of the family, the evolution of gender roles, and attitudes to sexuality in general" (p. 2).

Although our attention here focuses on debate over public policy, we must bear in mind that the substance of persuasive discourse produced in these debates bubbles up from our most fundamental cultural assumptions. Further, these beliefs and myths are dynamically created. They are not only the artifacts of the past, but a continuing creation produced through cultural production and struggle. Mass media, for instance, creates representations of gay and lesbian persons which then become suppositions in political discourse. Vito Russo (1987) in his analysis of lesbian and gay characters in film demonstrates the presence (and absence) of a range of images which flicker through popular culture. Similarly, sociologist Joshua Gamson (1998) shows how the changing guidelines for success in reaching mass audiences create new rules for understanding the behavior of both progay and antigay advocates. More generally, as philosopher Morris Kaplan (1997) points out, "a distinctive feature of modernity is that it supplements the juridical and repressive model of state action with a pervasive system of social relations that produces new institutional settings, modes of knowledge, and forms of subjectivity" (p. 71). Despite our emphasis on politics and the law, the widest definition of our topic is the creation of new social contexts, knowledges, and subjects through political communication. We do not avoid a discussion of cultural issues. Instead, we are focusing on the political aspects of the culture, including those fundamental beliefs which undergird the appeals and strategies which recurrently are expressed in the variant sexuality controversy. We leave to others the equally important subject of the influence of popular culture on political outcomes.

Our concentration on the process of antagonistic enjoinment further limits systematic discussion of the many factors which produced particular patterns of appeal and representation. A comprehensive account of discourse on variant sexuality public discourse would take into consideration the availability of models for imitation, adaptation to specific political opportunities, motives other than those involved in confrontation, and, perhaps of greatest importance, variation among institutional contexts in which progay and antigay discourses are produced.

On a variety of occasions throughout this analysis, we place adversarial influence within institutional context. For instance, institutional setting is important for the emergence of the progay/antigay contest, for the secularization of antigay rhetoric, for the production of different progay self-representations, and for the essentialization of gay identity in formal deliberative debate. Beyond this, we recognize that different institutional environments distribute power in unequal ways; they constitute diverse primary audiences and establish conflicting standards of rationality and acceptability. In brief, they encourage particular rhetorical strategies and discourage others. A comprehensive interpretation of discourse on variant sexuality would give prominence to such institutional influences. Our interest in foregrounding the effects of the antagonistic interdependence of progay and antigay advocates, however, leads us in this monograph to place institutional contexts in the background. This should not imply, however, that such contextual influence is beside the point of our analysis, but merely often in shadows around our main point.

Language, the most salient feature of culture, simultaneously enables and obscures public policy debate about variant sexuality. Discussions about the regulation of sexuality are conducted in a variety of lexicons which are deployed as weapons in struggles over specific issues. Each key word and phrase which threads through variant sexuality public issue contests contains a history, a strategy, and a critique. Choice of terms for use in engaging in public argument and for describing public discussion invariably signifies a commitment to a contested position and to a particular way of understanding sexuality. Among the crucial terms that come to mind is "variant sexuality," a frequently used phrase which has the virtue of nonjudgmental neutrality and inclusiveness. The term, however, could conceivably include groups such as pedophiles, a classification to which many gay activists would object. The word "sodomite" invokes a long history of denunciation and criminalization of sexuality. "Homosexual" is generally believed to medicalize same-sex erotic behavior, connoting the sense of pathology and possible treatment. The term "homosexuality" also sets up a homosexual/heterosexual binary which falsely structures perception of sexuality. Others object that "homosexual" wrongly constitutes a type of person rather than rightly naming only a behavior.

"Gay" or "lesbians and gay men" are terms often derided as being non-descriptive, opportunistically invented for political reasons, or too prescriptive of the kinds of persons named. The addition of "transgender" has the ambiguity of describing not only lesbians and gay men but cross-dressing heterosexuals. The term "bisexual" has been objected to on the grounds that it truly describes no actual sexual actors and that it inconveniently focuses attention on behavior rather than a fundamental class of persons. "Sexual orientation" is a generally accepted term, even though there has been objection that it is an ill-defined concept which naturalizes a certain kind of person. The word "queer," recently favored by some progay advocates and academics for its virtue of inclusiveness as well as its function both in reversing the valence of a traditional epithet and in subverting the received sexual order, is offensive to many lesbians and gay men precisely because it has long been used as a term of opprobrium, inviting discrimination and violence.

The language used to name those who oppose gay/lesbian political action is no less a terminological minefield. A number of terms imply that religion is the origin of antigay sentiment. Words such as "fundamentalist," "evangelical," and "new religious right" are frequently used pejoratively for individuals who oppose homosexual movements. However, such terms leave out opposition justified on secular grounds and suggest that religious opponents are merely a radical minority. The term "homophobe" to describe an individual who either dislikes homosexuals or opposes gay political action can be attacked as pathologizing proper moral views, as a diagnosis without basis, and as a mere epithet. "Bigot" and its variants has been frequently employed by progay advocates to describe their opponents, and has been rejected as simple name-calling by individuals who define themselves as "people of faith."

There is no means through which to compromise the innumerable semantic disagreements which mine the battlefield of public policy whose subject is same-sex sex. These disagreements are, in fact, useful artifacts marking boundaries between opposed groups as well as indicators of the deployment of particular rhetorical strategies. In examining these public policy debates, some conventions of usage, even though arbitrary, might provide clarity and consistency. In general, we propose to use the terms "progay" and "antigay" to denote opposing sides in public policy debate. Variants of the term "gay and lesbian" will refer to homosexuals within progay discourse. Similarly, the term "homosexual" will be used during analysis of antigay advocacy. Antigay advocates frequently will be called "traditionalists," a neutral term which suggests that antigay impulses have origin in both secular and religious beliefs.

1 Emergence of the Variant Sexuality Issue Culture

Public policy debate about homosexuality during the latter part of the 20th century strikingly contrasts with the limited public commentary in immediately preceding decades. Before the mid-20th century, there were indeed discussions about public policy toward homosexuality. Debate, however, was infrequent and one-sided, premised on the assumption that same-sex sex is both a sin and a menace to society. In both Germany and Great Britain in the late 19th and early 20th centuries, national legislatures deliberated antihomosexual measures, with results uniformly adverse to gay and lesbian people. A few writers constructed arguments to support repeal of laws which criminalized variant sexual conduct, but their work was either suppressed or limited in circulation (Crompton, 1985, p. 262).

That earlier narrow stream of information and injunction has today become a broad, roiling river of contentious opinion. Not only do legislators and judges wrestle with a growing volume of bills and cases centered on variant sexuality, but school boards, military tribunals, ecclesiastical bodies, and bureaucrats within government and in the private sector currently struggle over policies about variant sexuality and sexual identity. In short, as philosopher Richard Mohr (1994) remarks, "America seems to be at a turning point on gay issues; it is now at least acceptable to inquire about these issues in public discussion" (p. x).

Although this discussion of public policy has been carried forward in many venues, variant sexuality dramatically emerged as a set of political and judicial questions which currently occupies a significant place in ballot initiatives, legislative debate, and court cases. Whether homosexuality is to be discouraged or protected by government has recently become an extremely volatile political concern (Herman, 1997, p. 1). The erosion of the boundary between public and private spheres with respect to sexuality is an important change which has integrated both progay and antigay advocates into the political system. As a consequence, the regulation of sexuality has became an important subject at all levels of the political system. Debates on variant sexuality are now "fundamental sites for the establishment of an American politician's true conservative or progressive credentials" (Smith, 1994, p. 3).

Even a partial list of public controversies involving homosexuality suggests the daunting range of political and legal questions which are now under discussion. Public policy debate has occurred over,

- efforts to repeal sodomy laws and to rescind laws and limit police action against gay/lesbian public displays of affection, congregation of homosexuals, and gender discrepant dress
- censorship of gay/lesbian erotica and the circulation of material advocating homosexuality
- measures concerning exclusion from educational institutions of known homosexuals, gay rights advocates, and gay positive curricula
- prohibition of lesbians and gay men from being awarded custody of their children, adopting children, or serving as foster parents
- inclusion of "sexual orientation" in antidiscrimination laws, institutional policies, and "hate- crime" laws
- prohibition against gay and lesbian persons serving openly in the military
- approval of domestic partnership legislation and gay marriage
- constitutional provisions prohibiting sexual orientation nondiscrimination laws which have been approved through electoral and judicial processes
- prevention of harassment of lesbians and gay men in the workplace and discouragement of leniency toward gaybashers
- mandatory training in multiculturalism, including discussion of gay lifestyles.

In addition, religious groups are deeply divided about quasi-public questions concerning prohibitions against ordination of noncelibate gay/

lesbian clergy, edicts against the celebration of same-sex domestic commitments, and encouragement of church boycotts against corporations
thought to be sympathetic toward homosexuals.

Public deliberations about these issues have received extensive public-
ity. The media give regular, even dramatic, coverage to public policy questions concerning homosexuality. Journalist Edward Alwood (1996) reports that in the last decade, "coverage of gays and lesbians in major
newspapers, magazines, and television networks had become frequent
and practically routine" (p. 15). In addition, both proponents and opponents of policy reform to accommodate gay and lesbian citizens developed their own media in order to publicize and influence public debate
(Streitmatter, 1993). New technology significantly heightened the
amount of information available about gay politics, along with other aspects of homosexuality. Journalism professor Charles Kaiser (1997), for
instance, found that in 1996, an internet browser could find 62,902 documents mentioning queers, 251,592 concerning lesbians, and 663,239
about gays (p. 330).

Current enhanced public attention is not a sharp break with past concern about sexual and gender variation. Extensive discussion of homosexuality and its regulation is far from new in our own era. Recent works by
historians George Chauncey (1994) and John Loughery (1998) make
clear that coverage of the presence and suppression of homosexuality has
long been featured in both mass media and popular literature. In the past
several decades, however, a flood of information, opinion, and myth
about homosexuality has resulted in a fundamental shift in public attitude
away from the previously negative depiction adulterated by curiosity and
sensationalism to deep division in public opinion and among public advocates.

Polls confirm this shift, revealing a liberalizing trend, especially in the
current decade, toward gay and lesbian people. This trend creates a public
divided both about the morality of same-sex sex and about related public
policy questions. Political scientist Alan Yang's (1997) analysis of opinion
surveys conducted by 21 organizations between 1965 and 1996 reveals
that, while public disapproval of homosexuality remained remarkably
stable at the 70% level between 1973 and 1991, there was a 20% drop in
disapproval rates during the 1990s which results in a public "evenly split
on the morality of homosexuality" (p. 478). The public is also divided on
what types of civil protections and rights should be afforded to lesbians
and gay men. Majorities favor job protection, including in the military,

and free speech for gay people. Support for job protection, however, declines when professional roles involve children. Consistent with this position, a majority remains opposed by a more than two-to-one ratio to same-sex marriage as well as to adoption of children by same-sex couples (pp. 277-278). Given shifting views and the commitment of large numbers of individuals to each side in the progay/antigay public policy debate, a significant political opportunity is created for both progay and antigay advocates.

The nature of this opportunity is captured in social scientist Pierre Bourdieu's (1994) distinction between "doxa," universally accepted and unspoken truths, and "orthodoxies," dominant though contested opinions about the existing social order. Bourdieu argues that the common sense world is not expressed but assumed. He writes that tradition is silent, not only about the beliefs and behavior that it controls, but also about itself as a tradition (p. 163). A "doxic" understanding of the world is unaware that there are alternative views, and that groups can engage in competition and conflict over the legitimacy of these alternatives. (p. 163). In contrast, "it is when the social world loses its character as a natural phenomenon that the question of the natural or connected character . . . of social facts can be raised" (p. 164). Consequently, the "dominated classes have an interest in pushing back the limits of doxa and exposing the arbitrariness of the taken for granted . . . to undertake the work of conscious systematization and express rationalization which marks the passage from doxa to orthodoxy" (pp. 164-165). Opinion about variant sexuality has traced the arc from an unspoken certainty of the unnaturalness of homosexuality to a sharp contest between the orthodox advocates of a universal model of monogamous heterosexuality and the proponents of heterodox sexual variation whose central appeal is to the injustice of the state's enforcement of an arbitrary social ordering of sexual behavior.

Because lesbian and gay advocates now have a plausible opportunity to advance their case, variant sexuality has been transformed in our twentieth century society from a largely silenced aspect of human interaction into a topic for intense and lengthy public dispute. The political opportunity for advocates of gay/lesbian causes developed in the usual ways specified by social scientists. They gained allies, profited from elite fragmentation and conflict, and gained meaningful access to the political system (McAdam, 1996, pp. 26-29). Gay people developed allies in left-wing politics, other civil rights movements, as well as in the feminist movement. Important elites abandoned the traditionalist attitudes which had served as the principal justification for antigay policies. The gay/lesbian movement developed significant influence, especially among progressive and Democratic politicians. The increasing importance of homosexuality as a political topic thus lies in the emergence of extensive public support for advocates who favor decriminalization of private homosexual behavior, protection against discrimination arising from sexual orientation, and acceptance of the legal and ethical status of gay and lesbian associations and relationships (Kaplan, 1997, p. 14).

Progay advocacy has, of course, met with significant and determined opposition (D'Emilio, 1983, p. 58). What emerged from the gay/lesbian exploitation of their political opportunity was, to borrow a concept from rhetorical critics Kathryn M. Olson and G. Thomas Goodnight (1994), "an extended rhetorical engagement that critiques, resituates, and develops communication practices bridging the public and personal spheres" (p. 249). They observe that such social controversies introduce the public to facets of life "that are hidden away, habitually ignored, or routinely disconnected from public appearance" (p. 252). Strikingly new is the fact that lesbian and gay public policy advocacy has prompted the responsive "defense of heterosexuality and traditional gender identities, a task unthinkable in a previous era of homosexual pathologization" (Herman, 1994, p. 8). To paraphrase a cliche, the love which dared not defend its name has evolved through confrontation into an identity about which our society is irrepressibly loquacious.

The very abundance of communication about variant sexuality produces an incoherent montage of impressions which constitutes public knowledge about this subject. Such knowledge is a pastiche of representations created out of robust competition among various adversarial actors and agencies. Swirling together are names, images, and phrases: Robertson and Bennett; Kramer and Kushner; Helms and Frank; Bryant and Falwell; Milk and Gearhart; Rita Mae Brown and Schlafly; Navratilova and Louganis; memorial quilts and Washington marches; gay bashings, homicides, and suicides; Matthew Shepherd crucified on a Wyoming fence; people living with AIDS and the Gay Games; televangelistic denunciations and Ellen DeGeneres; the Christian Coalition and ACT-UP; "family values," "outing," and "we're here—we're queer." Such a collage forms a bewildering context for private quandary and spiritual uncertainty, no less than for the public policy disputes.

An obscuring cloud of factual assertions and appeals about variant sexuality has been created by clusters of organizations whose spokespersons use competing languages and logics to advance adversarial positions. Focus on the Family, the Traditional Values Coalition, and Concerned Women of America, along with hundreds of similar local organizations, are locked in combat with the Human Rights Campaign, the National Gay and Lesbian Task Force, the Lambda Legal Defense and Education Fund, and a myriad of other progay grassroots groups. Clarity is, of course, often the first victim as clusters of advocates work to frame issues in ways which facilitate both fundraising and victories in legislatures, courts, and in initiative contests.

Tracing the appearance of gay/lesbian and traditionalist actors and describing the development of a variant sexuality issue culture is a necessary prologue for subsequent description of the discourses scripted by these actors. Analysis of communication which developed between and within groups of actors, and criticism of the patterns of action which now characterize the symbolic world in which these actors speak requires preliminary description of a context which has only recently come into being.

The standard explanation for the unprecedented explosion of political communication about homosexuality in America and western Europe is that lesbians and gay men have revolted against the homophobia which consistently dominated western civilization. This revolt elicited a conservative backlash (Swan, 1997, p. xviii). The headline for this story would be "New Social Force Revolts Against Old Regime." This interpretation is accurate to the extent it recognizes that present circumstances create a historically unique moment making possible the mobilization of resources against public antihomosexual attitudes and policies. It is misleading, however, in its assumption that antihomosexual attitudes and policies are continuous characteristics of western civilization. Negative attitudes have varied in strength throughout the centuries. An answer which relies on antigay agitation understood as backlash, moreover, fails to notice that a tradition-building fundamentalist movement has now emerged for reasons only remotely connected to the subject of homosexuality. In a sense, the production of gay and lesbian people as political actors results from the material conditions of market-driven modern culture, whereas traditionalism with its antihomosexual component is a parallel reaction to the spirit, if not the substance, of modernity.

A more complete explanation of the development of policy discussion about variant sexuality might begin by recognizing the localized and episodic appearance of hostility to homosexuality. Opposition to the current wave of such hostility is possible only because lesbians and gay men have developed a strong sense of identity plus communication networks through which political opposition is mounted. The formation of active political response to progay efforts should be recognized as the attempt by a traditionalist interpretive community operating in adverse circumstances to seize an opportunity to reinforce its beliefs and to reinvigorate its hold on political and social power. The expansion of oppositional communication about homosexuality, consequently, is a result of the recent construction and convergence of two political formations, a homophile movement and a traditionalist movement. The intensity of the debate is heightened because both movements, though often relying on grassroots volunteers, make extensive use of professional media management organizations to disseminate complex discourses about public policy concerning gay/lesbian issues. Our thesis, then, is that currently we find a developing progay social force pitted against a transforming traditionalist social force, neither of which has a purchase on the power of political and social institutions.

The Invention of Progay/Antigay Discourses

The belief that homosexuality has been under attack everywhere and forever is intuitive to those raised in a society in which all major institutions—religious, educational, governmental, corporate, medical—have until recently been aligned against homosexuality. Further, a seamless history of homosexual oppression serves both sides in this contemporary political controversy. Traditionalists construct a narrative of longstanding social consensus opposed to the public representation of homosexuality as well as a nearly unbroken tradition of legislation against same-sex erotic behavior. Only in periods of extreme decadence, so this scenario goes, was control over homosexuality loosened, with inevitably destructive consequences. Conversely, progray advocates account for themselves within a narrative of steady movement toward freedom, playing enlightened warriors in revolt against a past of unrelieved prejudice (Gilbert, 1981, pp. 58, 66). Equally important, the isolation experienced in our own time by lesbians and gay men produced a conviction that silence and invisibility as characteristics of gay life could be projected into the past. They created an interpretation that "until gay liberation, lesbians and gay men were always the victims of systematic, undifferentiated, terrible oppression" (D'Emilio, 1992, p. 4).

Explanation of public debate over homosexuality as a sharp break from consistent suppression of gay and lesbian people, plausible and functional though it may be, must overcome the serious objection that hostility toward homosexuality has not been a continuity in human experience. Historian D. Michael Quinn (1996) accurately summarizes the historical and anthropological literature when he writes that "cross-cultural comparisons demonstrate that similar behaviors of gender and sexuality can have vastly different meanings to different people at different times" (p. 43). Sociologist David Greenberg (1988) adds a considerable body of evidence supporting the proposition that throughout the ancient world, male homosexuality was widely accepted as part of a general belief in human sexuality as a positive good (p. 184).

The convoluted history of hostility to homosexuality in the West defies easy summation. Scholars have offered facile interpretations tracing the source of homophobia to such single causes as patriarchy, a universal desire to suppress the homoerotic desire which exists in all persons, or to the rise of monotheism (Bronski, 1994, p. 10; Hoffman, 1984, p. 27; Mieli, 1980/1970, p. 23). These explanations are unpersuasive, however, because in the western experience, long periods of time have been characterized by relatively relaxed views of homoerotic behavior (Burg, 1981, p. 77). Such epochs of tolerance were punctuated by eras of rigorous suppression. Philosopher Elisabeth Young-Bruehl (1996) identifies three such periods: (a) the third century of the Christian era which brought to a close the Greco-Roman celebration of pederastic homosexuality, (b) the 13th century which ended a 600 year period during which homosexuality was widely tolerated, and (c) the 19th and 20th centuries which elaborated and institutionalized a range of strategies for the suppression of homosexuals (p. 436).

Each periodic appearance of strong antihomosexual belief and action can be explained by reference to specific developments. Greenberg (1988), for instance, attributes antihomosexual beliefs in the ancient world to the rise of an asceticism hostile to all forms of sexual pleasure, and the 13th century campaigns against homosexuality to intense class warfare (pp. 184, 298). The modern period of homosexual suppression, beginning roughly in the late 18th century, defies simple explanation through attribution to a single cause.

A wide range of interpretation has been offered for the intensity of antihomosexual practices in the past two centuries. Classicist Louis Crompton (1985) attributes mounting suppression of sodomy in the 19th century to a marked increase in xenophobia and to a generalized concern with social discipline, which resulted in a broad moral reform crusade. Weeks (1977) argues that attitudes toward homosexuality are inextricably bound to larger concerns about gender, family structure, and general attitudes toward sexuality. In his view, antihomosexuality is linked with the suppression of women, with the roles men and women are expected to act out in the family, and with the construction of erotophobic taboos (pp. 1, 5, 197). Chauncey (1994) traces the rise of compulsory heterosexuality to a crisis of middle-class masculinity. Throughout the nineteenth century, an increasingly industrialized and bureaucratic economy meant that many men's lives were less self-determined than those of their fathers. Consequently, sexual object choice—an exclusive desire for women—became a substitute for work-defined masculine independence. Defense of this definition necessitated the denigration of men who did not make this choice (p. 116).

A major advance in understanding the suppression of homosexuality lies in postmodern theoretician Michel Foucault's (1990) jump beyond psychological or structural explanations for attitudes toward sexuality to a definition of the "regime of power-knowledge-pleasure that sustains the discourse on human sexuality in our part of the world" (p. 6). Foucault denies the premise that the connection between power and sex ought to be understood as inherently repressive. Belief that homosexuality has traditionally been suppressed is a rhetorical device because, "if sex is repressed, that is, condemned to prohibition, nonexistence, and silence, then the mere fact that one is speaking about it has the appearance of deliberate transgression" (p. 6). Foucault finds in the historical record not a silencing of homosexuality in the past 200 years, but an explosion of discourses about sexuality. He argues that the "nineteenth century and our own have been rather the age of multiplication: a dispersion of sexualities, a strengthening of their disparate forms, a multiple implantation of 'perversions.' Our epoch has initiated sexual heterogeneities" (p. 6). The homosexual identity was created in the 19th century as a discourse which transformed the sodomite into a "personage, a past, a life, a life form, and a morphology. . . . The sodomite had been a temporary aberration; the homosexual was now a species" (p. 42).

To Foucault (1990), discourses of sexuality are means of control. In the elaboration of languages about sex, Foucault observes, "what one was seeking essentially was simply to conceal sex: a screen-discourse, a dispersion-avoidance" (p. 53). But the effect was otherwise, "since discourse is not only an instrument and effect of power, but also a hindrance, a stumbling-block, a point of resistance and a starting point for an opposing strategy" (p. 101). Social conflict over homosexuality became robust because discourse not only produces and transmits regulatory power but also exposes and undermines it. Foucault concludes that the multiplication of discourses about sexuality

> made possible a strong advance of social controls into this area of "perversity.". . . Importantly, it also was the condition for articulating a "reverse" discourse: homosexuality began to speak in its own behalf, to demand that its legitimacy or "naturality" be acknowledged, often in the same vocabulary. (p. 101)

An answer to the question of why homosexuality has become politicized in our society, therefore, does not lie in a progressivist scenario of enlightened agents struggling upward from a dark past of repression or a traditionalist narrative of decadence, but lies rather in the creation of a vocabulary which makes possible discussion of the gay/lesbian person as an identity, and which facilitates the circulation of adversarial positions about the gay/lesbian community and the movement which has grown from it.

Gay Identity, Community, and Culture

Central to the appearance of political debate over homosexuality is the emergence of a gay and lesbian identity around which individuals have mobilized. The continuous presence in history of such an identity cannot simply be assumed because relationships between nonconforming sexual actors and society have been vague and variable (Pronk, 1993, p. 199). A premise of current speculation on gay and lesbian identity is the concept that although homosexual erotic behavior has always been part of the human repertoire, homosexual identity is a comparatively recent phenomenon (Weeks, 1977, p. 3). Only in the latter half of the 19th century did a conception and an accompanying terminology emerge for the belief that homosexuality "was the characteristic of a particular type of person" (Weeks, 1981, p. 104).

This evolutionary development of the homosexual as an identity is lucidly described by literature professor David Halperin (1990) in his explanation of the emergence of the homosexual/heterosexual dichotomy in Western thought. He claims that only in the late middle ages did the notion surface that those who commit acts of sodomy might be a particular type of individual. In the 17th and 18th centuries, concern developed about men who were deviants in both sexual performance and gender behavior. This led to the 19th century's concern with sexual inversion, a concept which conflated gender discrepancy with variant sexual object choice. Only toward the end of the 19th century did there emerge the notion that gender and sexual behavior could be separated. Sexual desire for someone of the same sex was divorced from other kinds of gender nonconformity, a move which produced several effects. First, it laid the foundation for the production of the gay male as an individual like all other males except for sexual object choice. Second, the creation of this particular binary sexuality produced a class of persons composed of individuals who previously had not been grouped together: sexually passive with active males, men and women drawn to their own sex, gender conformists with gender deviants (p. 1-27).

The creation of the homosexual defined by sexual object choice was not, of course, completed at one time or, indeed, completed at all. As a variety of scholars have noted, the conflation of gender with sexuality continued for many years into the 20th century. Chauncey (1994) argues persuasively that in America before World War II, the belief was not hegemonic, as it now is, that sexuality is inevitably divided into homosexuality and heterosexuality, both defined by sexual practice. He asserts that this premise, now fundamental to public policy debate on the regulation of sexuality, only slowly and unevenly replaced the earlier division of men into gender discrepant "fairies" and "normal men." He writes that "homosexual behavior per se becomes the primary basis for labeling and self-identification of men as 'queer' only around the middle of the twentieth century; before then, most men were so labeled only if they displayed a much broader inversion of their ascribed gender status by assuming the sexual and other cultural roles ascribed to women" (p. 13). Feminist scholars Elizabeth Kennedy and Madeline Davis (1993) extend this view to variant sexuality among women. They note that until recently gender inversion determined lesbians' identities, "so that the butch was the lesbian. But from the mid-1950s on, women's attraction to women was the dominant way of defining and expressing lesbian identity, establishing commonality between butch and fem" (p. 385).

The concept of the homosexual as a distinct subject is not only recent, but also partial, especially in political and legal constructions of variant sexuality. A lesbian or gay person can still be construed as one who acts sinfully, against nature, out of an inverted gender, or from a sense of intimate friendship. As legal scholar Leo Flynn (1995) states, homosexuality has not completely replaced "earlier categories that assert themselves in vestigial form, submerged layers capable of disrupting the dominant discourse that has succeeded them." He believes that even though the dominant understanding centers on the homosexual/heterosexual binary, the "contemporary impact of the rhetoric and vision of otherwise anachronistic discourses is significant, and a multiplicity of overlapping systems of classification, each of varying strength, may interact in the narratives of law" (pp. 30-31).

Despite halting and uneven change in society's definition of sexuality, the creation of a gay identity was clearly the first step toward our current public policy debate over variant sexuality. This new identity formation hinged on a novel sexual regime produced by a "reorganization of male sexual categories and the transition from a world divided into 'fairies' and 'men' on the basis of gender persona to one divided into 'homosexuals' and 'heterosexuals' on the basis of sexual object-choice" (Chauncey, 1994, p. 358).

The emergence of a homosexual identity can also be explained by reference to changing conditions of economic production. Postmodern scholar Scott Bravman (1996), for example, argues that the development of industrial capitalism had profound impact on gender roles, family life, and ideologies of individualism (p. 335). Historian John D'Emilio (1992) explains this transition as a change produced by the rise of wage labor and the loss of the household as a site of economic production. The new capitalist economy thereby created circumstances that allowed some men and women the independence to organize their lives around emotional and erotic attraction to their own sex. This change was soon reflected in other ways, most noticeably in medicine, which responded to this method of arranging personal life by describing homosexuality as a condition inherent to the person. Then, in turn, the new medical model "affected the consciousness of the women and men who experienced homosexual desire, so that they came to define themselves through their erotic life" (pp. 7-8). This view was soon reflected by academics in the reification of the concept of the homosexual (Adam, 1985, p. 658).

A number of effects are produced by the creation of the homosexual as a "type of person." Sociologist Mary McIntosh (1990) points out that the intended consequence of the construction of a "homosexual role" is to segregate a group of deviants from others, thereby keeping their deviant practices contained within a relatively small group. In similar terms, journalist Frank Browning (1993) argues that secular and ecclesiastical authorities, having failed to suppress variant sexuality, have "elected to isolate and assign it to a distant category of 'other' people" (p. 220). This strategy, however, is a social control mechanism which also fixes identity, thus foreclosing the possibility of drifting back into normality (McIntosh, 1990, pp. 27-28). Out of such a legitimating process emerges an extension of identity in a politics which ethnicized sexuality, creating a group category whose members could collectively enter into political and cultural life (Kimmel, 1993, p. 573).

The creation of a gay collective subject is not universally accepted as an unalloyed good, even by those who favor a progay political program. Postmodern critic Slavoj Zizek (1989), for example, argues in Lacanian terms that becoming a subject inevitably involves misrecognition. He contends that the subject's symbolic representation

> always distorts the subject, that it is always a displacement, a failure—that the subject cannot find a signifier which would be "his own," that he is always saying too little or too much: in short, *something other* than what he wanted or intended to say. (p. 175)

Such concern with identity as always involving falsification is part of a postmodernist questioning of binary oppositions (Bersani, 1995, p. 34).

In stark contrast to suspicions about identity politics, there is a strong belief that adoption of a unifying identity works powerfully on behalf of the gay/lesbian community. This view is summarized by gay activist Robert Goss (1993), who asserts that creating and assuming an identity transforms "silence into power and the production of truth. . . . It breaks the cycle of hiddenness, isolation, anxiety, and pain that lesbians and gay men have experienced from internalized homophobia" (p. 36). Moreover, the primary effects of the emergence of a gay identity have been widely celebrated through claims about the appearance of a gay/lesbian "community" and acclaim for organizations which have successfully advanced that community's interests. Sociologist Steven Seidman (1993) points out that a unitary gay identity is fundamental to coalescing gay communities (p. 121). Further, as social activists Derek Cohen and Richard Dyer (1980) note, the creation of a social identity, even when that identity is not explicitly political, is a prerequisite for political action (p. 172). In turn, political involvement reflexively solidifies a sense of identity. Sociologist Bert Klandermans (1992), for instance, suggests that collective action involves participants in new identities that evolve from the beliefs which attracted individuals to the collective in the first place (p. 93).

As used by lesbians and gay men, the term "community" has many meanings, referring to a concept of unity among those sharing the same sexual identity, the aggregation of gays/lesbians, the institutions created by gay people, and the safe "spaces" carved out by deviant individuals (Weston, 1996, p. 123). The emergence of an organized gay culture has been noted in London as early as the late 18th century, evidenced by development of an argot and the opening of places of retreat and pleasure for men drawn to other men (Norton, 1992, p. 10). Only in the last century has the existence of such a community become general public knowledge (Weeks, 1981, p. 110). Chauncey (1994) extensively documents his belief that, beginning in the 1890s, a highly visible gay world took shape in New York City, a world consisting of gay neighborhoods, social events, and many commercial establishments (pp. 33-45). Out of this world developed a culture with its own language, customs, folk histories, and heroes.

This gay milieu was largely policed out of existence in the 1930s in an effort to eliminate the appearance of homosexuality in the public sphere (Chauncey, 1994, pp. 1-2, 9). World War II, as historian Martin Duberman (1993) demonstrates, reinvigorated gay life: "Many men and women who had grown up in rural areas or small towns and had regarded themselves as singular freaks, discovered in military service legions of others who shared their sexual orientation" (p. 76). These individuals frequently decided to resettle in large cities, thereby initiating a proliferation of gay life in urban enclaves (p. 76). There emerged first in these enclaves a variety of recreational centers, including bars, bath houses, social clubs, and bookstores. In major urban centers, a wider range of gay institutions developed later, including newspapers, theaters, sex clubs, community centers, and political organizations. With the AIDS epidemics, health care organizations flourished, along with fundraising and political mobilization for AIDS research and services (Kaplan, 1997, p. 37).

The building of loosely articulated gay communities throughout the United States and Western Europe can be understood as the result of the push of societal rejection of lesbians and gay men, and the pull of the gay world both as a solution to problems of visibility and an opportunity for a protected environment within which to live a full cultural life (Plummer, 1975, p. 167). Further, these communities were a conscious effort to develop a unitary lesbian and gay identity beyond self-presentation into an institutionally complete subculture (Seidman, 1993, p. 116). Finally, the development of the gay community can be understood as market driven. The most visible institutions of the community are the bars, restaurants, newspapers, and varied businesses of urban commercial districts (Warner, 1993, p. xvi).

There is considerable debate as to whether a "gay culture" developed within the gay community. Certainly, as sociologist Martin Levine (1992) concludes, the early gay world functioned as an impoverished cultural unit consisting largely of "socially isolated, self-hating social networks and gathering places" (p. 73). Browning (1993) asserts that gay male culture is only a transitional refuge against hatred or a temporary fragment of a self-conscious culture of desire (p. 8). Contradicting this position, other gay advocates maintain that though gay culture is not monolithic, it does constitute a "way of living" (Shepherd & Wallis, 1989, p. 15). In such a view, the social forms of gay culture are increasingly constituted by distinct social practices (Herdt & Boxer, 1992, p. 4). Given the heterogeneous composition of the gay community, the practices which it produces are strikingly diverse. As gay advocate Michael Bronski (1998) points out, "since the gay community is composed of women and men with a wide range of other identities—racial, national, class, ethnic, religious—its boundaries are open-ended" (p. 54).

Despite its fluidity and the broad range of its cultural practices, the modern lesbian and gay community consists minimally of social networks through which individuals who would not otherwise be in contact with each other can shape and articulate their understanding of themselves as homosexual subjects (Adam, 1987, p. 6). However the gay community and its culture may be construed, the creation of channels for extensive intragroup communication provided the basic condition for the transformation of some gay and lesbian people into political actors and for the organization of collective action (Taylor & Whittier, 1992, p. 104). Sociologist Carl Boggs (1986) asserts that gay political action developed out of

large and active subcultural environments in which individuals could produce collective demands "not only for a new kind of personal and community life but for the extension of civil rights to all areas of gay life" (p.
44). Such a community, no matter how fragile, provided the affinity
groups, free spaces, and prefigurative modes of collective action required
by high risk gay/lesbian politics (Gamson, 1992a, p. 62).

The appearance of gay and lesbian movements, which made political
demands for social change, certainly depended upon the prior creation of
gay identity and culture (Cruikshank, 1992, p. 2). While some individuals
might personally prefigure organized political resistance, however,
movements on behalf of the gay/lesbian community could only begin
"after a certain critical mass of collective awareness of oppression, and
a determination to end it, has been reached" (Duberman, 1993, p. 75).
Henry Gerber, a Chicago postal worker, founded the Society for Human
Rights in the early 1920s. His organizing effort attracted six members and
quickly ended in 1925 with his arrest on obscenity charges which were
later dismissed (Loughery, 1998, pp. 53-55). Bereft of the support of a social group and without a network to provide resources, effective political
campaigns could not develop.

The emergence of relatively stable gay organizations occurred first in
the subcultural enclaves which developed following World War II
(Duberman, 1993, p. 76). An initial phase of the drive to organize collective representation of homosexuals centered on homophile endeavors to
obtain limited legal reform. This effort was eclipsed in the late 1960s and
early 1970s by the gay liberation movement which militantly promoted
the cause of breaching rigid gender divisions and breaking sexual prohibitions. Following the general decline of New Left activism, liberationist activity was displaced by the gay civil rights movement whose goals, like
those of the homophile movement, were limited, but whose modes of action owed much to the defiant militancy of gay liberation (Weeks, 1977,
p. 6). While the gay civil rights movement currently dominates the representation of gay/lesbian political activism in the United States, "queer" organizations and advocates seeking a more inclusive politics have recently
emerged, advancing a poststructuralist critique of both society and a gay
movement based on a politics of identity (Seidman, 1993, p. 136).

The first discernible efforts to organize gay and lesbian collective action became visible in the early 1950s in an environment marked by tension between two developments. The first is the emergence of a rudimentary gay culture in America's urban centers. The second is a vigorous

campaign against homosexuality, begun in the 1930s, which intensified during the Cold War anticommunist hysteria. The milieu in which early gay movements coalesced was truly daunting. Even as opportunities to assume gay or lesbian identity were enhanced, the dangers of doing so increased (D'Emilio, 1992, p. 10). For almost all Americans, homosexuals, far from being an oppressed people, were understood as isolated individuals who threatened society's welfare by engaging in obscene sexual practices which violated accepted norms and common decency (D'Emilio, 1983, p. 9). Animosity toward gay people was heightened as they became a target for a widespread campaign to rebuild patterns of sexuality and gender undermined by depression and war (D'Emilio, 1989b, p. 236).

Thus, when Harry Hay and a small band of other Southern California gay men launched the Mattachine Society in 1951, neither the larger society nor even other homosexuals were responsive to their message (Loughery, 1998, p. 220). The founders of the Mattachine Society promulgated the belief that homosexuals constitute an oppressed cultural minority which should transform itself from an objective social category into a group acting in its common interests. The goal of the organization's founders was to stimulate consciousness of group identity, thereby mobilizing a large gay constituency and molding it into a cohesive political group (D'Emilio, 1983, pp. 63-65).

The radicalism of the early Mattachine Society, however, was inconsistent with the perceived realities of postwar gay life. In comparison to other minorities, the distinctive nature of gay culture was not obvious to most gay men and women. Moreover, given the increasing aggressiveness of conservative attacks on sexual "perverts," an appropriate strategy for even those few homosexuals who would participate in the homophile movement seemed to be to emphasize similarity rather than difference (D'Emilio, 1983, p. 75). Consequently, disagreement quickly arose within the Mattachine Society between the founders' minority group model of social action and newer members' emphasis on assimilation. At the third annual convention of the Society in 1953, a motion was passed to delete the words "homosexual," "ethic," and "culture" from the organization's statement of purpose. The majority believed that these words invited retribution from an offended public (Winters, 1997/1954, p. 317). The basis for the new homophile ideology is well summarized by Marilyn Rieger's declaration in 1953 that "we know that we are the same, no different than anyone else. Our only difference is an unimportant one to the heterosexual society, *unless we make it important*." For her, the only way to eliminate misconceptions about homosexuality was "by integrating . . . not as homosexuals, but as people, as men and women whose homosexuality is irrelevant to our ideals, our principles, our hopes and aspirations" (quoted in D'Emilio, 1983, p. 79).

The Mattachine Society was soon joined by a number of other homophile organizations. In 1952, activists who resented the assimilationist takeover of the Mattachine Society founded *ONE Magazine* which soon spun off One, Inc. and its educational arm, the One Institute (Loughery, 1998, pp. 234-237). In contrast to the reconstituted Mattachine Society, *ONE Magazine* took a militant civil rights stance, strongly decrying the injustice that "homosexuals do not have the civil rights assured all other citizens" (Blasius & Phelan, 1997, p. 309). The Daughters of Bilitis was organized in 1955 out of another tension, this one between the gay men who dominated the early homophile organizations and lesbians who believed that male concerns with police harassment had shoved women's interests to one side (D'Emilio, 1983, p. 105).

Despite the fact that a major emphasis of the homophile movements of the 1950s and early 1960s was education through publication of newsletters and magazines, the circulation of the principal gay/lesbian outlets was very limited. The combined circulation nationwide of the three leading publications—*The Mattachine Review, ONE Magazine,* and *The Ladder* was only 8,000 copies (Loughery, 1998, p. 262). Though the homophile organizations did not reach most lesbian and gay persons, they did reach influentials who initiated debate and presented themes which would continue to be important in the gay movement (e.g., minority group vs. unimportant characteristic; an oppressive system vs. individual prejudice; political action vs. educational work) (D'Emilio, 1983, pp. 3, 90). The militants of the 1950s made a beginning toward advancing a minority group vision in which lesbians and gay men joined to battle an oppressive system through collective action (p. 244).

In the 1960s, a militant philosophy and pattern of action, popularized by the visibility of the black civil rights crusade, became dominant in the movement. Civil rights became a master action frame for expressing gay and lesbian concerns (McAdam, 1994, pp. 41-42). The new militants carried with them a belief in equal rights for all minorities and an emphasis on direct action protest techniques (D'Emilio, 1983, p. 150). The rise of the New Left also had a powerful catalyzing influence on gay/lesbian collective action (Adam, Duyvendak, & Krouwel, 1999, p. 1). By 1968, the Fifth North American Conference of Homophile Organizations

(NACHO), despite continuing internal dissension, had articulated the slogan "Gay is Good." It adopted a "Gay Bill of Rights," demanding repeal of sodomy laws, the end of entrapment, elimination of employment discrimination based on sexual orientation, and the right to serve openly in the military (Loughery, 1998, p. 306). Equally important, the theme of gay militancy began to resonate within the culture, making possible the mobilization of large numbers of individuals who found activism consistent with the increasing visibility of lesbians and gay men (D'Emilio, 1983, pp. 176, 195).

In the late 1960s and early 1970s, gay liberationist leaders radicalized through their experiences in black and student organizations gave serious challenge to civil rights as the goal of gay collective action. Sociologist Barry Adam (1987) describes the leaders of gay liberation as motivated by their hatred of a corrupt establishment which led them to conclude that "civil rights had become passe: why petition to be let into a social system so deeply riven by racism, sexism, militarism, and heterosexism" (p. 76). An effect of the rise of gay liberation was to divide gay advocates into civil rights activists who wanted to reinforce the homosexual/heterosexual distinction and liberationists who wanted to erase this distinction as part of a global revolutionary crusade. Accompanying this ideological division was a divergence in political style, with civil rights advocates employing pressure group tactics against established institutions and liberationists emphasizing antiestablishment street protest (Bronski, 1998, p. 68; Padgug, 1989, p. 302). Gay liberationists also argued that the movement should promote gay pride in order to strike at what they perceived to be the cultural basis of homophobia. Gay liberation developed a coalition politics which emphasized the importance of joint action on behalf of all oppressed people. Consequently, liberationists not only demonstrated for gay causes, but on behalf of women, Third World countries, blacks, and farm workers (Shilts, 1993, p. 95).

At the center of gay liberation theory was the presupposition that human nature is polymorphous and androgynous. "Liberation politics aimed at freeing individuals from the constraints of a sex/gender system that locked them into mutually exclusive homo/hetero and feminine/masculine roles" (Rofes, 1996, p. 110). Rather than opposing specific forms of oppression, gay liberationists attacked the social structures which confined sexuality to monogamous heterosexual families (Adam, 1987, p. 78). At minimum, liberationists took the position that, instead of reinforcing the boundaries between homosexuals and heterosexuals, the movement had to present a "much broader challenge to the commonly held notions regarding sexuality that now prevail" (Birch, 1980, p. 86). More broadly, liberationists sought "not so much the rights of the homosexual, but the pleasures and joy in all their multiform ways of the whole body" (Weeks, 1980, p. 20). In addition, gay liberation emphasized a politics of visibility and the importance of creating a gay counterculture which would work in coalition with other revolutionary factions to end oppression (Vaid, 1995, p. 57). The utopian vision of gay liberation was captured in the slogan "Out of the closets and into the streets" (Bronski, 1998, pp. 68, 163).

The gay liberation movement lasted for only a few years during the 1970s. Liberationist organizations ceased to exist shortly after their founding, torn apart by internal discord and failure to continue to attract member support (Marcus, 1993, p. 257). The impetus behind gay liberation also weakened with the general decline of New Left movements in the late 1970s. As a result, reformist groups were left to occupy the field (Adam, 1987, p. 82). Leaders of the gay civil rights movement from the late 1970s to the present time, however, did not share the self-doubt and deference of the earlier homophile effort. Gay and lesbian civil rights leaders were emboldened by the growth of gay enclaves, increasing visibility, the doctrine of gay pride, and a modicum of media support and legislative success (Adam, 1987, pp. 97-99; Shilts, 1993, p. 213).

The lesbian and gay rights movement of the late 1980s and 1990s is distinguishable from its predecessors in several ways. First, civil rights now included not just protection of a behavior, but rights which attached to an identity (Bronski, 1995, p. 23). The right to have same-sex sex became less important than full citizenship as a gay or lesbian person. What gay activist Dennis Altman (1980) calls the "invention of the ethnic homosexual" led to widespread emphasis on equality as a substitute for the liberationist demand to release the homosexuality in everyone (p. 61). Second, the new civil rights movement did not emphasize the withdrawal of state power, but its extension to protect those who openly possessed a gay/lesbian identity and who wanted their "relational rights" recognized (Blasius, 1994, p. 132). Herman (1997) writes that the new gay/lesbian civil rights agenda required "state activism, not withdrawal, encompassing inclusion in antidiscrimination legislation, as well as spousal/family rights to marriage, pensions, and other forms of social entitlement" (p. 2).

Movement organizations which promote civil rights have not entirely dominated the representation of gay people in the public sphere. Aside from political activism, gay men and women endeavored to achieve social integration or cultural change. For some gay activists, cultural work is more important than politics because most lesbians and gay men, like everyone else, "drew upon popular culture for recognition and validation of their existence" (Bronski, 1998, p. 74). Recently, the most significant internal challenge to the lesbian and gay civil rights movement has come from activists and scholars who under the sign "queer" have challenged the ethnic identity model on which the new civil rights movement is built. "Queer" in its current political usage signifies a "politics and theory with a difference, typically a generational difference, but also a (asserted) difference of style, of strategy, of tactics, of ideology" (Walters, 1996, p. 833). This development can be understood as a protest by individuals who are marginalized in the mainstream gay movement dominated by a white, middle-class and, often, male cadre. Seidman (1993) characterizes this protest as a "revolt of the social periphery against the center, only this time the center was not mainstream America but a dominant gay culture" (p. 118).

Queer theory and activism frame culture as the chief battleground on which to fight against the regulation of sexuality. This frame requires putting aside identity politics. Culture must be changed, as English Professor Michael Warner (1993) argues, "because the logic of the sexual order is so deeply embedded by now in an indescribably wide range of social institutions. . . . Queer struggles aim not just at toleration or equal status but at challenging those institutions and accounts" (p. xiii). Such a view repeats themes earlier represented in gay liberation theory which celebrated the proliferation of many forms of intimate life (Seidman, 1993, p. 115). Queer political action followed the earlier liberationist modes of action by engaging in a "politics of carnival, transgression, and parody which leads to deconstruction, decentering, revisionist readings" (Stein & Plummer, 1996, p. 134). However, moving beyond a dialectic of difference based on sexual object choice, queer theory also brings attention to multiple differences: "Thus, the dominant liberationist opposition between gay/straight and gay/lesbian passes into divisions between, say white/black gay, black/Latino gay, middle-class/working class gay, or lesbian/lesbian S/M, and so on" (Seidman, 1993, p. 129). Within a culture which multiplies division, queer activism seeks to achieve unity by celebrating difference, subverting identity and attempting to mobilize on the basis of diversity, striving to value all individuals left powerless and unrepresented in the heteronormative social structure (Slagle, 1995, pp. 92-94). The goal of queer action, therefore, is to revolutionize the culture by challenging a gay politics founded on identity. Such an identity normalizes the gay/lesbian subject and thereby consolidates "heterosexuality and homosexuality as master categories of sexual and social identity" (Seidman, 1996, p. 12).

The evolution of gay/lesbian movements has not occurred because of specific incidents. Important events such as publication of studies by Kinsey, Pomeroy, and Martin (1948) and Hooker (1957) not only brought public attention to homosexuality, but raised serious questions about the accepted belief that homosexuals were few in number and emotionally disturbed. But more important, the emergence of gay networks and media made possible multiple and even divergent homophile movements. Occurrences such as the Stonewall Riot in 1969 only symbolized a broader drift of the entire society and the gay community to dramatic forms of militance. Through a continuing reciprocal relationship in which the formation of a rudimentary community made movement possible, and movement then shaped the culture of that community, specific forms of social action emerged which turned homosexuality into a topic of well publicized contention (Blasius, 1994, p. 129). As Adam (1987) asserts, "only by embracing it as an identity could homosexual desire be reorganized as a collectivity capable of defending itself from its enemies" (p. 107). However, this defense subsequently produced enemies in new form because the visibility and force of progay collective action elicited militant reaction. Even though many in the gay and lesbian community regard the movements through which they are represented as moderate reform efforts, traditionalist religious and political activists proclaimed that the organization of collective homosexual action threatened the foundation of sex roles, gender, the regulation of sex, and the nature of the citizen's proper relationship to government (Cruikshank, 1992, p. 2).

The Rise of Antigay Traditionalism

The antigay reaction to both gay civil rights gains and increasing cultural visibility of homosexual people has often been labeled a backlash, a response by the larger society which grows out of a general rejection of same-sex sex (Gallagher & Bull, 1996, p. xiii). Antigay political action, of course, cannot be considered solely a response to gay/lesbian efforts, but instead ought to be understood as a response to basic social processes which have created a "profound shift in the role of evangelicals in American life, a transition from cultural insiders to cultural outsiders" (Watson, 1997, p. 13). In general, the radical alteration during the second half of the 20th century of many institutions which individuals believe are foundational to their lives led inevitably to demands for a restoration of traditional modes of life (Bronski, 1998, p. 244). Religious historian Martin Marty (1984) writes that fundamentalism is a phenomenon which has recently become powerful and aggressive in response to a number of conditions including dislocations produced by modernity, a renewed desire to establish a fixed identity in a shifting world, a sense that value structures have disintegrated and must be restored, and the availability of new technology to narrowcast messages (p. 65). The fundamentalist impulse is not limited to the United States or the West, but is instead a worldwide "strategy, or set of strategies, by which beleaguered believers attempt to preserve their distinctive identity as a people or group" (Marty & Appleby, 1993, p. 1).

A key aspect of identity maintenance by fundamentalist groups is to endow boundaries with sacred power. Boundary building is not, of course, unique to fundamentalists. Anthropologist Mary Douglas (1978/1966) points out that all cultures create order by systematically imposing structure on chaotic experience. She asserts that "it is only by exaggerating the difference between within and without, above and below, male and female, with and against, that a semblance of order is created" (p. 3). Consequently, boundary anomalies are powerfully disruptive of order and, at the same time, potentially definitive of the boundaries which society seeks to maintain (pp. 4, 94, 121). If any society possesses a moral order consisting of more or less fixed boundaries, then various kinds of transgression necessarily evoke social reactions because people will go to great lengths to defend their symbolic worlds from chaos (Aho, 1990, p. 84). The religiously orthodox are chief among those persons who accept dogma which bestows special significance on their role in keeping intact traditional boundaries which they regard as timeless and sacred. For the orthodox, the necessity for building a tradition and keeping it unqualified arises from "their very identity and purpose as religious people (both collectively and individually). . . . For the orthodox, the symbolic boundaries mean everything" (Hunter, 1987, p. 158).

The fundamentalist impulse, based on a strong version of the human proclivity to bring order to experience through culture, has recently become prominent once again in American politics. Although religious in

foundational justification, what has been produced through political action is a cultural fundamentalism which, at core, is a protest against social
change in the form of the shifting social position of women, perceived
threats by public authorities to traditionalist values and institutions, acceptance of homosexuality, the loss of religious symbols in the public
sphere, and a general increase in sexual openness and freedom
(Blanchard, 1994, p. 41; Guth, 1996, p. 13). Mounting a defense against
perceived cultural chaos produced a populist vision of the institutions
which most needed defending: the traditional male-led family, a Biblical
moral code, and the self-reliant entrepreneur (Kazin, 1995, p. 256).

The strengthening of fundamentalism in American society can be understood as an effort on the part of the religiously and socially orthodox
to take advantage of action opportunities which have recently prolifer-
ated. Sociologist John Simpson (1992) maintains that the patriarchal-
heterosexual model accepted as inerrant by fundamentalists is antitheti-
cal to the belief that everyone should participate equally and freely in all
institutions. Consequently, when powerful pressure exists to eradicate
boundaries which have excluded women, homosexuals, and racial and
ethnic minority groups from full participation in the public sphere, an action opportunity arises for fundamentalists:

> Using the social logic of contrast, distinction, and difference, it can set itself
> apart and reinforce the boundaries separating it from those who advocate
> equality for all, irrespective of gender and sexual orientation. Constructed
> differences become a basis for oppositional action. (p. 25)

In this interpretation, the increasing visibility of fundamentalism is not
due to an increase in the popularity of its doctrines, but to exogenous
events which provide action opportunities to establish itself as a vital resource opposed to the extension and institutionalization of human rights.

Simpson's interpretation is plausible in that it accounts for the episodic
reappearance of fundamentalism in American life. Fundamentalists in the
1920s gained visibility by taking advantage of the action opportunities offered by issues concerning liquor, evolution, Bolshevism, Catholicism,
and the Social Gospel. International communism provided an important
target of opportunity in the 1950s. Events in the 1970s precipitated a resurgence of the fundamentalist impulse in America. Among the triggering
conditions which contributed to the revitalization and reorganization of
the New Christian Right were perceived threats posed by the feminist and

gay movements, the *Roe v. Wade* reproductive rights decision, local battles over textbook content, the national struggle over the Equal Rights Amendment, and contests with the Internal Revenue Service over the tax-exempt status of religious schools (Shaw, 1997, pp. 8-10).

Despite the diversity of causes which recently brought fundamentalism again into political engagement, generalizations can be drawn about the orthodox belief system. Social scientist Jerome Himmelstein (1990) argues correctly that, despite the disparate list of social changes traditionalists oppose, several common themes are clearly dominant. Among these are support for the constraints imposed by traditional roles and norms, and opposition to "emphasis on individual self-determination and self-fulfillment, and too much play for personal drives and whims" (p. 105). Underlying these themes is the notion that the foundations of American society—traditional morality, religion, community, and family—are under attack from liberals operating through government and the media (Himmelstein, 1983, p.16). In the words of evangelical leader Pat Robertson, the "centers of power in our culture—government, education, media, business, and philanthropy are firmly in the hands of secular humanists who are exerting every effort to debase and eliminate Bible-based Christianity from our society" (quoted in Cantor, 1994, p. 12).

The basic division between fundamentalists and those whom they identify as the enemies of American society has been thoroughly analyzed by sociologist James Davison Hunter. He argues (1991) that, given America's moral pluralism, fundamentalists are engaged in a competition to define social reality, a battle to "determine who is stronger, which alliance has the institutional resources capable of sustaining a particular definition of reality against the wishes of those who would project an alternate view of the world" (p. 158). Their construction of reality includes a commitment to a supernatural external authority which defines a "consistent, unchangeable measure of value, purpose, goodness, and identity, both personal and collective" (pp. 39, 43). The identity of communities which accept an orthodox external reality is deeply threatened by progressivist impulses which challenge and resymbolize historic faiths, thereby reordering basic relationships in society. These challenges have recently emerged from the new class of knowledge workers that dominates science based enterprises, the information industry, and public policy research. In contrast to fundamentalists, members of this new class both justify their beliefs and defend their behavior "solely on the basis of rationally deduced arguments and not on the basis of traditional societal authority—religious, bureaucratic, or familial" (Hunter, 1983a, pp. 107-108).

The new information class, condensed into the term "secular humanist," becomes a convenient explanation in traditionalist discourse for a wide range of social evils (Diamond, 1989, p. 85). In fundamentalist rhetoric, the production of an organized secular humanist opposition is at its core an attempt to create a good/evil dichotomy by polarizing religious belief against a vague philosophy of moral relativism (Daniels, Jensen, & Lichtenstein, 1985, p. 253). Attack on secular humanism, however, is only an expression of a more profound political effort to revitalize comprehensively a society which is radically disrupted (Capps, 1992, p. 200). The generalized goal of fundamentalist political action, then, has become the reoccupation of secular institutions by those who believe in a traditionalist social order (Diamond, 1989, p. 138).

Much of the disagreement which creates an action opportunity for traditionalists centers on a cluster of public issues which concerns, ironically, the private sphere. Marty (1984) asserts that fundamentalists have concentrated their efforts in gaining control over the "intimate zones of life in their own religious communities" (p. 5). Efforts to gain control over the private lives of believers, however, has led in a highly integrated modern society to demands for the establishment of rigid rules and boundaries universally enforced by state power. The result is contention over a cluster of public issues concerned with the body, the most private of concerns. Tracing back to the question of how the human body should be regulated are issues concerning sex education, the "right to die," abortion, pornography, vulgarity in the arts, sexual harassment, AIDS policy, and homosexuality. These issues are filtered into the public sphere through policy questions arising in institutions which have authority over the human body—the law, the church, the school, and the family (Hunter, 1994, p. 3).

The family has become a central focus for fundamentalist concern, a "symbol of social stability and traditional moral virtue" (Hunter, 1987, p. 76). For evangelicals, the family is a "potent and multifaceted symbol of many of their concerns, as well as common ground with non-evangelicals on the political right" (Watson, 1997, p. 22). Within traditionalist discourse, the family is the middle-class nuclear family raised to a supernatural plane where it is divinely ordained. In this understanding, all variations from the nuclear family become morally reprehensible (Hardacre, 1993, p. 135). Fundamentalist discourse about the family is designed to reinvigorate a fading version of marital relations, weakened parental authority, and the increasingly secularized institutions of education, religion, and entertainment which environ the family (Diamond, 1989, p. 84). A particular understanding of gender is crucial to the fundamentalist conception of the family in which differences between the sexes are clearly defined, and gender boundary crossing should be severely punished (Lienesch, 1993, p. 92). Differences are hierarchically ordered. Men are in natural authority over women who are defined by family roles as wives and mothers (Klatch, 1987, p. 9).

Reinforcement of masculinity and protection of children from corruptive influence are salient themes in traditionalist discourse which defends the family. In his analysis of religious books on family life, political scientist Michael Lienesch (1993) discovered that an important line of thought consists of reestablishing male dominion by denouncing the decline of masculinity. He observes that the authors of these books insist that clear distinctions between the sexes should not be breached. Homosexuality and androgynous behavior thus become significant threats to the performance of manhood necessary for the survival of the family. Similarly, sociologist James Aho (1990) finds that in the drama of New Christian Right rhetoric, the protagonist is invariably a male who must reject both the feminine and feminization (pp. 3, 172). The protection of children in the family has also become a major fundamentalist theme. Who shall control children's minds is clearly a valued prize (Diamond, 1989, p. 84). Accordingly, there is frequent emphasis in fundamentalist discourse on protecting children from institutions dominated by secular humanists who control public schools, the entertainment industry, and government bureaucracy. One of the chief dangers to children is the promotion of homosexuality through these institutions (LaHaye, 1982, pp. 22, 198-200).

Acting to defend or restore the rigidly gender-ordered family, traditionalists have embraced opposition to public policy changes favorable to homosexuals (Herman, 1997, p. 60).

Although attempts have been made to explain traditionalist opposition to homosexuality as merely exploitative—a mobilizing issue to raise money and recruit members—there is a cultural logic behind the centrality of gay issues for traditionalists. Symbolic negative attitudes toward variant sexuality are indicative of a conviction that the promotion of homosexuality is an attack on core values (Herek, 1984, p. 12). Claims on behalf of full citizenship for homosexuals, Hunter (1991) asserts, radically "challenge the traditional assumptions of what nature will allow, the boundaries of the moral order, and finally the ideals of middle-class family life" (p. 189). In attempting to organize against such a challenge, conservative political and religious leaders explain all attempts to establish sexual diversity "as threats, attacks, or insults even when they are not so intended and would not necessarily be so interpreted spontaneously" (Greenberg, 1988, p. 472).

Traditionalist opponents of homosexuality tend to coalesce around religious belief. Many surveys have demonstrated that religious orthodoxy and opposition to public policy changes favoring homosexuals is closely correlated with strong religious belief, leading to a conclusion that "antigay measures are, at their heart, orthodox Christian measures" (Herman, 1997, pp. 3, 167). The bulk of evidence clearly supports the impression that the "primary contestants against gay rights were religious traditionalists" (Button, Rienzo, & Wald, 1997, p. 177). Churches have supplied the workers who are active in a variety of moral campaigns, among them those directed at public policy issues concerning variant sexuality (Adam, 1987, p. 104). These campaigns have mobilized the discontent with secular culture felt by a growing number of evangelical Christians who have been organized into a rapidly expanding network of religious and cultural organizations (Himmelstein, 1990, p. 8). This expansion is made possible by the fervent embrace of modern means of communication by parachurch organizations which have spread opposition to modern secularism through state-of-the-art media and computer technology. Most visible in this effort has been the rise of televangelical ministries emphasizing social issues (Balmer, 1989, p. 64; Diamond, 1989, p. 2).

As an important element in traditionalist discourse, opposition to homosexuality is far from new. However, in the 1950s, homosexuality was only one among many manifestations of "sexual depravity" which traditionalists condemned, and this depravity was itself only one among many signs of cultural degeneration. In early traditionalist construction of the homosexual, the chief cause of concern was male same-sex acts. This discourse featured the homosexual as "tragic rather than dangerous; to be pitied, rather than vilified" (Herman, 1997, pp. 31, 42). Beginning in the late 1960s and 1970s, representation shifted in two ways. First, homosexuality ceased to be one of many sexual sins and became the cardinal sexual transgression. Second, concern shifted away from the individual homosexual and came to rest on the homosexual movement and its agenda. Herman observes that, beginning in the 1970s, homosexual militancy came to be portrayed as subverting Christianity by popularizing a "heresy increasingly sanctioned by the state in the form of decriminalization and the extension of civil rights" (p. 50).

Though some antigay activists are not evangelicals, the strategic moralism which evangelical fundamentalists bring to social issues such as homosexuality inject into cultural politics a profound sense of commitment (Lienesch, 1993, p. 12). As historian Charles Strozier (1994) observes, fundamentalist "certainty about ultimate issues lends ideological clarity to proximate concerns like gender equality, free speech, sexual choice, and curriculum change" (p. 252). Accompanying the cultural imperatives which traditionalists bring to the politics of morality is a sense of community which is equally or more important than specific doctrinal positions (Gellner, 1992, p. 3). Professor of religion Randall Balmer (1989) argues that evangelicals built a subculture for themselves as a defense against the larger American culture which had become hostile to them after the 1920s. To maintain this symbolically constructed subculture, evangelicals "smugly contrasted their world with the outside world in a kind of orgy of dualistic rhetoric" (p. 232). Those within the fundamentalist subculture were good, righteous and saved, but those without were portrayed as evil, secular, and damned. The fundamentalist subculture broke out of its boundaries only in the 1970s, when a "conservative mood swing looked congenial and when politicians promised, in effect, to impose the ethos of the evangelical subculture on *all* of American society" (p. 232).

Antigay traditionalists, along with other evangelical fundamentalists, embarked on political action committed to an expansive and activist state. They intended to "make the state act as a conservative moral leader, by example and by edict" (Herman, 1997, p. 171). For antigay activists, this meant that the state should discourage homosexuality through (a) enforcing laws against homosexual acts, representations, and associations, (b) withholding state protection from homosexual identities and relationships, and (c) denying homosexuals full citizenship. Specifically, this position led to demands for laws aimed at sodomy, pornography, and disorderly conduct; rejection of nondiscrimination ordinances based on sexual orientation; and refusal to allow openly homosexual persons to serve in the armed forces or to be employed as teachers. Support for an activist state, however, is inconsistent with the beliefs of the secular conservatives with whom traditionalists sought coalition. Religious moralism is not, of course, inevitably supportive of a conservative agenda. As historian Garry Wills (1990) points out, traditionalists have in other times worked toward an integration of evangelical moralism and a progressive politics (pp. 106-107). However, religious traditionalism in the second half of the 20th century made a firm alliance with conservative movements, creating a coalition with anticommunists, opponents of racial integration, and advocates of less government interference in the economy (Diamond, 1995, pp. 9-10).

The merger of moral traditionalists with economic and racial libertarians in a traditionalist movement was based on an internally consistent ideology. Social scientist Sara Diamond (1995) asserts that the conservative united front acted "to support the state as *enforcer* of order and to oppose the state as *distributor* of wealth and power downward and more equitably in society" (p. 9). Behind such a position lies belief in an organic social order which functions without conscious direction, the importance of private property and initiative, and resistance to the egalitarian impulse. In its antigay manifestation, this ideology supports the state as the agency for society's natural rejection of homosexuality. But it denies the state a role in imposing nondiscrimination policies which would limit individual expression of bias and encourage recognition of homosexuals as equal to heterosexuals.

Profound differences, however, threatened to divide libertarians and religious traditionalists (Klatch, 1987, p. 4). Himmelstein (1990) observes that libertarians promoted individualism and moral agnosticism. They favored a minimalist state assuring no more than negative freedom, and pure capitalism as the sovereign defense against collectivism. In contrast, traditionalists understood society as a web of community relationships which transcends individuals. Believing that a moral vacuum produced the collectivist state, they sought to fulfill a higher good which was more important than negative freedom, and they were wary of a capitalist system which went beyond small business and individual property owners. In taking these positions, traditionalists advanced views which their libertarian brethren could not easily abide:

> Totalitarianism arises in effect from too much individualism, not too little
> . . . the real danger is that the breakdown of social bonds and transcendent
> values will yield to a mass of rootless, atomized individuals preoccupied
> with material goals, who will ultimately yearn for the ersatz community and
> utopian lure of totalitarianism. (Himmelstein, 1990, pp. 53-54)

For traditionalists, the state must act to maintain community by enforcing on the individual positive values that produce social order.

The reconciliation of traditionalism and libertarianism within conservative ideology has not been complete, but a *modus vivendi* has been worked out which makes joint collective action possible. In the fusionist position which has produced a significant degree of unity in the New Right, loss of freedom was linked to loss of community and moral order. Moreover, economic relations were assigned to the realm of liberty, where God's invisible hand established order. In contrast, sexual and domestic relations were assigned to the realm of traditionalism, where the sinful individual unconstrained by government would create destructive disorder. Both government intervention in the economy and failure to support godly community values were equally subversive and fervently supported by the liberal archenemy (Himmelstein, 1990, pp. 45, 62).

This fusionist position works well in connection with antigay conservative advocacy. Traditionalists and libertarians may not fully comprehend one another's language, but both languages may circulate simultaneously as instruments for mobilizing support and persuading the general public. For traditionalists, homosexuality remains a sin contrary to community well-being, a transgression which the state must punish and, under no circumstances, encourage. Without having to accept fully this position, libertarians add that government attempts to promote homosexuality inevitably involve loss of freedom. From their perspective, nondiscrimination laws based on sexual orientation nullify the right to choose employees freely and to use property without restriction. Hate crime ordinances, they conclude, abridge freedom of thought and expression.

Although libertarians might not voice enthusiastic support for criminal sanctions against homosexuals, they join the traditionalist chorus in preventing government from legitimating homosexuality by granting "special rights." To the degree that progay movements have advanced beyond fighting against criminalization to asking for government recognition of civil and relational rights, the fusionist position has become increasingly powerful. The expanding place of antigay rhetoric in conservative campaigns may be attributable to the reconciling power of the homosexual as a representation of what is wrong with the liberal state which neglects its moral duty while promoting evil through the restriction of freedom

(Kaplan, 1997, p. 162). At the same time, there remains tension within the traditionalist movement between those who advocate antigay public policy positions out of fundamentalist religious motive and the "rights pragmatists" who subscribe to a libertarian position (Herman, 1997, p. 112).

In organizing antigay political action, however, religious traditionalists have a considerable advantage over their libertarian allies. Traditionalists can contribute to the present effort the dense organizational infrastructure of their subculture, which includes electronic ministries, networks of churches, and supradenominational organizations through which leaders, followers, and their resources can be mobilized in campaigns for public morality (Himmelstein, 1990, p. 98). Within this alliance, traditionalist antigay discourse proved a powerful force, while libertarian appeals could be employed opportunistically by religious and secular antigay advocates in addressing the public outside of the evangelical-fundamentalist subculture (R. Smith, 1997, p. 95).

For antigay crusades, no less than for progay efforts, the formulation of public claims in policy debate is largely in the hands of a host of organizations which have been developed to articulate political claims. Sociologist Robert Wuthnow (1994) provides an insightful analysis of the process by which organizations have become the representatives of traditionalism. He argues that because of the growing role of the state, discussions of public policy which have moral dimensions are increasingly carried on by professional advocates employed by organizations. Thus, "religious special interest groups proliferate to lobby Capitol Hill for various bills that have moral implications or affect the ability of religious organizations to carry on their basic ministries" (p. 94). Of course, organizational advocates are not unique to traditionalist organizations. Gay/lesbian political action is also dominated to a significant degree by advocacy organizations (Vaid, 1995, pp. 213-233). Despite the importance of grassroots efforts, such professionalized social movements have become the common form of recent collective effort (McCarthy & Zald, 1987, p. 373). Bourdieu (1991) correctly observes that politics in all its forms consists of efforts by professionals to speak on behalf of the non-professionals (p. 190). Not surprisingly, then, both progay and antigay public policy influence is significantly exercised through organizations led by cultural entrepreneurs.

Many effects are produced by the domination of debate over variant sexuality by organizations which use professional media relations techniques and lobbying skills. First, because of the professionalization of cultural politics, individuals cannot have a presence in public policy determination unless they speak through professional advocates who have acquired the right to represent them (Thompson, 1991, p. 26). As a consequence, organizations of professional advocates may become remote from their constituents both in ideology and strategy. Second, advocacy organizations generate a high degree of both external and internal competition which may prove divisive. Wuthnow (1994) notes that political organizations act in opposition to one another, "functioning as 'struggle groups' whose aim is to win some objective against the resistance of other groups with opposing objectives" (pp. 88-89). Internally, organizations must compete with one another to secure scarce resources from a limited constituency (p. 29). Externally, they are committed by self-interest to a conflict without end. Third, organizations, with their commitment both to self-preservation and to energizing their membership bases, systematically distort moral debate. The result is an intensification of polarities that makes the "rational exchange of opposing claims virtually impossible" (Hunter, 1994, p. 37).

In summary, what has developed in the United States in the past fifty years is a continuous and cacophonous public debate over variant sexuality. The origins of this debate cannot be simplified into gay/lesbian resistance to medieval customs or into righteous backlash against the promotion of sodomy. Although the depiction of the "eternal homosexual" in perpetual battle against exemplars of unchanging faith is a commonplace in the discourse of progay/antigay contests, this representation oversimplifies a considerably more complex story. Key to understanding this story is the emergence of the homosexual as a subject for diagnosis and of the gay/lesbian person as a political actor. Progay advocacy has been multivocal, changing over time in response to social context. Similarly, antigay advocacy has also been historically contingent and does not consist of support for a monolithic position. The representation of actors and of their contest in this ongoing controversy is sufficiently fluid to cause opponents to deeply influence one another. The question to be addressed now is how this influence can be analyzed.

2 Analysis of Communication in Contests Over Variant Sexuality

The discourses produced by progay and antigay advocates can be analyzed from many perspectives. While there is no sovereign program for structuring information about public debate on variant sexuality or drawing conclusions about it, we propose to employ a methodological sequence which will provide insights into mutual influence created by confrontation over homosexuality. Public policy discourse on variant sexuality can be analyzed from three related perspectives: (a) languaging strategies, (b) collective action, and (c) complex processes of interactional adjustment within an issue culture.

Language is marshaled into public policy struggle in many different forms. Advocates seek dominance for their lexicon, striving to naturalize their worldviews. They build arguments through language, employ ideographs, deploy condensation symbols, and spin narratives out of symbols. These uses of language are in the service of collective action. Interpretive communities in conjunction with the movements they spawn are central to the "culture war" metaphor of battles over variant sexuality policies. Such interpretation, however, neglects the dynamic of antagonistic enjoinment which through a movement/countermovement dialectic deeply influences both the creation of collective actors and the scripting of the drama in which they act. Movements endeavor to create change through the repertoire of communication patterns and technologies available to them, always seeking to promote collective action frames which mobilize and discipline followers and persuade a larger public. Advocates, often speaking in voices amplified by social movement organizations, bundle frames together in interpretive packages. The discourses which constitute these packages should not be considered in isolation. Taken together, they form an issue culture in which antagonists oppositionally cooperate in creating new identities, purposes, and relationships.

The struggle over public issues related to variant sexuality fundamentally concerns whether homosexuality should be excluded from all but stigmatized forms of public representation. This discussion quickly resolves itself into disagreement over whether the language of "sin, crime, and sickness" is more appropriate for homosexuality than a language of benign difference and civil rights. The appeals produced by both sides are quickly captured in slogans such as "no promo homo," "no special rights," "gay is good," and "We're here. We're queer. Get used to it." These slogans are supplemented by narratives which, for example, emphasize the loss of traditional families and communities or the violent consequences of antigay attitudes. The communities which employ these symbols and narratives understand themselves to be involved in movements which must use organizations and media relations practices to wage cultural war on the enemy. To consolidate their movement, progay advocates seek direct support from a network of lesbians and gay men rhetorically consolidated into a "gay community," which is then cast as a collective actor. In the same way, antigay advocates turn to evangelical religious communities and to libertarians of conservative bent. Both sides frame the issues of variant sexuality in partisan ways, as either a continuation of the epoch struggle for human freedom or an ongoing battle against decadence. In this process of oppositional framing, antagonistic advocates create an issue culture in which are represented gay and traditionalist identities and goals designed to influence public policy formation.

Languaging Strategies

In the past several decades, language has become central to the critical analysis of discourses which enter into public discussion and, more narrowly, to discourses which operate in debate over variant sexuality. A leading theoretician of political communication, Murray Edelman (1988), observes that the "most incisive twentieth century students of language converge from different premises on the conclusion that language is the key creator of the social worlds people experience, not a tool for describing objective reality" (p. 103). Cultural critic T. V. Reed identifies recognition of language's centrality to society with a growing acceptance of the proposition that "language uses people more fully than people use language" (p. 3). Interest in exploring the creation of discursive worlds leads critics to become deeply involved in the project of understanding every aspect of the world as text, with the result that the empirical search for objective reality becomes less important than attempts to discover the determinants and contingencies of historical-linguistic constructions (pp. 3, 7). This conclusion has led many rhetorical critics to accept the view that public debate should be conceived as "discursive symbolic action between rhetors and audiences by means of which humans negotiate social truth and power" (Iltis & Browne, 1990, p. 83).

Scholars in a variety of disciplines are involved in identifying changes in language which are tied to wider social and cultural shifts. Linguist Norman Fairclough (1992) believes that this approach not only brings greater attention to language as a social force, but also encourages recognition that "attempts to engineer the direction of change increasingly include attempts to change language practices" (p. 6). In the field of rhetorical criticism, a shift has occurred from conceiving communicative acts as occurring "subsequent to the construing of value and reality to the assertion of value and the meaning of materiality as qualities of the symbolic enactment of society" (Klumpp & Hollihan, 1989, p. 89).

Language is central to the process of public debate over social change. Hunter (1994) observes that "those who have the power to establish the language of public debate will have tremendous advantage in determining the debate's outcome" (p. 66). Rhetorical critic Celeste Condit (1990) extends this idea, observing that demands for social change are communicated through the medium of language which provides collective expression of social interests and conditions. Consequently, rhetoric "materializes ideas through the distribution of compelling vocabularies to large numbers of potent audience members or institutions" (p. 8).

Not surprising, then, almost any choice of language about variant sexuality will likely be contested because these choices invariably contain political strategies. Antigay advocates, for instance, condemn the progay movement for subverting the vocabulary of moral condemnation, for framing issues through such words as "gay" and "homophobia," and for appropriating the slogans of legitimate civil rights movements. Antigay advocate Enrique Rueda (1982), for example, argues that the homosexual movement seeks to profit illegitimately from the "appeal of such code words as human rights, privacy, minority rights, discrimination, dignity, and freedom" (pp. 68, 71, 76). In the same way, most of the terms used to refer to variant sexuality have been understood by gay advocates as constructing a language of domination and control. This understanding is present in Kaplan's (1997) conclusion that the categories of sexual classification and identification "were imposed by diverse social authorities working together to exercise control over individuals" (p. 80).

The power of language and, consequently, the importance of controlling language, emerge from its capacity to create and rank classifications. Sociologists Robert Hodge and Gunther Kress (1993) believe that a "classification system constrains thought, giving a basic unity to everything expressed within it, whatever its content, and making alternative systems of classification seem incommensurable" (p. 64). Through reshaping language, proponents of particular positions on social questions resignify what is at issue, thereby creating new knowledge. In the process of reconfiguring language, the "social production of new definitions in problematic areas produces both 'explanations' and 'justification' " (Hall, 1993, p. 72). In this way, the introduction of the word "gay" has both the power to explain same-sex erotic behavior and to justify that behavior as natural to the species of person who engages in it. Conversely, the definition of "family" as a procreative unit establishes the essence of the sexually acceptable and, at the same time, packages within that explanation reasons for rejecting homosexuality. By promoting to dominance terms favorable to them, advocates stake out claims to power over how social relations ought to be understood and evaluated (Herman, 1994, p. 64).

The rhetoric of social relations can be understood, therefore, as struggle over a structure of domination and subordination, in which

> dominant classes attempt to "naturalize" the meanings that serve their interests into the "common sense" of the society as a whole, whereas subordinate classes resist this process in various ways, and to varying degrees, and try to make meanings that serve their interests. (Fiske, 1992, p. 255)

In the debate over public policy concerning variant sexuality, the effort to defend a language which stigmatizes gay people can be understood as a method of shoring up dominance through insult. At the same time, efforts to reverse the valence of stigmatizing terms (e.g., turning "queer" into a positive label), can be understood as service to the interests of gay and lesbian people.

Struggle over language is recognized as a central feature of confrontation between traditionalist and progressive advocates. Each side denies the legitimacy of the other's pattern of speech. Consequently, language, as the ordering and valuing of symbols in society, becomes a "politicized dimension of the culture war" (Hunter, 1991, p. 184). For some observers, making claims to linguistic legitimacy seems dysfunctional because attempts to control symbols of legitimacy is strongly antidemocratic, challenging the right of others to produce speech (Hunter, 1983b, p. 162). Significantly, language itself is truncated in the struggle to achieve control as consequential social issues are often reduced to soundbite, aphorism, cliche, and slogan (Hunter, 1994, p. 9). Certainly, some of the advocacy produced around homosexuality does degenerate into exchanges featuring such terms as "homophobe," "bigot," "unnatural," "theocrat," "sex obsessed," and "special rights."

The terminology employed in public debate on variant sexuality can be understood more positively, however, as an attempt to reconstitute culture by changing meanings within language. A terministic analysis of rhetoric focuses on movement in language, especially the "ideographs, culture types, characterizations, myths, metaphors, narratives, and *topoi* employed in public discourse to argue collective being into existence" (Condit & Lucaites, 1991, p. 1). A number of approaches are available to communication analysts who would examine language produced in the variant sexuality debate. They might be concerned with ideographs, condensation symbols, supersaturated symbolic acts, and deployment of key terms.

Ideographs can be understood as terms central to a culture which warrant power, excuse eccentric or antisocial acts, and "guide behavior and belief into channels easily recognized by a community as acceptable and laudable" (McGee, 1980b, p. 15). Such terms are invoked differently in various rhetorical cultures. Tracing the history of such usage in any particular rhetorical culture can create a sense of "how social and political problems are constituted and negotiated through public discourse" (Condit & Lucaites, 1993, p. xii). Certainly, the manipulation of culturally constitutive terms such as "sin" and "rights" is a prominent feature of both antigay and progay discourses. The notion that same-sex erotic behavior is a "sin" circulates throughout antigay rhetoric, and the elaborate denial of the term's applicability is a constant in progay appeals. The ideograph "rights" assumes a number of different meanings in this debate, taking various shapes when described as "minority rights," "rights of the majority," and "special rights."

Another approach to the language of the variant sexuality debate lies in Murray Edelman's (1964) conception of condensation symbols: verbal acts that condense into symbolic representation such themes as patriotism, anxiety about social decline, the group's history, and hope for future achievement (p. 6). Condensation symbols do not have reference to objective experience, but arise out of the psychological needs of audiences for expressive vehicles of threat or reassurance. The deployment of condensation symbols fixes, simplifies, and distorts situations in order to mesh with a cognitive style which resists ambiguity or complexity (pp. 7, 11, 31). Much of the debate over homosexuality seems to consist of invoking such condensation symbols. For example, the terms "unnatural," "abominable," "privacy," and "diversity" function to simplify a variety of feelings by condensing them into a single expression.

In similar fashion, anthropologist Karen McCarthy Brown's (1994) concept of supersaturated symbolic acts points to another function of discourse in addressing at many different levels questions of social order and morality (p. 182). For example, the defense of the term "family" functions within traditionalist discourse to invoke a nostalgic vision of domestic perfection, and to draw a boundary between acceptable and unacceptable sexual behavior. In the same way, "diversity" serves progay advocates as a way of expressing rejection of traditional forms of social conformity, tolerance for idiosyncratic behavior, and the grounds for making alliances with other disempowered groups.

Terministic analysis provides yet another way of entering into the language of contestation over variant sexuality. This concept follows from the suggestion by rhetorical critics Charles J. Stewart, Craig Allen Smith, and Robert E. Denton (1994) that established social orders use terministic control to maintain power (p. 134). The corollary is that oppositional collectives seek legitimacy and power by providing new meaning for old terms or by inventing new terms (Smith & Windes, 1993, p. 49). "Sodomy" serves as a term of control. "Sexual orientation" serves as a means of reordering perceptions of the nature and cause of variant sexuality.

The analysis of terms used in public debate, while useful in itself, does not exhaust the possible approaches to the production of language in contests over public policy. For instance, significance can be attached to whether appeals are generated following rules for signaling assurance of situated rationality and recognition of accepted means of persuasion. Scholars, for instance, point out that "even the dominator's style of *elocution* is imposed on society as the first sign of competence. Deemed to be more convincing and more intelligent, this speech stands out clearly from the uncertain *tone* of the dominated" (Noel, 1994, p. 38). In antigay rhetoric, the cadences of religious oratory seem to place truth claims within a credible genre. The stylistic eccentricities of postmodern expression give to some progay advocates a similar reassuring familiarity.

Many attempts to establish dominance in contests over variant sexuality take the form of arguments. Thus, antigay advocates offer argument from principle applied to example (homosexuality is immoral), from definition (homosexuality is a sin), from analogy (homosexuality is like drug addiction), from effect to cause (homosexuality is a psychological disturbance), from examples to generalization (homosexuals are child molesters), and from cause (homosexuality produces disease). Similarly, progay advocates offer claims based on principle (gay people deserve equal rights), from cause (bigotry causes antigay violence), from sign (gays are wealthy and well educated), and from analogy (gays are the same as African Americans). In addition, much of the discussion in contests over sexuality involves refutation of claims made by the other side: denial by antigays that they are bigoted, assertion that being gay is not a choice.

However, both students of argument and many progay advocates have reservations about the power of rational discourse to change social beliefs and values. In general, advocates in moral argument seem to follow a pattern of reasoning which philosophers Albert Jonsen and Stephen Toulmin (1988) call "geometrical" moral reasoning based on universal principles which "can be deduced from some comprehensive *super*principle that captures all essentials of moral action and reflection in a single formula" (p. 293). Given different principles and incompatible intended outcomes, opposing advocates cannot agree about "what counts as data or whether a particular piece of data supports, refutes, or is irrelevant to a hypothesis" (Pearce & Littlejohn, 1997, p. 16). Absent common ground, advocates engaged in moral argument only pretend to be talking with each other when, in fact, they are simply hurling at each other slogans, cliches, and aphorisms (Hunter, 1994, pp. 8-9). Social scientists Donald Mathews and Jane De Hart (1990) observe of moral argument that incomprehension and avoidance of opposing arguments result from refusal to understand the fundamental strands of meaning which hold together the arguments of the opponent (p. 222). Legal scholar Richard Posner (1992) suggests that argument often only leads to the conclusion that opponents inhabit different moral universes, "and there is no arguing between universes" (p. 230). Viewed another way, discourses shield themselves against challenge by establishing a single authoritative text, through repetition, and by "organizing it as a discipline with an institutionalized domain of enunciations, methods, propositions, and set rules" (Therborn, 1980, p. 84).

Gay advocates tend to agree that argumentative processes do not ordinarily change public policy toward variant sexuality. Mohr (1988) asserts that arguments are not an adequate defense for gay civil rights because, in many areas of discussion, prejudice is the "social lens through which all is categorized, interpreted, and assessed. At that level, where reality, meaning, and value are preconfigured in society's hardwiring, argument will not work" (p. 2). Even when antigay arguments are refuted, new claims are propounded in defense of a prerational rejection of homosexuality (Bawer, 1993, p. 112). Viewed another way, argument becomes merely a seductive evidence game whose only effect is not to remove prejudice but simply to reinforce the structure of the game itself (Smith, 1994, pp. 191-192). In the end, the only approach to a structure of claims and counterclaims may be not to play the game at all. As Duberman (1997/1977) observes of antigay advocates, "to treat their insulting simplicities as legitimate arguments and to dignify their smarmy psyches with a rational probe feels like an exercise in self-hatred—a smiling curtsy to the descending ax" (p. 445).

Narrative is an alternate way in which progay and antigay advocates organize language. Rhetorician Walter Fisher (1987) defines narrative as:

> Stories meant to give order to human experience and to induce others to dwell in them in order to establish ways of living in common, in intellectual and spiritual communities in which there is confirmation for the story that constitutes one's life. (p. 63)

According to Fisher, narrative is persuasive even though it does not follow argumentative form. Narration is a form of persuasion in which individuals assess moral reasoning by the standards of narrative probability (coherence) and fidelity (consistent with experience). He sees narratives as moral constructs which are often intended to influence untrained thinkers and which combine intellect and imagination as well as reason and emotion (pp. 64, 68, 71). Stories of homosexual child molestation and of gay bashing, for example, can be evaluated through narrative analysis.

In analyzing discourse, narratives can be considered fundamental constituents of social life as well as basic units of persuasion. Sociologists Margaret Somers and Gloria Gibson (1994) assert that social life is storied." They observe that stories direct action because:

> People construct identities (however multiple and changing) by locating themselves or being located within a repertoire of emplotted stories . . . and that people are guided to act in certain ways, and not others, on the basis of the projections, expectations, and memories derived from a multiplicity but ultimately limited repertoire of available social, public, and cultural narratives. (pp. 38-39)

These units are "constructed as characterizations—universalized depictions of important agents, acts, scenes, purposes, or methods" (p. 14).

At the most general level, narratives create social cohesion because they draw on a storehouse of stories which constitute the central dramatic resources of a society (McIntyre, 1981, p. 201). Public religion, for example, depends on narrative for the articulation of connections between private feelings and public claims (Wuthnow, 1994, p. 164). However, narrative also functions in divisive ways which produce public dispute. According to sociologist Harrison White (1992), identity is essentially presented in accounts that are developed from story lines which are held in common within a culture (p. 314). Different identities can come into collision even though they are produced from common sources. For instance, heroic struggle for freedom (religious or sexual) is a recurrent plot line in both progay and antigay appeals. Further, movements produce metanarratives of resistance that create tensions between accounts which justify change and the more established narratives. (Reed, 1992, p. 16). The narrative of true love functions in progay same-sex marriage appeals no less than in appeals establishing the value of the traditional family. Once narratives are developed which define a particular identity or movement, they regularly function to seal off collectivities from other groups. Rhetorical critic Barnett Pearce (1989) suggests that in oppositional situations, the stories of each group "are richer, more elegant, and capable of more rhetorical eloquence than those seen in the interaction between them" (p. 174).

Both antigay and progay appeals rely heavily on narratives. Among the leading antigay narratives are those which center on the decline of national morality, the loss of masculine vigor, and child molestation (Dobson & Bauer, 1990, pp. 3, 106; Douglass, 1997, pp. 28-29; Podhoretz, 1977, p. 30). Progay advocates frequently offer a narrative of liberation in which lesbians and gay men fight for their rights, or in stories of early childhood experience which demonstrate biological assignment of a gay identity (Sullivan, 1995, p. 17).

Interpretive Communities, Culture War, and Social Movements

Languaging strategies do not exist apart from social structures. Consequently, verbal action ought to be incorporated into a larger understanding of the social processes which underlie contests over variant sexuality. Analysis of the symbols, arguments, and narrations of public policy opponents cannot be undertaken apart from a painstaking study of the "moral orders from which the discourse arises and ways in which such axioms give rise to interpretation and action" (Pearce, Littlejohn, & Alexander, 1987, p. 172). Processes of sustaining a moral order develop within the social production of culture which provides a link between objective social behavior and symbolic constructions (Eder, 1993, p. viii). The cultures in confrontation over variant sexuality can be understood both through the concept of interpretive communities engaged in culture wars and through theories of collective action.

An entry point into a culturalist understanding of political contests involving variant sexuality is to recognize that in many public policy disputes a collision is occurring between rival interpretive communities. Efforts at social change do not occur in a vacuum, but evolve out of and join together in existing associations and groups which have "leaders, members, meeting places, an activity routine, lines of communication, social bonds, shared beliefs, symbols, and a common language, cemented over a period of years" (Oberschall, 1993, p. 24). Stewart and his colleagues (1994) generalize that political behavior consists of the "struggle among interpretive communities to establish their own interpretive structures as legitimate so as to define social and political realities for everybody else" (p. 34). They describe an interpretive community as a group of individuals who are bonded together in agreement about how to understand the world. This consensus consists of a common social interpretive structure manifested in " 'languages' to coordinate their symbolizing, 'logics' to coordinate their reasoning, 'ideologies' to coordinate their preferencing, and 'laws' to coordinate their need fulfillment activities" (p. 32). Interpretive communities come into collision because legitimating one interpretive structure necessarily disadvantages others (p. 33). Acceptance of a gay-positive set of public policies, for example, devalues the language of moral condemnation and the traditions through which many individuals define themselves and construct their relationships. Conversely, the maintenance of ideologies which reject homoeroticism clearly marginalizes the habits of heart and mind of gay and lesbian persons.

An effect of the appearance of multiple interpretive communities within a single political system is the emergence of moral pluralism, the coexistence of incompatible systems of ultimate value based on particularistic patterns of social attachment and identity. Political scientist Donald Moon (1993) points out that group efforts to publicly express their distinctive identities and to organize their lives around familiar traditions and values, and to protect their integrity and existence over time "are among the most important and intractable sources of political conflict in the world today" (p. 24). Within Western nations, both gay/lesbian and traditionalist interpretive communities have coalesced which accept attitudes, beliefs, behaviors, and ways of being crystallized into identities (Noel, 1994, p. 5). Gay/lesbian communities tend to favor a rights-oriented conception of society which values the individual as an independent unit of action, affirms individual differences, and seeks to promote the dignity of individual actors. Traditionalists favor a virtues-oriented order which promotes the community as the source of action and community welfare as the transcendent social goal (Pearce & Littlejohn, 1997, p. 59). Within the contest over variant sexuality public policy, for advocates to claim that homoeroticism ought to be a protected form of individual action is consistent with a rights-oriented understanding of moral order but is incomprehensible within a traditionalist order based on virtue (p. 59).

The concept of "culture war" is an extension of the idea that interpretive communities are social entities which articulate discourse on sexuality. Along with variant sexuality, the culture war which many commentators believe is taking place in Western societies consists of a series of

public controversies over abortion, affirmative action, sexual harassment, pornography, federal funding for the arts, and censorship of the
media (Hunter, 1994, p. 3). All of these conflicts are symptomatic of a
deeper struggle over the "first principles of how we will order our lives together; a struggle to define the purpose of our major institutions, and in
all of this, a struggle to shape the identity of the nation as a whole"
(Hunter, 1994, p. 4). This deeper struggle develops from a basic social division which has grown from the institutional and political expressions of
two different cultural belief systems central to which are distinct ways of
understanding morality, perceiving reality, and drawing conclusions.
Hunter (1991) concludes that "each side of the cultural divide, then,
speaks with a different moral vocabulary. Each side operates out of a different mode of debate and persuasion. Each side represents the tendencies of a separate and competing moral galaxy. They are, indeed, 'worlds
apart' " (p. 128).

An important insight of a culture war approach to the discourse generated by interpretive communities struggling over variant sexuality is that
the conflict which is produced usually resists compromise and containment (Dickstein, 1993, p. 540). Because much of the debate is about ultimate beliefs, conflict is more easily sustained than compromise, reconciliation, and consensus. As a result, a rhetoric of moral antagonism for
traditionalists centers on a "wrathful God, who is above all concerned
with righteousness, justice, fierce combat against the scourge of evil, and
the warriors of good in their fight for God's kingdom" (Wuthnow, 1994,
p. 98). Such absolutist rhetoric is shared by many progressives because, as
Hunter (1991) asserts, the discourse of cultural warfare is religious even
"when those who promote a position are hostile to traditional forms of
religious expression" (p. 62).

Given an understanding of cultural confrontation as a form of warfare,
each side appreciates that an alternative view is not a free floating
evaluative act but an "attack upon the moral worth and survivability of
the culture itself" (Balthrop, 1984, p. 350). The response must then be in
the form of "reciprocated diatribe" which is characterized by both unde-
veloped and simplistic appeals and by a disinclination of opponents to appreciate each other's world views, much less to engage them (Pearce et al.,
1987, p. 177). Many of these appeals focus on the oppositional other, the
opponent. As Hunter (1991) asserts, "neutralizing the opposition through
a strategy of public ridicule, derision, and insult has become just as important as making credible claims for the world that each side champions"

(p. 136). The product of such a strategy is a rhetoric of vilification in which opponents are cast in an exclusively negative light through the attribution of unrestrained power and diabolic motives (Vanderford, 1989, p. 166).

The interpretive community/culture war perspective on confrontation over variant sexuality emphasizes the stability of interpretive communities, their monolithic nature, and the connections among a variety of social issues. This perspective also brings attention to the fact that collective action is based on interlocking sets of institutions, small groups, and social networks (Tarrow, 1994, pp. 21-22). Oppositional discourse on variant sexuality, however, cannot be understood fully as a clash of stable interpretive communities. The appeals, strategies, and constituencies of each side of the debate undergo change. The evolution of specific persuasive appeals about same-sex eroticism cannot be subsumed entirely under generalizations about Manichean cultural battle. Neither antigay nor progay advocates express single traditionalist or progressive world views and their advocacy does not consist merely of specific application of fundamental antagonistic principles.

A dynamic concept of social movement provides an important corrective to the idea that culture clash is an expression of relatively fixed social beliefs. Herman (1997) observes that it is helpful to understand social movements as "fluid, dynamic, contradictory, and contingent, rather than simply as forces meeting counterforces in the evolutionary spiral for supremacy " (p. 196). As movements struggle to mobilize consensus, new issues appear and innovative modes of action are adopted, organizations are reassessed, beliefs and ideologies replace one another, and even desirable outcomes are reformulated (Klandermans, 1992, p. 91). The concept of movement projects a constantly changing field of social action in which competing organizations create and transform meaning, identities, and relationships of cooperation and confrontation.

There is doubtless truth in the argument that movement rhetoric is confrontational in form and that every battle is a "clash between right and wrong, good and evil, saints and sinners, victims and victimizers" (Stewart, 1991, p. 67). However, the "right, good, and saintly" undergo constant redescription as movements endeavor to achieve both their instrumental end of integration into the polity and their expressive goals. The instrumental aspect of movement action, featured in resource mobilization theory, emphasizes rational calculation by movement participants. The expressive dimensions of collective action highlight the creation of identity and consciousness of both solidarity and autonomy (Gamson,

1989, p. 353). Instrumentally, movements don't challenge society as a whole. They oppose varied forms of social closure and exclusion "by thematizing issues excluded from normal societal and political decision-making, and by articulating the grievances of groups who are themselves excluded" (Scott, 1990, p. 150). At the same time, social movement environments provide individual contact with sympathetic persons by creating social bonds and an ethic of solidarity (p. 126). Both progay and antigay movements can be seen as performing instrumental and expressive functions. Each has concerns excluded from the public sphere. Both provide networks of association and identification through which a sense of empowerment and purpose are created.

Movements occur when groups of individuals discover that they have opportunity to express collective interests through cooperative effort. While some aspects of political opportunity (e.g., institutions and traditions) are relatively stable, other aspects, such as elite alignment, public policy, or style of political discourse, are dynamic (Gamson & Meyer, 1996). Movements exploit opportunity by engaging a wide variety of institutions including government, organized religion, mass media, the market, medicine, higher education, and science (Epstein, 1999, p. 31).

In their political operation, movements work in three identity fields which Hunt, Benford, and Snow (1994) classify as protagonists, antagonists, and bystanders (p. 186). Protagonists include adherents, the constituencies of the movement, and potential beneficiaries of its successful action. Antagonists are opponents of the movement and their allies. Bystanders are elements of the community which are initially uninvolved but who may become active in influencing outcomes (McAdam & Snow, 1997, pp. xxiii-xxiv). Persuasive messages generated by movements are intended to mobilize constituents and potential beneficiaries. Other persuasive messages are aimed at the opponents' allies, seeking to create division in the enemy camp. Bystanders are also targeted as movements seek to attract elite support, form coalitions, and shape generalized public opinion.

From another perspective, progay and antigay movements can be understood as collective actors engaged in a constant effort to produce and reproduce themselves within a public space. In sociologist Klaus Eder's (1993) formulation, collective action cannot be represented solely by using the dominant perspective that movements are phenomena objectively defined by indicators such as attitudes or the organizational patterning of resources. Instead, movements are *"constructed* in the public space, and their function has to be understood within the process of the public construction of a collective actor" (p. 4). This view of movements is consistent with McGee's (1980a) proposal that "movement" should be understood as a set of meanings rather than an objective reality. Consequently, movements can be conceived as rhetorical claims to significance rather than as an objective phenomenon (p. 233). Certainly, both traditionalists and progays make claim that they are powerful social actors brought into being to accomplish a significant social purpose.

However, objective artifacts of collective action cannot be dismissed as insignificant. Resources, organizations, and texts of public expression are vital indicators of collective representation. Social scientist Alberto Melucci (1985) believes that movements cannot survive in complex societies without channels of representation and without institutional actors able to translate collective patterns of thought and action into policies. Such representation is the "only condition of preserving movements from atomization or from marginal violence" (p. 815). Consequently, both traditionalists and progays have built dense networks of social movement organizations.

Although movements can be considered as both objective collectivities and as conscious rhetorical claims to significance, movement explained as a process of producing personal meaning is helpful in comprehending the evolving and varying identity claims of both progay and antigay collective actors. The powerful drive to establish a sense of self through taking on social identities has long been recognized (Snow & Anderson, 1987, p. 1365). Recently, the concept of identity has become important in exploring the mobilization of socially embedded individuals into action groups which perceive themselves to be movements. Sociologist Alan Scott (1990) defines movement as constituted by individuals who share not only common interests but a common identity as well (p. 6). This view is elaborated by sociologists Verta Taylor and Nancy Whittier (1992), who explain that "collective identity is the shared definition of a group that derives from members' common interests, experiences, and solidarity" (p. 104). Such a socially created identity can be understood as consisting of boundaries that fix differences among groups, consciousness that provides interpretive frameworks for assessing relationships among groups, and means of negotiation that concern the symbols and actions through which groups simultaneously resist and restructure established forms of hierarchy (p. 111). The construction of identity is a complex and dynamic process as movements acting under a variety of influences simultaneously celebrate and suppress a wide range of differences (Bernstein, 1997, p. 532).

   Key to this new identity oriented social movement paradigm is recognition that a common structural location does not bring collective political subjects into being. Rather, social movement action creates identity. Scholars grant that movements create new activist identities from existing roles (Friedman & McAdam, 1992, p. 162). In order to comprehend the way in which roles are transformed, however, one must "analyze the social and political struggle that created the identity" (Taylor & Whittier, 1992, pp. 109-110). A beginning in this analysis is to recognize, as sociologist William Gamson (1992b) does, that "being a collective agent implies being a part of a 'we' who can do something" (p. 84). In the process of dynamic movement action, identity is elaborated and negotiated over time, making questions of identity important to internal discourse. Further, identity construction often involves disputes not only with antagonists but with protagonists as well. As Joshua Gamson (1997) observes, "the *us* is solidified not just against an external *them* but also against *thems* inside, as particular subgroups battle to gain or retain legitimate *us* standing" (p. 180). In general, then, establishing a collective identity is crucial to making claims on society as a whole and to producing a rhetoric of identity in which one's own nature and virtue are valorized while the representations of adversarial groups are denigrated. Both progay and antigay advocates, therefore, produce external identity discourses which influence adversaries.

   A number of scholars employ the concept of identity as a means for distinguishing "new social movements" from older forms of collective action. Some analysts have objected to the use of this term because it privileges a narrow range of western, middle class movements focused on peace, ecology, and feminism (Gamson, 1992a, p. 58). Despite this limitation, political scientist Timothy Luke (1989) suggests that what is new about a variety of recent movements is that they have rejected an older politics of resource distribution in favor of a new politics of cultural identity (p. 207). New movements, according to Boggs (1986), "exist at the intersection of state and civil society rather than in the factory or the traditional system of production alone" (p. 63). The new movements centered on identity pose challenges to the "operant cultural codes of the existing state and corporate order" (Luke, 1989, p. 207). The nature of progay and antigay advocacy considered as social movement can be conceptualized as the struggle of outsiders against central institutions and elites who, respectively, reject the irrationalism of traditionalist thought and deny the usefulness of gay/lesbian identity. Despite their occasional claims to power, most participants in the conflict over sexuality, then, are fighting battles for access, voice, and control (p. 220). Consequently, like other new social movements, both progay and antigay collective efforts raise issues about centralization and decentralization, identity and difference, hierarchy and equality, and social representations (Reed, 1992, p. 14).

While antagonistic collective actors struggling to gain definitional control over sexuality have parallel goals with respect to the dominant social code, they also exist in the relation of movement and countermovement. As originally conceived, countermovements oppose social change in general, not necessarily another movement (Lo, 1982, p. 118). In later conceptions, movement and countermovement became interactive. Each is the grievance which, at least in part, motivates the other. Sociologist Sidney Tarrow (1994) points out that "movements not only create opportunities for themselves and their allies; they also create opportunities for others" (p. 97). The dynamic interplay of movement and countermovement has not been investigated in depth. However, it is clear that much movement discourse is directed at confronting and delegitimating its corresponding countermovement (Zald & Useem, 1987, pp. 247-248). In the process of interaction, movement and countermovement influence one another (Lo, 1982, p. 119). Progay and antigay movements have formed such an interdependent oppositional relationship. Advocates on both sides attempt to undo the results of opponents' efforts, engaging in a loosely coupled tango of mutual recrimination, and responding to each other's strategies by adopting new definitions of reality, types of rhetorical appeals, and even purposes.

In many instances, prolonged struggle occurs between conflicting organizations and social networks. Rather than conceiving one movement as a reaction to the other, both can be conceived as opposing movements. Such opposing movements are vitally important to each other in that they exercise mutual influence and alter the situation in which each side acts. As sociologists David Meyer and Suzanne Staggenborg (1996) observe, the "opposing movement is a critical component in the structure of political opportunity the other side faces" (p. 1632). Gay/lesbian and traditionalist movements have certainly established an oppositional relationship in which each side deeply influences the other.

Rhetorical critics have noticed that antagonistic enjoinment is a characteristic of social movement. They have observed that "confrontational rhetoric enables the movement to define itself to its members as well as to the outside world" (Short, 1991, p. 174). Rhetorician Parke Burgess (1970) argues that moral discussion is inherently dialectical because if a demand system is advanced by one group, another group which finds that system abhorrent emerges to attack it (p. 121). According to rhetorical critic Robert Cathcart (1983), moral conflict is definitive of rhetorical movements because awareness of movement is generated by "dialectical enjoinment" (p. 72). Although there is some doubt about whether moral confrontation defines all rhetorical movement, it does identify a general theme which has been usefully employed in various forms by a number of rhetorical critics (Smith & Windes, 1975, p. 142). Cathcart's concern is principally with struggle between establishment and movement. But in one of the earliest formulations of rhetorical theory of movements, critic Leland Griffin (1952) advanced the notion of conflict between movements, highlighting the clash between aggressor and defendant rhetors (p. 185). Rhetorician Barbara Warnick (1977) uses this concept to suggest that conservative resistance movements can clearly be classified as countermovements (p. 257). Rhetorical critics, however, as we mentioned in the Introduction, have not gone far in identifying the effects of dialectical enjoinment on the production of movement subjects and their discourses.

The plasticity of movements (i.e., their tendency to reconstitute themselves in interaction with their symbolic environments), is best grasped through the concept of framing. As previously noted, frames are patterns for organizing thought about issues (Gamson, 1992a, p. 71). In the process of framing, advocates "select some aspects of a perceived reality and make them more salient in a communicating text, in such a way as to promote a particular problem definition, causal interpretation, moral evaluation, and/or treatment recommendation for the item described" (Entman, 1993, p. 52). The function of frames is to interpret problems and suggest "action pathways" to address problems (Zald, 1996, p. 265). An emphasis on framing brings attention to cognitive processes and provides a correction to the treatment of meanings and ideas as prediscursive givens "rather than as social production that arise during the course of interactive processes" (Snow & Benford, 1992, p. 136). Movements can be understood as signifying agents involved in the "amplification and extension of extant meanings, the transformation of old meanings, and the generation of new meanings" (p. 136). Thus, rather than seeing the belief systems of movements as superimposed patterns of thought or as the inevitable expression of grievances, the appeals of movements can be understood as a continual process of framing work (Tarrow, 1994, p.22). Such work often leads to bitter contention within movements as social actors advance a variety of goals and strategies (Gamson & Meyer, 1996, pp. 283-284).

Movement rhetoric properly can be conceived as a process of projecting collective action frames which involves naming grievances, establishing connections among grievances, and "constructing larger frames of meaning that will resonate with a population's cultural predispositions and communicate a uniform message to powerholders and others" (Tarrow, 1994, p. 122). Movements endeavor to achieve frame alignment between individual and movement interpretive frames through a process of bridging, amplification, extension, and transformation (Snow, Rockford, Worden, & Benford, 1986, p. 476). In the heat of controversy, oppositional forces convert cultural symbols into the collective action frames necessary to mobilize support (Tarrow, 1994, p. 133). At the same time, adversaries reflexively modify frames in response to adversarial messages (Simons, 1994, p. 469). As we shall see, progay advocates have oscillated in framing "gay rights" as either claims to privacy or claims to public representation. Traditionalists have similarly shifted between framing homosexuality as individual sin or as social subversion.

Movements do not need to invent *de noveau* their action frames, nor do they need to discover novel forms for representing themselves in the public sphere. In order to affect social change, movements engage in a limited range of actions which can be considered their "repertoire of contention" (Tilly, 1978, p. 151). Each society "has a stock of familiar forms of action that are known by both potential challengers and their opponents which become habitual aspects of their interaction" (Tarrow, 1994, p. 19). Such forms of collective action become routinized in movement organizations. In the current controversy over variant sexuality, the major forms of special interest politics are everywhere present as the favored repertoire of collective action: lobbying, direct mail campaigns, the use of referenda, the endorsement and mobilization of other institutions, coalition building, internet information dissemination and, above all, the employment of mass media.

Profoundly influenced by the mass media, social movement organizations, at the same time, influence how the media frame issues, define grievances, and depict episodes of collective action. Equally important, the mass media are the sites where adversarial movements meet. Klandermans (1992) correctly asserts that in public discourse, "arguments evolve in response to counterarguments, new information, and new events. Media discourse has now become a crucial element in this evolutionary process" (pp. 87-88). Media organizations, however, do not directly transmit movement messages, but augment collective action frames with their own frames. Collective actors must compete with media framing devices through which the messages on which movements depend are filtered (Tarrow, 1994, p. 23). Thus, collective action frames interact with media frames, that is, those "persistent patterns of cognition, interpretation, and presentation, of selection, emphasis, and exclusion, by which symbol-handlers routinely organize discourse, whether verbal or visual" (Gitlin, 1980, p. 3). As a result, movements spend considerable energy adjusting their discourse in response to both their adversaries and to the media which convey their discourse to the public and to decision makers.

Issue Cultures and Interpretive Packages

The concept of issue culture and interpretive package refine the notion of interpretive community and present an entry into the communicative action of social movements by highlighting the instability of discourses on controversial public issues, the uniqueness of specific conflicts, and differences among allied advocates. Sociologists William Gamson and Andre Modigliani (1989) argue that a culture develops around every public issue. They define such an issue culture as a set of language practices that evolves over time and which consists of the "metaphors, catchphrases, visual images, moral appeals, and other symbolic devices that characterize this discourse" (pp. 1-2). In an issue culture, advocates organize symbolic actions into clusters so that they are perceived not as individual symbols but as "interpretive packages" (p. 2). A number of interpretive packages develop on most public issues. This is the essence of the concept of public debate since dispute over many policies can be understood as "symbolic contests over which among several interpretations will prevail" (p. 2). Interpretive packages provide meaning for a public policy field by deploying condensation symbols that provide a shorthand representation of the core frame which is at the center of the package (p. 3). Each interpretive package has sponsors (i.e., individuals, organizations, and movements) striving to make their interpretive package the dominant source of meaning within an issue culture. However, opinion within any interpretive package is not monolithic. Each interpretive package develops a "range of positions, rather than any single one, allowing for a degree of controversy among those who share a common frame" (p. 3).

Gamson and Modigliani's formulation of interpretive package and issue culture synthesizes developments in interpretive social science which bring attention to symbolic repertoires of collective behavior, condensation symbols, and frame analysis.

Contests between progay and antigay advocates can be understood as efforts to gain support for rival interpretive packages which frame same-sex orientation and behaviors as either sin, sickness, and crime, or as neutral difference and positive identity. When opportunity occurs to make variant sexuality a contested subject, coalitions of organizations, joined by movement clusters, sponsor antagonistic interpretive packages in order to impose a dominant meaning on a public dispute. In conflicts over inclusion of gay supportive material in sex education courses, for example, a variety of opposing organizations compete to define what issues are being contested: parental rights, morality, affirmation of individual difference, or academic freedom. Advancing a particular view does not require either antigay or progay advocates to share monolithic belief systems. To the contrary, Gamson and Modigliani's (1989) approach highlights a changing constellation of situated appeals and stresses that adherents of any one package contend among themselves over appropriate lines of rhetorical action. With respect to sex education, parental rights advocates may attempt to push aside religious moralists, or gay and lesbian advocates may seek to highlight sexuality and ignore academic freedom.

Understanding the dynamics of interpretive packages requires investigation into how rhetorical strategy is influenced by interactions among sponsors of rival interpretive packages.

Pearce and his colleagues (1987), for example, observe that although confrontational rhetorical forms have been analyzed, the structure of interaction between groups in conflict has been largely ignored (pp. 173-174). William Gamson (1992b) provides a way of understanding such interaction by emphasizing the dialectic nature of thematic appeals, noting that conventional themes in a society are inevitably accompanied by counterthemes which are adversarial. Consequently, he writes, that themes and counterthemes "are paired with each other so that whenever one is invoked, the other is present in latent form, ready to be activated with the proper cue" (p. 135). This concept can be pushed further by observing that in the progay/antigay dialectic, each theme provokes an oppositional countertheme. "Gay rights" necessarily produces "special rights." "Sodomy is sin" invokes "gay is good."

The sponsors of adversarial interpretive packages influence one another more profoundly than simply by eliciting a counterthematic position. Within an issue culture, opposition influences not only the production of adversarial themes, but also shapes the very nature of who are in combat over what issues, and in what relationships. Oppositional discourse in public controversy over variant sexuality shapes presentation of collection identity, influences definition of controversy, and contributes to establishing plausible connections between antagonists. Progay and antigay advocates are not simply preformed actors who confront one another. They are forged as particular kinds of collective subjects within the ritualistic combat which is the central binding force of their issue culture.

To illustrate, the extent to which the gay/lesbian community is represented as sexualized is deeply influenced by the presence of conflict, as is the extent to which traditionalists represent themselves as a "loving opposition." At the same time, the attempt to shape a collective self in the heat of conflict produces disagreement within communities over strategic representation. Representational alternatives carry advantages and disadvantages for persons differently situated, therefore, rivals within communities can gather adherents by asserting the superiority of one form of collective strategy over another. Thus, progays engage in sharp conflict over their origin and nature, while traditionalists dispute whether to present themselves as condemnatory or therapeutic.

We believe that interaction and reciprocal influence among progay and antigay advocates can be analyzed by examining symbolic appeals, collective action frames, and interpretive packages developed in the variant sexuality issue culture. The following three chapters seek to explain mutual influence in confrontation through employing this interpretive approach. Chapter 3 describes the principal interpretive packages which are sponsored within the variant sexuality issue culture. The influence of adversarial symbolic action on identity and strategy within these packages is examined in Chapter 4. Chapter 5 analyzes internal divisions exacerbated by confrontation, an analysis that explores the differences among rival interpretive packages which are designed to influence variant sexuality policy.

3 Appeals in Progay and Traditionalist Discourses

This chapter describes the interpretive packages which are dominant in the increasing number of debates over public policy toward variant sexuality. Present through the specificity and pattern of these appeals is the discourse to which publics are exposed when they are drawn into the variant sexuality issue culture. These packages consist of appeals expressed in symbolic acts which are, in the broadest sense, arguments. As sociologist Stephen Ellingson (1997) points out, discursive struggles occur at the level of arguments which function as the building blocks of partisan discourses (p. 271). He notes that such arguments are "both the means by which speakers create and justify their diagnoses and solutions and the carriers of economic, political, or moral goals and interests that motivate public debate" (p. 271). Taken together, the process of propounding arguments serves a combination of goals, including advancing rival definitions of conflict, contesting basic conceptions and challenging categories, bringing into question or reinforcing specific beliefs, and discrediting arguments advanced by opponents (p. 272).

The task of describing progay and antigay appeals, though daunting, is more easily accomplished than it may first appear. While the same pattern of appeals is not duplicated in each contest between gay/lesbian and traditionalist advocates, a limited number of appeals recurrently surface in different combinations in most of these contests. For example, in recent years, the theme of "no special rights" has appeared prominently in some antigay texts while in other texts, both homosexuality as "sin" and the "seduction of the child" have been featured. Similarly, the defense of same-sex sex has been prominent in some gay/lesbian campaigns, while absent in others. The extent to which particular appeals are produced, emphasized, and connected to specific policy issues varies significantly, depending upon the subject of the contest, the particular constituency to which advocacy is directed, the institutional setting in which discussion occurs, the ideological position of advocates, and tactical considerations. In this chapter, however, we are concerned primarily with describing particular appeals which thread through the variant sexuality issue culture. We also recognize that there is a variety of interpretive packages available to partisans on each side. For the moment, however, our concern is with those appeals which the literature reveals to be most dominant across a variety of settings in which policy decisions are taken.

Such appeals fall readily into two general classifications. First, appeals are presented concerning whether public policy should allow discrimination against homosexuals. Traditionalists argue that there is a reasonable basis for discrimination against homosexuals, while progay advocates maintain that such discrimination is unwarranted and impermissible. Second, appeals are presented concerning whether public policy should actively protect lesbians and gay men from discrimination. Gay/lesbian advocates maintain that protection is warranted, while traditionalists claim that government action on behalf of homosexuals is neither necessary nor constitutional. Put another way, traditionalist discourse consists of antihomosexual appeals plus an attack on the public policy program of homosexual movements. In contrast, gay/lesbian discourse consists of the refutation of antigay appeals and justification of public policy favorable to the interests of lesbians and gay men.

Ironically, the most encompassing ground for disagreement between traditionalist and gay/lesbian advocates arises out of agreement to distinguish between but to link private behavior and public action. The binary ideographic term "private/public" provides the generic frame through which the variant sexuality issue culture produces a wide variety of appeals. The play of "private" against "public" is so complex that many variations on this binary term are sounded. While there is a common ground in the progay and traditionalist understanding of the relationship between private and public spheres, each side draws dramatically different conclusions from this binary.

In defending a traditionalist understanding of the state's expansive role in restricting homosexual conduct and suppressing gay/lesbian orientation, the British legal scholar John Finnis (1994) relies strictly on the private/public dichotomy. Finnis has been extensively involved in American legal matters, most notably as a state witness defending Colorado's Amendment 2 in federal court (Keen & Goldberg, 1998, p. 162). Finnis grants that government cannot legitimately make "secret and truly consensual adult acts of vice a punishable offence against the state's laws" (p. 1076). His dominant theme, however, is based on the premise that the state "should deliberately and publicly identify, encourage, facilitate and support the truly worthwhile (including moral virtue), and hinder the harmful and evil" (p. 1076). The distinction he draws between government regulation of public conduct as opposed to private behavior is warranted by a construction of the state's responsibility for maintaining virtue, which he asserts is auxiliary to that of parents and nongovernmental associations. In that auxiliary role, the state should, "by its criminal prohibitions and sanctions (as well as other laws and policies), assist people with parental responsibilities to educate children and young people in virtue and to discourage their vices" (p. 1076). As a consequence, government's responsibility is to create a

> milieu in which and by which all citizens are encouraged and helped or discouraged and undermined, in their resistance to being lured by temptation into falling away from their own aspirations to be people of integrated good character, and to be autonomous, self- controlled persons rather than slaves to impulse and sensual gratification. (p. 1053)

With respect to public action, Finnis (1994) argues, the state "does have the authority to discourage, say, homosexual conduct and 'orientation' (i.e., overtly manifested active willingness to engage in homosexual conduct)" (p. 1049). The state should do so because homosexual behavior is intrinsically a moral wrong. Government must actively discourage the "deliberate decision so to orient one's public *behavior* as to express or *manifest* one's active interest in and endorsement of homosexual *conduct* and/or forms of life which presumptively involve such conduct" (p. 1053). For Finnis, the domain of the private is small, limited to truly secret liaisons, while the domain of the public is so extensive as to allow the state to prohibit "advertising or marketing of homosexual services, the maintenance of places of resort for homosexual activity, or the promotion of homosexual 'lifestyles' via education and public media of communication" (p. 1076).

In most gay/lesbian discourse, the theme is played that a clear dividing line should be maintained between private and public. For example, the struggle against sodomy laws is waged largely in terms of the constitutional privacy rights of homosexuals (Gross, 1993, p. 33; Kaplan, 1997, p. 27). Similarly, civil rights for gay people are often advanced on the premise that homosexuality is a purely private matter which has no place in the public sphere (Miller, 1998, pp.52-53). A secondary position is also advanced, however, which hinges on the belief that there is a close linkage between private and public manifestations of homosexuality. Progay advocates Michael Nava and Robert Dawidoff (1994) state this position by claiming that there is no self-evident or clearly marked division between private and public life. The two merge because "law, custom, and public policy promote specific models of acceptable private life by rewarding some forms of relationships between people and punishing others" (p. xiii).

Gay/lesbian and traditionalist advocates agree that there is some relationship between the public and the private, but their conclusions about the substance of public policy are diametrically opposed. Finnis (1994) argues that law should support the moral judgment that homosexuality is morally wrong because such a judgment is not a "manifestation of mere hostility to a hated minority, or of purely religious, theological, and sectarian belief" (p. 1055). Accordingly, he supports "laws, regulations, and policies [which] discriminate (i.e., distinguish between heterosexual and homosexual conduct adversely to the latter)" (p. 1049). For gay advocates, discrimination against persons on the basis of sexual orientation is impermissible and unwarranted precisely because it is only motivated by a farrago of private hostility and personal beliefs which should never enter into public policy decision making. In analyzing a series of court cases as well as government policy, Mohr (1992) concludes that under the morality which Finnis wants the law to enforce lies merely the beast of popular prejudice. With respect to the Supreme Court's decision that sodomy laws are constitutional, he notes that the "court's sole articulated reason for upholding the law against this challenge was that the law expressed a legitimate state interest in that it promoted 'morality.' The Court made clear that what it meant by 'morality' was simply 'majority sentiments' . . . about morality" (p. 59). Mohr also finds that discrimination against gays and lesbians in almost all cases, and with respect to a wide range of policies, is based on an appeal to "amassed private prejudices" which courts, in other contexts, have consistently found to be illegitimate justification for discrimination (p. 61).

The private/public binary, in short, is an implicitly agreed upon ideographic construct which produces two central issues around which public policy is debated. The first issue is whether homosexuality is in some sense a "private evil" which public policy must limit or merely a "neutral difference" whose suppression implements unfounded belief. The second issue is whether public policy can permissibly be used to inhibit discrimination against lesbians and gay men.

Whether homosexuality is morally acceptable, then, is a question to be addressed prior to determining whether public policy can discriminate against homosexuals or protect lesbians and gay men. Thus, the core frames of antigay and progay interpretive packages concern the nature of homosexuality and the character of gay persons. In describing these frames, we will first discuss questions of public policy discouragement of homosexuality and then describe appeals concerning the public policy protection of gay and lesbian people.

Justification for the Discouragement of Homosexuality.

Because of cultural tradition and strategic advantage in fund raising and media, traditionalists have succeeded in advancing reasons for discouraging homosexuality to which gay/lesbian advocacy is largely a response (Gallagher & Bull, 1996, p. 23). Our discussion of persuasive appeals in discourse on variant sexuality begins, therefore, with the traditionalist interpretive package. Antigays endeavor to demonstrate that variant sexuality should be legally discouraged for religious and secular reasons. They support a lexicon in which homosexuality is "sinful," "immoral," "criminal," "mentally disturbed," "pathogenic," "corruptive of the young," and "socially disruptive."

Homosexuality as sin is a theme frequently invoked in antigay discourse. Evangelist James Robison declares in denunciatory style that homosexual behavior is "perversion of the highest order. It is against God, against God's word, against society, against nature" (quoted in Lienesch, 1993, p. 84). Antigay activist Anita Bryant (1977), drawing on Leviticus, asserts that "we believe in the word of God, and there it says that homosexuality is abominable." She also reminds her audience that:

> God warns us not to forget the cities of Sodom and Gomorrah and their
> neighboring towns, all full of lust of every kind, including lust of men for
> other men. Those cities were destroyed by fire and continue to be a warning
> to us that there is a hell in which sinners are punished. (p. 17)

Such themes continue to surface in antigay texts. Antigay attorney Roger
Magnuson declared in 1985 that the "biblical view of homosexual behavior could not be clearer. It is, quite simply, an abomination" (p. 53). In
1994, antigay advocates Tim and Beverly LaHaye concluded that the "Bible's condemnation of the homosexual lifestyle was not given by God in
mean-spiritedness but rather is divine instruction for the good of the individual and of humanity" (p. 14).

The most virulent denunciations of homosexuality have come from religious fringe groups such as the Westboro Baptist Church of Topeka,
Kansas, which lets its views be known in its web address, www.
godhatesfags.org. From these groups come demands for the death penalty
for homosexuality and declaration that true intolerance consists of the
suppression of those who know that this is God's will (Peters, 1996). Such
views, however, are not limited to the remote past or to small sects. Robertson declared in 1998 on his religious mainstream program, *The 700
Club,* that the city of Orlando, Florida, risked earthquakes, hurricanes,
terrorist bombs "and possibly a meteor" for allowing gay organizations to
display rainbow flags in support of sexual diversity. He warned Orlando
citizens that "you're right in the way of some serious hurricanes and I
don't think I'd be waving those [gay pride] flags in God's face if I were
you" ("Orlando," 1998, p. A15).

Although much of the denunciation of homosexuality as sin is based
solely on citation of biblical texts, some religious appeals provide more
elaborate argument. Psychologist Stanton Jones (1993) asserts that there
is a strong basis for condemning homosexuality within the context of
Christian sexual ethics. Sex is rightly used only within heterosexual marriage; therefore, chastity is mandatory for both homosexuals and unmar-
ried heterosexuals. This is not a trivial mandate because marriage is "a living parable, a concrete symbol, that models for the world the mystical
union of Christ and his people" (p. 21). On different grounds but with the
same outcome, talk show host Dennis Praeger (1993) claims that the Ju-
daic prohibitions on homosexuality "demanded that all sexual activity be

channeled into marriage" (p. 61). This demand was rational because "Torah's prohibition of homosexuality was a major part of its liberation of the human being from the bonds of unrestrained sexuality and of women from being peripheral to men's lives" (p. 63).

Traditionalists have, with some resentment, recognized that the audience for biblical appeals condemning sodomy is limited. Tim and Beverly LaHaye (1994) ruefully observe that "it is not politically correct to invoke biblical teaching about homosexuality" (p. 14). Consequently, traditionalists often introduce a second level of moral argument which adamantly maintains that same-sex sex is unnatural. Magnuson (1994), for instance, asserts that homosexuality is not natural simply because it is a frequent behavior engaged in by high status persons. "It is natural like incest, drunkenness, adultery, egotism, lying, greed, or rape is [*sic*] natural" (p. 66). On one level, traditionalists use "unnatural" to mean abnormal in the sense of not being socially accepted (Pronk, 1993, p. 139). However, the most frequent usage has strong religious overtones, suggesting that homosexuality is unnatural because it is a " 'distortion' of the *normative* order of creation and therefore wrong" (p. 96). On this basis, antigay advocates assert that "we must be concerned not only with the questions of statistical normalcy, from a so-called 'objective' viewpoint, but even more importantly, with what constitutes 'normal' from a moral viewpoint" (Burtoft, 1995, p. 26). This position is based on the premise that procreation orders sexuality and for that reason the "intention to reproduce is the criterion for the moral quality of the act; it serves as the criterion for what is 'natural' in the moral sense. And because homosexual acts do not satisfy that criterion they are (morally) unnatural" (Pronk, 1993, p. 234). In addition, homosexuality can be understood as unnatural because it is the result of gender confusion. As Bryant (1977) declared, "God has ordained sexual identities innate in male and female; so homosexuality is a twisting of divine order" (p. 107). Or, in the cliched words of Congressman William Dannemeyer, "God's plan for man was Adam and Eve, not Adam and Steve" (quoted in Clendinen & Nagourney, 1999, p. 519).

Depiction of homosexuality as sinful and unnatural undergirds the position that the practice of homosexuality ought to be a crime. Magnuson (1985) asserts that because homosexuality "is an offense against nature as well as against revealed religion, it is properly legislated against by lawmakers" (p. 53). Such explicit connections between religion, morality, and the criminalization of homosexuality are not unusual. In the 18th century, Blackstone wrote that sodomy should be a capital offence, on the basis of

> the voice of nature and of reason, and the express law of God. . . . Of which we have a signal instance, long before the Jewish dispensation, by the destruction of two cities by fire from heaven. . . . And our antient law in some degree imitated this punishment, by commanding such miscreants to be burnt to death. (quoted in Crompton, 1985, pp. 14-15)

Traditionalists emphasize that sodomy laws have a long lineage. Sodomy was a crime in all the thirteen original states (Magnuson, 1994, p. 93). Such laws are a proper terminological classification of homosexual behavior and perform valuable inhibitory functions. Dannemeyer (1989) argues that "we have laws on the books outlawing rape and child molestation because we believe these things are wrong. We should likewise reaffirm our belief in the immorality of Sodom" (p. 217). These laws, he declares, are the "highest expression of communal morality, not just in matters of life and property but in matters of sexual conduct as well" (p. 12). In addition, such laws protect "society against public effrontery, the flaunting of patently immoral conduct" (p. 12). More positively, sodomy laws "affirm a normative way of life for all Americans that they are born and nurtured in traditional families" (p. 218). Most important, perhaps, sodomy laws are a major impediment to the passage of measures favoring homosexuals. As Magnuson notes, homosexuals will have a difficult time achieving social and legal acceptance "when society has already decided to make what they do criminal and punishable by imprisonment" (p. 93).

The depiction of lesbians and gay men as pathological came in the 20th century to supplement a vocabulary of condemnation featuring "sin" and "crime." In general, the antigay psychological literature "presents homosexuals as pathetic and unfulfilled; lesbians and gay men constantly seek parental substitutes as love objects—a tragic and doomed quest" (Herman, 1997, p. 71). Such a description was the standard view of homosexuality throughout much of the twentieth century. Psychotherapist Charles Silverstein (1991) notes that "not a single professional book published before the 1970s contradicted the accepted idea that homosexuality was a serious and obdurate disorder" (p. 5). Psychiatrist Charles Socarides (1968) summarized the dominant view by maintaining that the homosexual lifestyle, is filled with aggression, destruction, and self-deceit. It is a masquerade of life in which certain psychic energies are neutralized and held in a somewhat quiescent state. However, the unconscious manifestations of hate, destructiveness, incest and fear are always threatening to break through. (p. 8)

Consequently, Socarides claims:

Instead of union, cooperation, solace, stimulation, enrichment, healthy challenge and fulfillment, there are only destruction, mutual defeat, exploitation of the partner and the self, oral-sadistic incorporation, aggressive onslaughts, attempts to alleviate anxiety and a pseudo-solution to the aggressive and libidinal urges which dominate and thwart the individual. (p. 8)

At the center of a psychology which presents homosexuality as disease is acceptance of the natural universality of heterosexuality. Socarides (1978) writes that the

male-female design is taught to the child from birth and is culturally ingrained through the marital order. This design is anatomically determined, as it derives from cells which evolved phylogenetically into organ systems and finally into two classes of individuals reciprocally adapted to each other. This is the evolutionary development of human beings. (p. 5)

In short, he insists, homosexuality is a disturbance of the healthy existing order. Psychiatrist Joseph Nicolosi (1991) describes the homosexual condition as "a developmental problem—and one that often results from early problems between father and son. . . . Failure in relationship with father may result in failure to internalize male gender-identity" (p. xvi). Reflecting a similar view, Socarides (1995) believes that "something frightened these people very early in life. Something went wrong in their childhood, some disturbance in the formation of their sexual identity." He also believes that child molestation causes homosexuality because "most homosexuals have been abused as infants, or in their early childhood" (p. 87).

Conversion therapy, based on the concept that gay people can, through appropriate interventions, become heterosexuals, has long been a staple of the traditionalist approach in psychotherapy. Sociologist Kenneth Plummer (1975) asserts that "such visible control of deviance becomes another effective means by which a social order tangibly displays its potency" (p. 120). Conversion of homosexuals has grown into a major element in antigay efforts. As recently as the summer of 1998, 15 different religious groups including the Christian Coalition and the Family Research Council ran a series of advertisement in American national newspapers explaining the possibility and highlighting the results of conversion therapy (Ghent, 1998, p. 25).

The theme of mental illness has been further augmented in recent years with depiction of homosexuals as "disease carriers." Rueda (1982) sounded the keynote for this appeal by describing the "homosexual community as a reservoir of disease for the rest of society" (p. 49). Homosexuals are diseased, so this argument runs, because they are inherently promiscuous and because they engage in dangerous sexual practices. As Herman (1997) notes, antigay advocates emphasize the gay male engaged in sexual behavior which is an "extraordinary combination of power, degradation, excitement, pleasure, savagery, and bacchanalian hedonism" (p. 81). Because homosexuals are far more promiscuous than heterosexuals, psychologist Larry Burtoft (1995) declares, they are far more prone to disease. "As the number of multiple partners increases, so does the danger and incidence of disease" (p. 36). Gay sexual behavior is not only promiscuous but also degraded. The antigay discourse of disease routinely contains narrations "detailing how gay men ingest pounds of feces during their lifetimes and pour urine on each other during parties" (Gallagher, 1994, p. 396).

The AIDS epidemic is, of course, the leading topic for dramatic depiction of the diseased homosexual. This disease has emerged as one of the primary reasons justifying strict laws suppressing homosexual conduct in the interest of both the general population and homosexuals themselves. Dannemeyer (1989) argues that

> it has only been with the legalization of this unhealthy behavior and the increased tolerance of the normal population that these various diseases have become problematic and even epidemic. We have done homosexuals themselves the greatest injustice by permitting such license, since they have become the chief victims of their own misbehavior. (p. 221)

As Burtoft (1995) concludes, "given the tragically high rate of disease and short life spans of homosexuals, clearly their sexual behavior poses a public health risk. If for no other reason than this, homosexual acts deserve public censure" (p. 49). The term "diseased" thus condenses a variety of indictments of homosexuality.

Allied to the "disease" appeal is the invocation of a sexual aesthetic which consists of repulsive and threatening images. Anthropologist Gayle Rubin (1993) observes that "most people find it difficult to grasp that whatever they like to do sexually will be thoroughly repulsive to someone else" (p.15). Consequently, philosopher Michael Ruse (1988) argues that antigay advocates can draw on strong negative feelings about homosexuality, especially male same-sex eroticism. Bryant (1977), for example, recounts that "I opened the mail one day . . . and there before my eyes was the most hideous thing I had ever seen—a picture of two nude men committing an act of homosexuality" (p. 67). Pat Buchanan finds that such visceral recoil from homosexuality "is the natural reaction of a healthy society wishing to protect itself" (The Other Minority, 1992, p. 7).

Another recurrent theme running through antigay literature is the seduction of the young. This theme condenses belief that individual homosexuals molest young people with the sense that public knowledge of homosexuality will influence young people to experiment with variant sexuality. Herman (1997) observes that children are depicted as having a "malleable sexuality, vulnerable to persuasion. Homosexuals are represented as predators, subverting God's plan for youth" (p. 79). Bryant (1977) compressed both meanings into the slogan "homosexuals cannot reproduce—so they must recruit. And to freshen their ranks, they must recruit the youth of America" (p. 62). The theme of child molestation has been richly elaborated in the antigay literature. Rueda (1982), for instance, asserts that the "existence of child-centered pornography ("kiddie porn") and very young homosexual child prostitutes, as well as a number of instances in which homosexuals have been convicted of seducing children, are clear indications that for a substantial number of homosexuals, children are the sexual object of choice" (p. 176). Equally important is the idea that homosexuality if not hidden will entice young people into sin and disease. If homosexuals are allowed to live openly, children will quickly realize that this hedonistic lifestyle is a socially approved lifestyle. As LaHaye (1982) declaims, the "truth is . . . that unless it is culturally branded as wrong, homosexuality will offer a credible option to impressionable young people" (p. 200). Thus, dangers of conversion to homosexuality have become an important frame for antigay action.

The theme of the seduction of the child is amplified in the figure of the homosexual school teacher. Bryant (1977) declares, "public approval of admitted homosexual teachers could encourage more homosexuality by inducing pupils into looking upon it as an acceptable life-style. And second, a particularly deviant-minded teacher could sexually molest children" (p. 114). Max Rafferty, former California Superintendent of Public Instruction, took for granted that "a homosexual in a school job was as out of the question as a heroin addict working in a drugstore" and noted that young people would quickly infer that "if it's okay to put a pervert in charge of the educational destinies of school children, then it must be okay to be a pervert" (quoted in Bryant, 1977, p. 142).

The seduction of the child appeal has been recently expressed more moderately, but with much the same effect. Psychologist E. L. Patullo (1992), for instance, believes that society should protect young "waverers," the many individuals "who fall somewhere in the middle of the continuum" of human sexuality (p. 21). Protection requires that "we guard against doing anything which might mislead wavering children into perceiving society as indifferent to the sexual orientation they develop" (p. 22). Society must strongly signal its preference for heterosexuality because "in a wholly nondiscriminatory world, the advantages of homosexuality would not be obvious" (p. 22). In general, protecting those who might waver into homosexuality should prevent government from "giving homosexuals a special status and making it illegal to discriminate in any way on grounds of sexual orientation" (p. 23). In addition, Patullo would deny homosexual couples adoption rights and, in custody cases involving natural parents, he would discriminate in favor of a straight person over a gay one, other things being equal" (p. 23). He concludes:

> Schools should also be able to insist that homosexual elementary- and secondary-school teachers not flaunt their sexual orientation in ways likely to influence their pupils. Nor should schools be forced to authorize the formation of gay and lesbian student organizations, let alone to propagandize their pupils. (p. 23)

The appeals summarized above are often stitched together in the "collapse of civilization" narrative which is a central figure in traditionalist discourse. Although there are many variations to this narrative, homosexuality is essentially represented as introducing chaos into culture in the sense that variant sexuality challenges established boundaries. As we discussed earlier, channeling behavior into approved forms is central to traditionalist belief. A common theme of traditionalist discourse is opposition to excessive freedom, lack of constraint, and rampant individualism (Himmelstein, 1990, p. 105). Consequently, the traditionalist view of homosexuality focuses on the "inevitability of a symbolic order based on a logic of limits, margins, borders, and boundaries," expressed in a "language and law of defense and protection: heterosexuality both secures itself from what it sees as the continual predatory encroachments of its contaminated other, homosexuality" (Fuss, 1991, pp. 1-2).

The religious version of the collapse of civilization narrative depicts a God angry at homosexuality as an agency for destroying civilization. LaHaye (1978) declares:

> [The] day we legalize homosexuality and accept it as a normal way of life, we will cross over the line into human depravity and degeneracy, and God will "give us up" as he did the Sodomites, the Romans, and the many others whose rejection of his standard of morality caused their destruction. (p. 202)

Such a theme of God's wrath against a sinful society continues to appear in antigay discourse (Magnuson, 1994, p. 18).

The secular version of the same theme depicts permissive societies dying of natural causes. Fear of a wrathful God is unnecessary to advance these arguments. Religious antigay discourse can evoke Sodom's fire, Onan's sin, Leviticus, St. Paul, and death as the "wages of sin." In secular form, society collapses because of the naturally corrosive effects of the wrong people sleeping with each other. Socarides (1995), for instance, asserts:

> Our sexual folkways are a product of the human race's long evolutionary march, which has established certain patterns that were found to work. They make possible the cooperative existence of human beings with one another. . . . Not all cultures survive. The majority have not, and anthropologists tell us that serious flaws in sexual codes and institutions have undoubtedly played a significant role in many a culture's demise. (p. 289)

This position is exaggerated and popularized by such advocates as James Dobson, prominent antigay advocate and leader of Focus on the Family, who declares that "robbed of sexual standards, society will unravel like a ball of twine. That is the legacy of Rome and more than 2,000 civilizations that have come and gone on this earth" (Dobson & Bauer, 1990, p. 55).

Civilization's collapse through approval of homosexuality bundles together in an interpretive package several of the appeals discussed so far. An increasingly larger homosexual population of non-procreative and diseased persons leads inevitably to social decline. In addition, approval of homosexuality will result in effeminacy. Essayist Norman Podhoretz (1977) argues that pacifism is inevitably linked to homosexuality, asserting that this was true in England between the world wars, and in the United States during the Vietnam War (pp. 30-31). For Magnuson (1994), effeminacy extends beyond foreign policy to infect every aspect of civilization. He asserts that the increasing acceptance of homosexuality warps every aspect of society:

> The clothes we wear, the music we listen to, the preaching we hear from our pulpits, the treatment given our children, the lives lived by homosexuals themselves. We live, as philosopher Richard Weaver once said, in an increasingly effeminate culture. (p. 157)

In addition, approval of homosexuality pushes America down the "slippery slope" to destruction through unbridled hedonism. A recurrent theme appears in traditionalist discourse that there is a pressing need to enforce a line "between sexual order and chaos" resulting in the fear that if "anything is permitted to cross this erotic DMZ, the barrier against scary sex will crumble and something unspeakable will skitter across" (Rubin, 1993, p. 14). As Browning (1993) points out, the problem posed by homosexuality is a "universal impulse toward wildness, an impulse that if allowed to go unchecked would proliferate into a thousand jungles of desire" (p. 100). Antigay religious leader Jerry Falwell (1980) expresses this fear by wondering "if homosexuality is deemed normal, how long will it be before rape, adultery, alcoholism, drug addiction, and incest are labeled as normal" (pp. 183-184).

The most important strain in the often repeated "collapse of civilization" theme is that homosexuality will destroy the family on which society is based. As Georgia Attorney General Michael Bowers declared, "Homosexual sodomy is anathema of the basic units of our society—marriage and the family" (quoted in Clendinen & Nagourney, 1999, p. 535). Burtoft (1995) summarizes the argument, "Homosexual sexuality is necessarily incapable of creating and deepening the physical and emotional unity upon which strong marriages, strong families and, therefore, strong societies are built" (p. 51). Put another way, homosexuality "is essentially antifamily. It encourages promiscuous sexuality, a self-centered morality, and socially irresponsible behavior that exacts huge costs from society" (Magnuson, 1994, p. 92). Such a line of inferences has long been present in antigay discourse. For example, Bryant (1977) employs George Gilder's popular book on the decline of family to "prove single men are the chief source of crime and social disruption. He argues convincingly that marriage is essential to male socialization in the modern world" (p. 53).

Social scientist Rebecca Klatch (1987) capsulizes the antigay interpretive package which links the evils of homosexuality, the collapse of the family, and the end of civilization, writing that, in the traditionalist world view, the "ideal society is one in which individuals are integrated into a moral community, bound together by faith, by common moral values, and by obeying the dictates of the family, the church, and God" (p. 24). Essential to civilization is an unchanging conception of gender roles "which, divinely ordained, are essential to the survival of the family and to the maintenance of a moral, ordered society" (p. 46). Attack from any quarter on gender roles is understood to be an assault on the social order, but homosexuality is the "ultimate fear underlying this concern over confused gender roles" (p. 47).

In summary, the antigay interpretive package includes religious and sectarian claims that the state can discriminate in order to exclude expression of homosexuality from the public sphere. Although homosexuality is characterized as a social evil, specific appeals are framed through the general belief that social approval, acceptance, or legitimation of homosexuality in any form will destroy the community. The fundamental basis for opposition to homosexuality, therefore, is that sodomy, defined ambiguously as all forms of nonprocreative sex, "has been viewed historically, at least in the West, as constitutively disruptive of essence. In this way it has proven to be infinitely adaptable as a figure for the disruption or destabilization of any foundational order" (Edelman, 1994, p. 100).

Refutation of Antigay Appeals

Gay and lesbian advocates have generally been defensive respondents to the interlocking set of traditionalist appeals. They are faced with the task of attempting to demonstrate that long accepted claims are fundamental distortions, simply wrong or inapplicable. The progay case consists of an interpretive package which establishes that same-sex sex and gay/lesbian identities are consistent with religious belief and morality. Homosexual behavior is natural and not productive of disease. Openly gay men and women are not threatening to the young, and do not disrupt society.

The progay religious response has produced a large literature on the theme that religious precepts have been used to reinforce cultural prejudice. In the mid-1950s, theologian Derrick Bailey (1955) wrote tentatively that it might

> be well for us frankly to face the fact that rationalization of sexual prejudices, animated by false notions of sexual privilege, has played no inconsiderable part in forming the tradition which we have inherited and probably controls opinion and policy today in the matter of homosexuality to a greater extent than is commonly realized. (p. 162)

The progay response to traditionalist religious condemnation of homosexuality has been an effort to describe antihomosexual doctrine as woefully prejudiced and a transparent rationalization for the exercise of social power. Theologian and pastor William Sloan Coffin declared that "it is not Scripture that creates hostility to homosexuality, but rather hostility to homosexuality that prompts certain Christians to retain a few passages from an otherwise discarded law code" (quoted in Doupe, 1992, p. 188).

On the level of biblical texts, gay/lesbian advocates seek to demonstrate that the Bible has been misunderstood and misused regarding homosexual acts and gay identity. In an analysis which deeply influenced subsequent progay discourse, historian John Boswell (1980) concludes that the "effect of Christian Scripture on attitudes toward homosexuality could be described as moot. The most judicious historical perspective might be that it had no effect at all. The source of antigay feelings among Christians must be sought elsewhere" (p. 116). This view is based on the premise that it was not until the middle ages that Christians distorted the meaning of the few biblical passages which could conceivably be understood to refer to homosexuality. Boswell maintains that in the Levitical condemnation of homosexual acts, abomination "does not usually signify something intrinsically evil, like rape or theft (discussed elsewhere in Leviticus), but something which is ritually unclean for Jews, like eating pork or engaging in intercourse during menstruation, both of which are prohibited in these same chapters" (p. 100). He argues on both the basis of textual analysis and later biblical references that the sin of sodomy was inhospitality to strangers rather than homosexual activity (pp. 94-95). Further, the "New Testament takes no demonstrable position on homosexuality" (p. 117). Boswell also suggests that passages currently cited as condemning homosexuality are either mistranslations or passages which condemn the homosexual acts committed by persons who are naturally heterosexual (pp. 109-111). Based on this analysis, he contends that supposed biblical injunctions are not the cause of intolerance toward homosexuality. He concludes:

> If religious strictures are used to justify oppression by people who regularly disregard precepts of equal gravity from the same moral code, or if prohibitions which restrain a disliked minority are upheld in their most literal sense as absolutely inviolable while comparable precepts affecting the majority are relaxed or reinterpreted, one must suspect something other than religious belief as the motivating cause of the oppression. (Boswell, 1980, p. 7)

Antigay advocates are further accused of ignoring Biblical passages which encourage tolerance, acceptance, and universal love.

Recent progay commentators have traced the motivation for religious opposition to homosexuality to cultural prejudice rather than biblical text, seeking to frame antigay belief as prejudice rather than doctrine. Scripture is read through antigay cultural beliefs. For example, theologian Pim Pronk (1993) asserts that the Bible is primarily cited "to explain, give ground to, and excuse our own attitude to homosexuals. But a need for that attitude can in no way simply be derived from or be read in the Bible" (p. xiii). Instead, Mohr (1994) concludes, it is "not that the Bible is being used to ground condemnation of homosexuality as much as society's dislike of homosexuality is being used to interpret the Bible" (p. 9). The traditionalist advocate is engaged in what gay evangelical Mel White (1994) calls "selective literalism, choosing to interpret literally only those texts that suit his predetermined purposes, in this case honoring the ancient, evil, ignorant spirit of superstition and hatred against gay and lesbian people" (p. 238). In an open letter to Jerry Falwell, White (1999) asserts that Biblical verses condemning homosexuality should be balanced against the fundamental Biblical message:

> The Scriptures are still clear about fighting injustice and standing against the immoral and dehumanizing traditions of man. Why can't you apply *those* Scriptures to us instead of the six verses you misuse over and over again to clobber and condemn GLBT people. (p. 26)

A key theme which has recently emerged in progay writing is a condemnation of cultural Christianity which the Harvard theologian Peter Gomes (1996) describes as interpreting the Bible through the lens of contemporary beliefs and anxieties. He asserts:

> In reading and interpreting the Bible, the great temptation is to use it as the moral sanction for our own culture. In making an idol of the culture, we seduce the Bible into its service, and reduce the will and word of God to a mere artifact of things as we know them. (p. 48)

He further explains:

> For those who hold to the intimate relationship between the Bible and culture, the Bible often becomes an icon of that culture. The culture seems itself mirrored in the Bible, the Bible is understood to be the norm by which the culture is defined, and this often results in the Bible's use as a textbook of the status quo. (p. 58)

As a result, he notes, almost every effort to create social change has been opposed on a biblical basis. Such change is consistently understood as "not simply tinkering with the culture, it is tinkering with the Bible, and therefore tinkering with God" (p. 58). Gomes traces religious condemnation to the demands of the medieval and modern church rather than to the Bible, asserting:

> What the homosexual did was different, and hence the homosexual was different, and in a religious world that increasingly prized conformity in all things, but particularly in sexual matters, the difference branded the homosexual as a threat to the moral order, the equivalent of the heretic in the church or a traitor in the state. (p. 169)

Taking a different tact which leads to the same conclusion, Goss (1993) contends that "Christianity has institutionalized a particular discourse and practice of heterosexist power relations . . . [which] have actively contributed to homophobic oppression and violence" (p. xvi).

Progay advocates take the position that homosexuality is in no sense "unnatural." In the late 1940s, novelist and essayist James Baldwin (1997/1949) declared that "if we are going to be natural then this [homosexuality] is a part of nature; if we refuse to accept this, then we have rejected nature and must find other criterion" (p. 236). Rather than being an independent ground of judgment against homosexuality, progay advocates construe natural law as simply an expression of religious belief. Nava and Dawidoff (1994) point out that as "natural" is used in antigay discourse, it is a religious and not a biological term. They assert that the

> claim that homosexuality is unnatural is an ideological assertion grounded in religious opinion. Religious condemnation of homosexuality as "against nature" derives from the work of theologians, whose understanding of nature is not the result of a scientific attempt to understand the processes of the world. (p. 46)

Further, theologically based natural law, understood as the prohibition of nonprocreative sex acts, has lost its persuasive force because, as progay essayist Andrew Sullivan (1995) observes, "there are many features of contemporary Western society that violate the centrality of monogamous procreation to sexual intercourse just as powerfully as toleration of homosexuality" (p. 53).

The progay position on the "naturalness" of homosexuality takes two forms. On the one hand, homosexuality and gay persons can be understood as natural. Hence, Nava and Dawidoff (1994) assert that homosexuality is the "natural predisposition of a minority of human beings" (p. xii). Taking another approach, biologist Bruce Bagemihl (1999) marshals extensive data to suggest that homosexuality is common in nature because a wide variety of species engage in homosexual acts. On the other hand, progay advocates argue that no sexuality is natural. Postmodern social scientist Anna Marie Smith (1994) extrapolates the work of Judith Butler to conclude that "any apparently prediscursive being is a constructed fiction which legitimates the extensions of intensifications of disciplinary strategies" (p. 104). In particular application, Butler "by conceptualizing gender as the effect of performative practices . . . undermines the distinction between 'natural' and 'unnatural' articulations" (p. 104). This is to say that no form of sexuality can claim status as anything other than a social convention. Consequently, heterosexuality is not natural in the sense of being normal. To the contrary, normal heterosexuality "fundamentally depends for its production upon extensive familial, educational, medical, moral and legal intervention" (p. 104).

The concept that homosexuality should be considered criminal is regarded by progay advocates as subsidiary to other antigay appeals. They do not doubt that sodomy laws serve to suppress homosexual behavior and to stigmatize gay persons. Instead, they take the position that this effect, far from being salutary, constitutes a serious and fundamental injustice. Nava and Dawidoff (1994) argue:

> Sodomy laws, however lax or intermittent their enforcement, are the foundation of discrimination. . . . They justify second-class citizenship and cannot be looked upon honestly without acknowledging that they still stigmatize certain citizens, making them virtual outlaws, and encourage and reinforce prejudice and violence against those citizens whether or not they break the law. (p. 3)

For progay advocates, sodomy laws exist "not out of a concern with the *actions* of gay people, but with their *status*" (Mohr, 1988, p. 59). Such laws, designed only to insult and degrade a category of citizens, do not constitute an independent justification for further public policy discrimination.

Progay literature consistently contends that lesbians and gay men are not psychologically disturbed. One component of this literature centers on the claims that "psychology's use of disease terminology to characterize socially and politically deviant behavior functions, as many researchers have pointed out, as a powerful form of social control" (Kitzinger, 1987, p. 32). The use of mental illness to characterize homosexuality has often been explained as a substitute for religious terminology. Kaplan (1997) argues, for instance, that "at a time of increasing secularization, and within a constitutional context of religious pluralism, models of mental health have figured importantly as vehicles, sometimes as disguises, for ethical judgment and authority" (p. 33). Psychiatrist Ronald Bayer (1981) points out that modern psychologists and psychotherapists "in place of a Divinely determined standard for sexuality . . . put one thought to exist in nature" (p. 18). The argument is also advanced that gender bias deeply motivates the antigay psychiatric position because it "derives from an initial gynecophobic stance in psychoanalysis and that the fear and denigration of women which hover at the perimeter of analytic discourse became displaced onto the theory of male homosexuality" (Lewes, 1988, p. 21).

Functioning as moral categorization, the pathologization of homosexuality blinded mental health professionals to the possibility that homosexual orientation is a normal human variation. For example, pioneering gay activist Frank Kameny (1997/1969) argues with respect to the etiology of homosexuality that, "if no non-pathological alternatives are even considered, homosexuality *will* be found to be pathological, or to result from a disturbed or defective background" (p. 368).

Progay advocates point out that justifications for state action on the ground that homosexuality is a mental illness have lost force because they "no longer command support from authorized experts in the fields of psychiatry and psychology" (Kaplan, 1997, p. 33). Psychologist Kenneth Lewes (1988) maintains that "there can be no doubt that some forms of homosexuality are psychopathological, but the same is true for heterosexuality" (p. 22). Consequently, the description of homosexuality as mental illness

> was not based, as scientific theories supposedly are, on an unbiased inspection and ordering of its data, but on the confluence of that approach with historical accident, unexamined moral and social judgment, and the vagaries of the history of psychoanalysis and psychoanalytic discourse at various points in its history. (Lewes, 1988, p. 230)

In this view, the "status of homosexuality is a political question, representing a historically rooted, socially determined choice regarding the ends of human sexuality" (Bayer, 1981, p. 4).

Progay critics recognize the potency of the connection between homosexuality and disease. Rhetorician James Chesebro (1994), for example, notes:

> AIDS has become a critical factor in altering political trends. It has functioned as a rationale for political oppression, isolated gay males from the mainstream of society, and provided a foundation for reversing the civil, legal, and social rights secured by gay males and lesbians in the 1960s and 1970s. (p. 80)

Gay advocates have attacked the scientific rigor of those who would link disease to homosexuality, claiming that traditionalists were using faulty methods in the pursuit of predetermined conclusions (Gallagher & Bull, 1996, p. 116). Generally, progay advocates describe traditionalist researchers as woefully inadequate "scientists" whose influence with policy makers is greatly disproportionate to their sham results (Pietrzyk, 1994, pp. 10-12). Moreover, claims about disease caused by homosexual practices have been applicable only to men, ignoring women's far different (and safer) sexual practices (Herman, 1997, p. 92). Finally, progay writers reduce the traditionalist disease appeal to a rhetorical figure. Smith

(1994), for example, argues that the "hegemonic interpretation of the AIDS phenomenon, which equates AIDS with male homosexuality with promiscuity with death, is actually a strategic response to perceived threats of subversion of the heterosexual patriarchal order through the advances of the radical sexual liberation and feminist movements" (p. 198).

Progay advocates have responded strongly to the traditionalist attack on homosexuals for sexually molesting and recruiting children. Apart from the claim that gay people molest children no more often, or even less frequently, than heterosexuals, progay advocates contend that the "notion that gays are sexual predators is a projection of antihomosexual sexual obsession. It is also fueled by the majority's refusal to recognize homosexuality as equally natural, if not as common, as heterosexuality and bisexuality" (Nava & Dawidoff, 1994, p. 37). The argument is advanced that because variation in sexual orientation is natural, produced by an individual's genetic makeup and/or early childhood experience, it is impossible to recruit young people into homosexuality. Posner (1992), for instance, observes that the "formation of homosexual preference, at least in males, appears to be deeply rooted in genetic, hormonal, and (or) developmental factors unlikely to be offset by purely social influences" (p. 203). This premise is used to rebut suggestions that school children can be recruited into homosexuality (DeCecco, 1981, p. 34).

Progay advocates dismiss the notion that homosexuality subverts civilization, arguing that such a charge "functions to displace (possibly irresolvable) social problems from their actual source to a remote and (society hopes) manageable one" (Mohr, 1994, p. 3). Traditionalist discourse on the family operates to "displace the cause for the breakdown of the family onto an external figure . . . [to support] the phantasmatic representation of the family as an antagonism-free space" (Smith, 1994, p. 222). In a similar vein, Nava and Dawidoff (1994) assert that the "family to which these moralists refer was the rhetorical invention of the 1950s; it was done in not by gays but by its own failures as an economic, parenting, emotional, mythic, and moral unit" (p. 24).

The contention is also advanced that gays and lesbians, in fact, do not threaten the family at all. Goss (1993) claims that "homosexuality threatens only what traditional values are based upon—the dualistic politics of gender and sexual identity" (p. 2). Moreover, progay advocates assert that gay and lesbian people want to defend the family because so many of them are in families with their own children. They cite, for example, reports that lesbians are as likely to be mothers as heterosexual women (LeVay & Nonas, 1995, p. 110). Mohr (1994) puts the matter another way, reporting that "around 6 percent of the U.S. population is made up of gay and lesbian families with children" (p. 39). Consequently, traditionalists are the real enemies of strong family life because no "conceivable purpose can be served for these children by barring to their gay and lesbian parents the mutual cohesion, emotional security, and economic benefit that are ideally promoted by legal marriage" (p. 39). The traditionalist depiction of gay/lesbian attack on the family is a fundamental distortion because "it is homophobia that strains family relationships by restricting communication among family members" (Blumenfeld, 1992, p. 10).

Running beneath specific progay refutation of anti-homosexual claims is the effort to frame lesbians and gay men as persons unjustly stigmatized. As gay English professor Alan Helms (1995) remembers, the reverberations of a lexicon of antigay epithets and characterizations:

> Sounded even in our dreams, inducing a kind of concentration camp mentality. We were disposable, the scum of the earth, living crimes against nature . . . and we knew that socially, religiously, legally, psychoanalytically, and in every other way that mattered, we were beyond the pale of what was considered acceptably human. (p. 75)

Such systematic denigration of lesbians and gay men has been represented as unfair because they are both good citizens and decent people entitled to the same rights everyone else enjoys. From the earliest days of the homophile movement, the notion was present in discourse and public performance that, in the words of homophile activist Dorr Legg (1997/1958), "I am glad to be a homosexual, proud of it" (p. 326). In recent years, argument has been advanced that the lesbians and gay men perform important social functions (Sullivan, 1995, pp. 200-204). A defensive posture, however, remains dominant in the progay interpretive package. Smith (1994) laments that "there remains a tremendous absence in the [progay] discourse . . . [of] the argument that homosexuality *can* and *ought to be* promoted" (p. 238).

Gay/Lesbian Public Policy Claims

Most broadly stated, gay/lesbian advocates have collectively created an interpretive package which supports the end of public discrimination against individuals of variant sexuality. More precisely, they seek (a) the end of state action against homosexual behavior (abolition of sodomy laws); (b) the prohibition of state discrimination against gay people (exclusion from the military, denial of same-sex marriage); and (c) the use of state power to discourage discrimination by individuals and other non-governmental groups (equal housing and employment nondiscrimination measures).

Progay public policy appeals assume many forms, but they are unified by the concept that society should address harms which are done, publicly and privately, to lesbians and gay men. The overarching proposition which packages these harms together is that "discrimination on the basis of sexual orientation affects lesbians and gay men in a wide range of contexts in both the public and private sectors" (*Sexual orientation*, 1990, p. 161). The first set of harms involves denial of personal freedom. Political scientist Mark Blasius (1994) asserts that the "source of a relational right, then, resides in individuals' need for relational freedom—the freedom to choose their sexual-affectional relations with others—in order to constitute themselves as ethical beings" (p. 141). The second set of harms occurs when gay and lesbian people are denied full citizenship (i.e., the right to participate as equals in civil society). The most salient and controversial current denials of citizenship are the military ban on service by known homosexuals and the prohibition of same sex marriage (pp. 25-63). The third set of harms concerns discrimination against gay and lesbian Americans "in virtually every area of civil life. Seeking health care, employment, housing, access to public facilities, homosexuals encounter discrimination simply by identifying themselves as gay or lesbian" (Nava & Dawidoff, 1994, p. xiv).

Gay advocates maintain that these harms are serious. Most directly, systematic discrimination against lesbians and gay men "perpetuates a vicious cycle of anti-gay violence and abuse" (*Sexual orientation*, 1990, p. 31). Further, they are denied specific benefits such as those which are a part of the right to marry (Eskridge, 1996, pp. 66-70). Equally important, gay and lesbian citizens are essentially dishonored as participants in society. In general, the "legal and social status of homosexuals in our society amounts to a condition of second-class citizenship" (Kaplan, 1997, p. x).

Blasius (1994) argues that lesbians and gay men suffer a "social death" which is

> significantly manifest in their rejection from families of birth, the society's unwillingness to allow them to marry and rear children, censorship of their production of artifacts that could transmit culture across generations, and inability to contract laterally for housing, employment, and essential services *as* lesbian or gay. (p. 32)

From another perspective, Mohr (1994) contends that denial of protection and equality to gay individuals is a rejection of their status as persons. Thus, "being fired or being physically attacked because one is gay is a harm, but even more so it is a degradation. Gay oppression is mainly the denial of gay dignity" (p. 59).

As Kaplan (1997) points out, correction of harms produced by antigay public policy accomplishes three primary goals:

> (1) decriminalization of homosexual activities between consenting adults; (2) the prohibition of discrimination against lesbians and gays in employment, housing, education, and public accommodations; and (3) the legal and social recognition of the ethical status of lesbian and gay relationships and community institutions. (p. 14)

A long list of legislation has been proposed, and innumerable court cases filed as partial steps toward achieving these goals.

Although a wide range of justification is offered by progay advocates for why public policy should be modified to incorporate gay positive changes, the progay interpretive package hinges on the ideographs "rights" and "liberty," resolving itself into claims for protection for rights to a decent life, stable relationships, and political expression and for individual liberty. In addition, gay and lesbian advocates maintain that because of a history of discrimination, equal protection of the law requires that state action with regard to gay/lesbian people requires heightened scrutiny.

With respect to individual rights, Kaplan (1997) observes that the extension of gay and lesbian rights necessarily hinges on "fundamental conceptions of individual liberty as established in constitutional texts and practices within modern democracy. It invokes liberal conceptions of personal freedom and moral autonomy" (p. 5). In balancing rights, personal freedom is given heavy weight. Consequently, "opposition to gay rights

represents the continuing efforts of those who mistrust individual freedom as the basis of a just society" (Nava & Dawidoff, 1994, p. 10). In
the pursuit of happiness, "gays and lesbians are fighting for the right to secure the conditions under which they may lead ordinary, civilized lives"
(p. 27). Among these conditions are the right to association with others of
one's choice, essentially a claim "to individuate oneself through relationships" (Blasius, 1994, p. 139). Kaplan (1997) agrees that "respect for individual freedom requires the existence of a plurality of voluntary 'intimate associations' through which individuals shape their lives and define
their personal identities" (p. 3).

In progay discourse, the most important associational rights concern
political action. Kaplan (1997) argues:

> Political equality for unpopular minorities can be secured only if they are
> protected against retaliation for exerting their civil rights by laws that pro-
> hibit discrimination against them in employment, housing, education, and
> other critical areas of social and economic activity. (p. x)

Mohr (1994) adds that an individual who "is a member of an invisible minority and who must remain invisible, hidden, and secreted in respect to
her minority status . . . is effectively denied all political power except the
right to vote" (p. 89). Broadening this concept, rhetorician Paul Siegel
(1991) anchors the associational right of gay and lesbian people in freedom of expression. He observes that gay and lesbian advocacy against discrimination and for protection

> almost invariably involve[s] issues of freedom of expression . . . ranging
> from classic "access to a forum" controversies to those concerning symbolic
> conduct and freedom of association (including marriage and child custody
> law), employment discrimination, and proscriptions against deviant sexual
> conduct. In each category, claims to a right of freedom of expression are
> manifest. (Siegel, 1991, p. 203)

Progay advocates assert that society should be particularly careful to
protect the civil rights of gay and lesbian citizens because of a long history
of discrimination and exclusion from the political process (*Sexual orientation,* 1990, p. 57). Mohr (1994) argues, for example, that gays and lesbians should be accorded "suspect" class status because they have long
been treated in discriminatory fashion. He asserts that "this treatment justifies the application to gays of the moral sense of minority, and in turn

ought to invoke the constitutional norms the culture thinks appropriate for minority status, especially enhanced constitutional protection" (p. 72).

As this summary suggests, the gay/lesbian interpretive package on public policy issues is predominantly "rights" based. Justification for gay positive public policy is expressed in terms of protection against discrimination on both individual and collective levels.

Traditionalist Public Policy Claims

Traditionalists assume the role of protective defender against what they pejoratively term the "homosexual agenda." They recognize that gay/lesbian social movement organizations have made significant progress in modifying public policy. Podhoretz (1996), for example, dolefully judges that "what set the process in motion through which homosexuality would eventually be legitimated in every sense was its transformation from a private condition into a political movement" (p. 35). In response to the emergence of gay/lesbian advocacy, traditionalists urge countermobilization. Many have asserted that homosexuals are mobilizing to achieve the goal of "total acceptance and legal sanction of their behavior and lifestyle, and they have made inroads seemingly everywhere" (Magnuson, 1994, p. 13).

As discussed earlier in this chapter, traditionalist public policy positions are based in staunch antihomosexual views. Discrimination is justified as the only available means to keep homosexuality excluded from the public sphere. Thus, opposition to the gay movement interlocks easily with this discourse of anti-homosexuality. What is alleged to be wrong with homosexual movements is that they promote sin, crime, sickness, recruitment, and social disorder. This position is supplemented with the elaboration that discrimination occurs only against visible lesbians and gay men. Bryant (1977) maintains that "homosexuals do not suffer discrimination when they keep their perversions in the privacy of their own homes. They can hold any job, transact any business, join any organization—so long as they do not flaunt their homosexuality" (p. 62). Joining this position, Rueda (1982) asserts that discrimination only "arises when individuals who are affected by what, in the estimation of the social majority, is a repugnant and potentially disruptive condition, contend openly and aggressively that this is not so" (p. 131). In traditionalist discourse, discrimination is the fault of the homosexual movement which insists on defending homosexuality and thereby making it visible.

The role of homosexual movements in creating public issues out of private behavior is condemned by traditionalists on a number of grounds. First, such movements ease entry into the homosexual subculture which, in turn, has the effect of "objectively decreasing the individual's freedom even as it provides him with a sense of liberation" (Rueda, 1982, p. 46). Involvement in movements for homosexual civil privileges is nothing more than a "freeing of the homosexual to seek the complete satisfaction of his sexual appetites without the restrictions which children, family responsibility, and the tenets of the Judeo-Christian ethic impose on heterosexuals" (p. 46). Second, realization of the "homosexual agenda" would facilitate more extensive recruitment of the young. LaHaye (1978) argues that "we cannot give the unhappy gays the acceptance they demand without sentencing millions of innocent youths to a lifetime of this misery" (p. 190). Third, social acceptance is precisely the goal of homosexual political activism. Magnuson (1985), for instance, claims that because there is no compelling necessity to make public policy changes, legal changes are not the motivation for homosexual activism, "but simply a way station enroute to what homosexuals really want: full social acceptance" (p. 40). Fourth, achievement of the public policy objectives of the homosexual movement will only lead to protections for other forms of perversion (Magnuson, 1994, p. 95). If homosexuality were to be a protected category under civil rights law, "then what is to stop the adulterer from claiming 'adulterer rights,' the murderer from shouting 'murderer rights,' the thief to claim 'extortionist' rights,' and a rebellious young person to insist on 'rebellious-child rights' " (Bryant, 1977, p. 35).

Two related ideographic frames in traditionalist discourse have become increasingly prominent in recent years. First, the protections sought by homosexuals are demands for unconstitutional "special rights." Second, public policy outlawing discrimination against homosexuals infringes on the rights of other citizens. Each of these appeals was present in early traditionalist opposition to the gay rights movement. Bryant (1977), for example, opposed the Dade County, Florida, nondiscrimination ordinance on both grounds and argued:

> If this ordinance is allowed to become law, you will, in fact, be infringing on my rights and discriminating against me as a citizen and a mother to teach

my children and set examples and to point to others as examples of God's moral code as stated in the Holy Scriptures. (p. 16)

Further, the ordinance simply constituted "privileges to homosexuals in areas of housing, public accommodation, and employment" (p. 13). During the same period, Falwell (1981) said that "we do not oppose civil rights for homosexuals. We do oppose 'special rights' for homosexuals who have chosen a perverted life-style rather than a traditional life-style" (p. 189). Such an appeal was used in a 1982 campaign to oppose inclusion of gays in a nondiscrimination ordinance led by the Committee to Oppose Special Rights for Homosexuals (Gallagher & Bull, 1996, p. 111). Throughout the traditionalist response to homosexual movements runs a deep-seated concern with deprivation of rights, an anxiety manifested as a libertarian appeal for freedom to act in areas of vital interest. Within this frame, "prohibitions on sexual orientation discrimination, it was argued, would curtail individual liberties unjustifiably" (Herman, 1997, p. 3).

The "special rights" argument begins with the premise that homosexuals share equal protection of the law with all other persons. As Magnuson (1994) puts it, homosexual persons are protected by the Constitution and statutes: "They have the same status before the law as do other citizens" (p. 30). The next step is to assert that the only characteristic which defines homosexuals as a group is the type of sexual activity in which they engage. Civil rights issues are framed as protection for deviant behavior: "Does the inclination to practice anal or oral sodomy (or related sexual practices) with members of the same sex merit special legal safeguards?" (p. 31). Traditionalists answer with a resounding "no" based on their analysis of what constitutes "minority status" meriting the granting of rights beyond that afforded to all citizens.

Placed within the frame of antihomosexual appeals, special protection for homosexual persons in any form is unwarranted. Combining religious and criminal condemnation, Burtoft (1995) writes that "since the Supreme Court has ruled as constitutional the states' right to criminalize sodomy, it is unreasonable to grant special rights to a group for whom sodomy is the primary identifiable characteristic" (p. 72). Further, bundling together the appeals in favor of antihomosexual discrimination, any denial of the right to make distinctions between heterosexuals and homosexuals becomes irrational. Magnuson (1994) provides the controlling generalization: "Reasonable people—for reasons of deep-seated moral conviction, of health, of psychological stability, or of common sense—may wish to take a person's homosexual lifestyle into account in their decision-making, all without the slightest tinge of bigotry or irrationality" (p. 101).

The core of the "special rights" argument, however, is a distinction between groups in society which deserve special protection and homosexuals who, lacking the immutable defining characteristics of such groups, do not deserve those protections. In essence, "special rights" rhetoric is based on what legal scholar Jane Schacter (1994) calls a "discourse of equivalents" which emphasizes the issue of "whether lesbians and gay men are sufficiently 'like' other protected groups, and whether sexual orientation is sufficiently 'like' race, gender, disability, religion, or national origin to merit the legal protection of civil rights laws" (p. 285). In traditionalist discourse, according to Schacter, homosexuals are unlike groups which rightfully deserve special protection because they do not have an appropriate "status," have not suffered harm, and are not politically powerless (Jeremiah Films, 1993).

With respect to status for special protection, traditionalists maintain that civil rights protection has historically been given only to " 'discrete and insular' minorities who share an immutable *status*. That status was generally unrelated to behavior, traditional perceptions of moral character, [and] public health" (Magnuson, 1994, p. 46). Race, according to Magnuson, is the model for such a status. "Race tells us nothing about a person's lifestyle or behavior. Removing race as a criterion of social decision-making therefore makes sense to all but the most arbitrary decision-maker" (p. 46). In this argument, homosexuals choose to perform acts of sodomy, and because these choices have moral dimensions which ought to be socially recognized, special protection should not be granted.

Further, homosexuals have not been harmed by society in the same way that other protected groups have been damaged. Herman (1997) summarizes this argument, "First, gays are immensely wealthy; second, the gay movement is not only one of the most powerful in the country, but lesbians and gay men as individuals hold vast amounts of political power and unfairly wield it over others" (p. 116). In this appeal, evidence is introduced that gay people are economically better off than most Americans and that they have unlimited political access (Burtoft, 1995, pp. 69-71).

The "special rights" argument leads easily to the claim that homosexuals are seeking inclusion in affirmative action (Levin, 1997, p. 41).

For instance, Magnuson asserts that gay rights success "bears with it the possibility of increasing demands for affirmative action, using the successes of the civil rights movement generally as a model" (p. 38).

Reverse discrimination leads to the vision of deprivation of rights at the center of the "special rights" argument. The core belief is that only in the most pressing and unusual circumstances should society limit citizens' economic and political decision making. An especially strong emotional overtone is often produced within this appeal by situating the alleged deprivation of rights as close as possible to home and children. LaHaye (1978), for instance, writes that as a result of gay rights legislation:

> You will not be able to refuse to rent your home to mating homosexuals, even if your straight children are being raised next door. . . . And worst of all, as a straight taxpayer you could not object if your son or daughter happens to draw a homosexual teacher. (p. 196)

More recently, using the same premise, Magnuson (1994) maintains that the creation of rights can easily lead to the loss of courses of action based on sound moral principles:

> If a homosexual has a right to teach sex education courses in a public school, the school has a duty to allow him to do so, and the parent of a child in that school loses his right to have a say in the moral caliber of a person who teaches his child. (p. 106)

Invoking the same thought used long before by Bryant, Magnuson concludes that, in general, "gay rights laws are coercive to people of conscience" (p. 108). Further, legal protection for homosexual behavior violates fundamental constitutional guarantees. Burtoft (1995) claims that such laws:

> Rob other citizens of their rights to freedom of conscience, freedom of speech, and freedom of association. What's more, to lose the right to discriminate against homosexuality is to also lose the right to protect personal health, as is currently the case with the protected status of people infected with AIDS. (p. 71)

Progay Refutation of Traditionalist Opposition

Progay advocates characterize traditionalist discourse on the gay and lesbian movement as profoundly deceptive. They contend that traditionalists have misrepresented the effect of discrimination. Gay essayist Bruce
Bawer (1993), for instance, claims that what the gay rights movement
seeks "is to abolish the inequities that homosexuals have to live with and
that make it difficult for them to live honestly" (p. 25). Discriminatory
laws do not "keep a single gay person from being gay; they can only keep
him from being honest about it" (p. 25). The result is not an enforced gay
invisibility, but a compulsory silence

> on the part of the majority of gays who, feeling compelled by the ubiquity of
> prejudice to hide their homosexuality, have rendered themselves powerless
> to challenge those false representations—that has kept most Americans
> confused and ill-informed about the basic truths of homosexuality and gay
> life. (Bawer, 1993, p. 25)

Progay advocates also deny the assertion that only visible gays and lesbians are harmed by discrimination. Nava and Dawidoff (1994) claim
that "homosexuality, in this society, is the sole criterion by which the fit-
ness of gays and lesbians is judged in virtually every aspect of civil life"
(p. 60). Rights to employment and promotion, military service, marriage,
and child custody are judged by this criterion. "The deprivation of these
rights does not depend on whether a person announces his homosexuality
or is discovered in his secret; homosexuality, not visibility, is the
disqualifier" (p. 60).

According to progay advocates, the traditionalist case is deeply flawed
by a contradiction. As gay activist Urvashi Vaid (1995) asserts, traditionalist discourse "undermines the gay and lesbian civil rights quest in two
conflicting ways: by denying discrimination against gay people and by defending it" (p. 330). The older terminology of "sin," "sickness," "crime,"
and "social collapse" constitutes the justification of discrimination; the
newer rhetoric of "special rights" denies its existence.

The "special rights" argument has been of considerable concern to
progay advocates who recognize its potentially strong persuasive power.
Vaid (1995) claims that the "most damaging weapon in the right's arsenal
is its use of 'special rights' rhetoric" (p. 330). She cites polling data that
demonstrates that half of voters in states which had gay public policy

questions on their ballots accepted the proposition that lesbians and gay men were seeking "special rights." The popular response of progay advocates is to claim that there is nothing special to the rights which they seek. Nava and Dawidoff (1994) maintain:

> Anti-discrimination laws do no more than prevent gays and lesbians from being fired from their jobs and denied housing or medical care because they are gay. These can be deemed as "special rights" only if a job, food to eat, a place to live, and medical attention are unusual demands. (p. 70)

A more complex refutation of the "special rights" appeal is offered by Schacter (1994), who maintains that this appeal is based on a "misguided search for sameness [which] undermines the foundation of all civil rights law" (pp. 295-296). She asserts that the premise of "special rights" discourse is that "the entry barrier for civil rights protection can be overcome only if the forms and phenomenology of discrimination against lesbians and gay men are the same as for other protected groups" (p. 296). In her view, such a representation "ignores the history of civil rights laws as open-textured and ever-evolving products of changing legal and social norms" (p. 296). Consequently, she concludes that the special rights argument should be dismissed because the common ground between lesbians and gay men and other groups already protected "can be found at a higher level of generality: social subordination and stigmatization subject lesbians and gay men—like other subordinated groups—to systematic exclusion and disadvantage at the hands of dominant groups" (p. 298).

In Schacter's (1994) analysis, the phrase "special rights" also serves as a code to undermine all civil rights protections. She contends that through this phrase "opponents of gay rights not only tap into an existing reservoir of anxiety and antagonisms, but they strengthen the association of civil rights laws with quotas, reverse discrimination, minority domination, and balkanization" (p. 306). This view is seconded by Kaplan (1997) who believes that no group could qualify for civil rights protection by the standards imposed by the "special rights" frame. "The standards were so loose and legally untenable that they could deny virtually anyone's rights" (p. 112). According to Kaplan, Jews could be excluded on the basis of economic power, and religious believers on the grounds that they engage in a chosen behavior (p. 112).

At its core, Schacter (1994) argues, the power of "special rights" as a political strategy lies in symbolically condensing "the idea of reverse discrimination and the related notion that civil rights are a disguised vehicle by which 'powerful special interests groups' manipulate the democratic process to abuse a defenseless, besieged majority" (p. 302). Attempts have been made by progay advocates to oppose this evocation through both denial and analysis of the libertarian position which underlies the theme of "special rights." Bawer (1993), for instance, decries traditionalist attempts to "raise the specter of affirmative-action quotas and recruitment programs for gays in government jobs, the military, college admissions, and the like" on the ground that "quotas and recruitment programs do not figure in any of the gay-rights bills that have passed various state and local legislatures" (p. 147). Despite such attempts to reframe "rights," however, a strong residue remains of the claim that civil rights laws in general, and especially gay civil rights laws, "thwart, rather than promote, equality by jeopardizing the freedom and prerogatives of the dominant group" (Schacter, 1994, p. 312).

Most progay advocates have not responded to the libertarian argument that nondiscrimination laws abridge the freedom of all citizens. Two related analytic responses, however, have been offered. The primary response is that libertarian objections confuse truly private choices with decisions which have wide social impact. Kaplan (1997) grants that proponents of the minimal state are correct that antidiscrimination laws prohibit individuals from exercising their prejudices in all realms, but he maintains that "their objection conflates individual freedom of association, the right to choose your friends, with the collective economic and social power of large-scale employers, financial institutions, real estate enterprises, and the like" (p. 15). Discrimination in the public sphere can be prohibited, whereas private discrimination cannot.

A second, more limited response has been to suggest that nondiscrimination law be confined only to agencies of the state. Sullivan (1995), for example, concedes that "liberals are curiously blind to the illiberal dimensions of their program: they wish, after all, to deny others the rights to complete freedom of contract and to complete freedom of expression, in order to protect a specific minority" (p. 137). In order to defend this position, liberals "argue that their primary concern is not to preserve liberty, but to create a society which holds certain values dear . . . and to use the laws to educate people in this fashion" (p. 137). Sullivan vigorously rejects the liberal position because its effect is to limit the freedom of many in order to expand the liberty of a few. He believes that a consistent position is to affirm a "simple and limited principle: All *public* (as opposed to private) discrimination against homosexuals be ended and that every right and responsibility that heterosexuals enjoy as public citizens be extended to those who grow up and find themselves emotionally different" (p. 171). He contends that the result would be "no cures, or re-education, no wrenching private litigation, no political imposition of tolerance; merely a political attempt to enshrine formal public equality, whatever happens in the culture and society at large" (p. 171). Thus, Sullivan radically modifies the Finnis (1994) position with which this discussion began: Public discrimination, especially by government, is impermissible, but truly private discrimination, though wrong, is simply beyond the law's reach.

In this description of progay and antigay interpretive packages, mutual influence between antagonists takes the assertion/response form characteristic of public debate. Progays are encouraged to include in their package an elaborate response to antigay condemnatory use of condensation symbols, arguments, and narratives. The increasing visibility of collective action on behalf of gay/lesbian subjects initiates an attempt to frame negatively all forms of homosexual activism. Such a frame, in turn, calls forth the deployment of a variety of symbolic responses to this attempt to malign the gay/lesbian movement. The mutual influence between progay and traditionalist movement actors, however, is far more fundamental than the "case building" usual in debate. The interpretive packages of both movements also construct competing representations of collective actors and of the contest in which they are involved, attempting to achieve dominance by creating both the cast and the plot.

4 Antagonistic Construction of Identity and Conflict

The clash of appeals summarized in the previous chapter forms the surface of a more fundamental contest of representation in which traditionalists and progay advocates strategically construct themselves, their relationships to their antagonists, and their position in the public sphere. These contests of representation provide the structure for the variant sexuality issue culture. We will argue that both progays and antigays seek to cast their opponents in the worst light and themselves in the most favorable. What emerges, then, is what Smith (1994) describes as a "competition for legitimation and normalization through [which] the fundamentally political strategy of representation brings competing claims into a mutually subversive battle" (p. 93). Note, for instance, that embedded in many traditionalist appeals are biblical or natural law claims that homosexuals are defective and despicable. Progay appeals carry the message that antigay texts are steeped in ignorance, authoritarianism, and self-interest. Further, appeals of both progay and traditionalist advocates make implicit claims for their side's legitimacy as defender of order, and cast aspersions on their opponents as aggressors against the established political culture.

Traditionalist and progay constructions of self, other, motive, and social position emphasize their differences one from another. Although there may be similarities between progay and antigay tactics, relative location in the political system, and their marginality, a variety of reasons compel each group of advocates to emphasize difference over similarity. The reasons include the need to create drama through contrast in order to mobilize followers and the tendency of the media to push representational contests to their extremes (Smith & Windes, 1997, p. 31). Accordingly, the contest over representation is enacted less to arrive at consensus, and more to create and project a dominant interpretive package.

Attempts to construct a dominating frame require both antigay and progay advocates to draw upon cultural resources in order to "legitimate their involvement and solutions, while casting aspersions on their opponents' positions" (R. Williams, 1995, p. 126). Choice of cultural resources to facilitate mobilization is limited by the repertoire of political symbols available within the larger culture. Further, control over these symbols is tenuous and every interpretation can produce a rival. In this sense, "who controls cultural resources is a contest over who sets the terms of their meaning. Part of every public political struggle is the battle over whose 'framing' of an issue is authoritative" (p. 128). Opposing movements not only contend for "power and influence, but also for primacy in identifying the relevant issues and actors in a given political struggle" (Meyer & Staggenborg, 1996, p. 1635).

Within struggles to establish interpretive dominance, advocates of different positions on variant sexuality most strikingly shape representation of collective identity. Both progay and traditionalist advocates cast themselves in ways diametrically opposed to the forms in which they are represented by their adversaries. While both sides converge on certain sites of contestation, each side defines its place in society, its relation to the public good, and its motives in ways formulated to gain strategic advantage in a drama which is being interactively scripted. Progay and antigay advocates confirm sociologist Mary Bernstein's (1997) general proposition that "expressions of identity can be deployed at the collective level as a political strategy, which can be aimed at cultural or instrumental goals" (p. 535).

Identity in Antagonistic Encounter

Social identity has been broadly defined as an individual's "knowledge of his membership in a social group (or groups) together with the value and emotional significance attached to that membership" (Tajfel, 1981, p. 255). This knowledge is perceived as objective because an individual "recognizes his identity in socially defined terms and these definitions become reality as he lives in society" (Berger, 1966, p. 107). In everyday life, identities are understood as natural, "perceived by others as having an unproblematic continuity" (White, 1992, p. 6). Unproblematic identity is both the effect and cause of social stability because, as novelist and essayist Monique Wittig (1992) concludes, "as long as oppositions (differences) appear to be given, already there, before all thought, 'natural'— there is no conflict and no struggle—there is no dialectic, there is no change, no movement" (p. 3).

In the politics of representation, social identities become epistemological strategies in which the ascription and ownership of characteristics become inextricably involved in struggles for power. Political scientist Shane Phelan (1989) argues forcefully that "identity formation . . . is a matter not only of ontology but also of *strategy*" (p. 136). Strategic identity claims are based on assertion of difference (Connolly, 1991, p. ix). Differences are dynamic, constantly changing as collectivities adjust to one another (Highwater, 1997, p. 197). Strategic claims to and about identity through the projection of difference are inherently political and public in character because "they involve refusing, diminishing or displacing identities others wish to recognize in others" (Calhoun, 1994a, p. 21). Identities become markers of political allegiance fabricated out of "decisions about who we want to be aligned with, carved out in ongoing negotiations with the available repertoire" (Sinfield, 1994, p. 72).

Identity is established in interpretive packages by constructing protagonists and antagonists. William Gamson (1992b) argues that identity is a central component of collective action. The *"identity component* refers to the process of defining this 'we,' typically in opposition to some 'they' who have different interests or values. Without an adversarial component, the potential target of collective action is likely to remain an abstraction" (p. 7). Because struggle for dominance requires obtaining favorable judgment for oneself and condemnation for one's opponent, drama is created through ascribing persona and motives to collective actors. Hunter (1991) asserts that establishing identity in social struggle requires a protagonist to monopolize legitimation symbols and an enemy to be discredited as culturally marginal (p. 136). Communication scholar Cindy Patton (1993) points out that the new-right/gay-movement oppositional dyad not only helped consolidate the internal identities of each group, but was also used by each to promote general societal *dis*identification with the other: if neither group could reasonably hope to recruit many outsiders to its identity, promoting disidentification produced at least temporary allies. (p. 145)

Interpretive packages, consequently, contain collective self-characterizations which are, to a significant extent, responses to antagonistic depiction.

In public controversy over variant sexuality, rival interpretive packages describe both progay and antigay collective actors. These descriptions are powerfully influenced by knowledge of antagonistic representations. On the one side, progay self-representation is pushed by antigay depiction toward immutable, fixed identity and nonerotic self-presentation, and away from an understanding of gay behavior as merely a choice of erotic style. On the other, antigay self-presentation is forced by progay depiction toward civility and secular argument, and away from vituperative denunciation and moral appeals. In short, antagonistic depiction becomes a transformative force.

Antigay Depiction and Progay Response

Two key issues arise out of the depiction of homosexuals in antigay texts and gay/lesbian representation in progay works. The first concerns mutability. In antigay texts, homosexuality is a chosen behavior which can be modified or extinguished, whereas in progay texts, a gay or lesbian sexual orientation is an immutable identity determined by genetics or early childhood experience. The second issue concerns definition. In antigay texts, homosexuals are defined by their behavior (i.e., engaging in homosexual acts). Conversely, progay texts feature homosexual activity as only one aspect of the total personality of gay and lesbian persons. This is, of course, a description of dominant positions. As we argue in Chapter 5, other strategies are contained within rival antigay and progay interpretive packages which cause considerable divisiveness among advocates allied in achieving similar outcomes.

Rhetorical critic Barry Brummett (1981) employs Burkeian analysis to describe issues concerning mutability and definition. He argues that the clash between antigay and progay rhetoric lies in a diametrically opposed use of the act/agent ratio. Within this framework, traditionalists claim that a "person is what he or she is through his/her actions or the actions of others. People are essentially malleable. Therefore, actions are primary and *agents are derivative*" (p. 293). Conversely, progay appeals "feature the *agent*: people are what they are and must be dealt with on their own grounds. *Acts are derivative* from agents, people do what they do because of the kinds of people they find themselves to be" (p. 293). This position is in strong reaction to the traditionalist emphasis on act which demands that "agents are responsible for who they are, that people make themselves through their actions" (p. 296). The twofold conclusion is inevitable that homosexuality is a chosen behavior and that homosexuals are defined only by engaging in same-sex sex. The opposed position, produced by a terministic emphasis on agent, stresses the "right *to be* gay and to be protected in that state of being from discrimination" (p. 294). In this construction, lesbians and gay men do not choose nor can they change their sexual orientation. Further, they are not to be defined solely through their sexual behavior.

Traditionalist and progay advocates mutually reinforce one another in their respective positions on the mutability of sexuality. Vaid (1995) understands the disagreement as developing out of the antigay theme that because homosexuals "choose to engage in gay behavior . . . we are not entitled to legal protection" (p. 334). In refutation, gay advocates usually respond to this characterization with an assertion that "homosexuality is innate" (p. 334). Herman (1997), on the other hand, traces the emergence of this question to an original gay/lesbian use of immutability. Traditionalists accepted the centrality of mutability as a vital political issue, "largely because the mainstream lesbian and gay rights movement had made it so" (p. 72).

No matter the direction of influence, each side seizes on mutability as an important issue. Biologist Simon LeVay (1996), supporting the progay position, uses survey results to show that "attitudes toward gays and lesbians are inextricably tied up with beliefs about what causes to be homosexual" (p. 2). He describes a *New York Times*/CBS poll which shows the public equally divided on whether homosexuality is a choice, and reveals that those who believe that there is no choice of whether to be homosexual are considerably more gay-positive than those who believe in choice (p. 2). On this basis, LeVay concludes that "beliefs about the causation of homosexuality clearly *do* influence attitudes toward gay people"

(p. 5). Antigay advocates seem to be in agreement. Herman (1997) observes that they proceed

> on the understanding that if people think homosexuality has a biological
> foundation then . . . [they] will be less likely, and less able, to stand in the
> way of protective law reform. Sexuality, like race and sex, will be seen to be
> beyond the individual's control, and therefore not the appropriate subject
> of discrimination. (p. 74)

The central depiction of lesbians and gay men in traditionalist texts is that they are people who have chosen to be homosexual or have chosen to act on their homosexual inclination. At its simplest, the antigay proposition is that "homosexuals are made, not born!" (LaHaye, 1978, p. 90). A satisfying explanation has to be offered, then, for how homosexuals are made. In a general way, the notion is advanced by traditionalists that homosexuality is simply a bad habit which can be resisted or broken. Dannemeyer (1989), for example, claims that a substantial body of evidence demonstrates that homosexuality "is not undeniably an inherited 'orientation,' but is probably a bad habit acquired in early childhood or puberty" (p. 11). This position recently received widespread notice when it was articulated by Senator Trent Lott (Mitchell, 1998). In elaboration of this view, LaHaye (1978) asserts that homosexual behavior becomes habitual through a spiral of reinforcement (pp. 90-91).

In the traditionalist frame, engaging in homosexual behavior is indisputedly not biologically determined. Magnuson (1994) points out that even if genetic factors are involved in creating homosexual desires, "some homosexuals choose to act on them while others do not" (p. 89). Praeger (1993) asks "if homosexuality is biologically determined, how are we to account for the vastly differing numbers of homosexuals in different societies?" He answers that social attitudes determine the number of individuals who choose to act on homosexual impulses (p. 74). The mutability of sexuality is further supported by the assertion that many persons with homosexual inclination can avoid homosexual behavior entirely. LaHaye (1978), for instance, claims that "most of those with a predisposition toward homosexuality have never had a homosexual experience, and more than 80 percent of those who have such a predisposition are *not homosexual*" (p. 77). Mutability is also demonstrated by conversion from homosexuality to heterosexuality. The claim is frequently made in traditionalist literature that "change is possible for the homosexual who has a sincere desire to do so" (Magnuson, 1994, p. 85). Even in the face of low conversion rates, Burtoft (1995) asserts, the "fact that change is possible is the fundamentally important issue. Since it is, there is both hope for individuals who desire change and irrefutable proof that homosexuality is not an immutable, unchangeable fact rooted in the physical constitution" (p. 45).

Finally, even if homosexuality is only partially mutable, society should not condone homosexual acts. Burtoft (1995) argues that

> Even if future research identifies some biological factor in homosexuality, it does not follow that homosexuality ought to be socially accepted or judged as desirable. There are many genetically determined conditions which, precisely because they are destructive to human health, are not considered desirable for either individuals or society. (p. 30)

Religious belief reinforces the contention that homosexuality is a choice. For traditionalists, "anti-immutability did not exist in the Bible; the sins of Sodom were behavioral, not ontological. Homosexual behavior is thus a modern and, in their view, a human invention" (Herman, 1997, p. 73). Goss (1993) summarizes the biblical argument based on creationism: "Homosexual tendencies are one of the many disorders that [have] beset a fallen humanity. How could God condemn a behavior and not provide a means of escape? Therefore, homosexuals are made, not born" (p. 11). This argument then combines with the conversion position. "If homosexuals are not born but socially made, they can be unmade. God defines homosexuality as sinful abomination. Therefore, if homosexuality is an act of sin, it can be repented of" (p. 11).

The choice position is also consistent with the narrative of the seduction of the child. If children have a malleable sexuality, then homosexuality is, to a significant extent, the product of homosexual molestation. LaHaye (1978) writes that "only God knows how many 'chickens' one 'hawk' can entice into homosexuality in a lifetime. But since it is impossible for homosexuals to propagate, they must recruit to enjoy companionship, sex, or both" (pp. 93-94). His conclusion is that a society lenient with homosexuals will influence children into behavior which causes individuals to become practicing homosexuals.

Traditionalists define homosexuality as no more than a category of sexual behavior, and homosexuals as simply individuals who engage in that behavior. For example, Magnuson (1994) asserts that the only defining characteristic of the homosexual minority "is the inclination to commit sodomy with members of the same sex" (p. 95). For Rueda (1982), being a member of the homosexual subculture simply means "centering one's life on one's sexual peculiarities" (p. 46). Consequently, antigay advocates reason that homosexuals are not a distinct group and should therefore not be protected against discrimination (Esterberg, 1997, p. 27).

The gay/lesbian response to traditionalist appeals based on mutability and definition by sexual behavior is to create an immutable identity which lies outside the volition of the individual. The public policy appeals which dominate gay/lesbian discourse produce a naturalized gay subject working for a place within an unquestioned gender and civic order. Media scholar Larry Gross (1993) asserts that the "preponderance of lesbian and gay political rhetoric, both within the community and externally, reflects an essentialist position, insisting that one doesn't 'choose' to be gay, but 'recognizes and accepts' that one is so" (p. 113). Such tracts on gay politics as Kirk and Madsen's (1989) *After the Ball,* Nava and Dawidoff's (1994) *Created Equal,* Bawer's (1993) *Place at the Table,* and Sullivan's (1995) *Virtually Normal* share an understanding of the natural and unitary identity of gay people. Sullivan, for example, asserts that the

> homosexual experience . . . reaches into the core of what makes a human being who he or she is. . . . The truth is that, for the overwhelming majority of adults, the condition of homosexuality is as involuntary as heterosexuality is for heterosexuals. Such an orientation is evident from the very beginning of the formation of a person's emotional identity. (p. 17)

The dominant account of gay/lesbian identity in political discourse has frequently been labeled "essentialist." Such an essentialist identity construes homosexuality as a real, lifelong trait defining a distinct type of person—the gay man and lesbian. This essential orientation is natural, transhistorical, and transcultural. An essentialist view "necessitates the location of sexuality within the individual as a fixed essence, leading to a classic division of individual and society and to a variety of psychological determinisms, and, often enough, to a full-blown biological determinism as well" (Padgug, 1990, p. 50). In the essentialist view, sexual categories are understood "as universal, static, and permanent, suitable for analysis of all human beings and all societies" (p. 50). This understanding is based on a concept of sexuality as "an overpowering force in the individual that shapes not only the personal but the social life as well. It is seen as a driving, instinctual force, whose characteristics are built into the biology of the human animal" (Weeks, 1981, pp. 1-2).

Essentialist rhetoric deployed by progay advocates can best be understood in contrast to constructionist interpretations which explain homosexuality as fictive, not real; socially constructed through language, not natural or biological; involving a degree of choice, not simply discovery of an internal essence. Constructionists, as Boswell (1990) observes, "have in common the view that 'sexuality' is an artifact or 'construct' of human society and therefore specific to any given social situation" (p. 135). More specifically, philosopher Edward Stein (1990) summarizes the contrasts by suggesting that "essentialists hold that a person's sexual orientation is a culture-independent, objective and intrinsic property while social constructionists think it is culture-dependent, relational and, perhaps, not objective" (p. 325).

Opposition influences whether the gay subject is understood as a homosexual by nature or by social construction. Apart from substantive arguments in favor of essentialism and its resonance with the experiential understanding of many gay and lesbian persons, the legitimating potential of an essential identity suits it to a situation dominated by public controversy. Robert Bray, a leading gay advocate, asserts that essentialism "strikes at the heart of people who oppose gay rights and think we don't deserve our rights because we're choosing to be the way we are" (quoted in Kimmel, 1993, p. 577).

An essentialist understanding of gay and lesbian people has a striking advantage given the vocabulary of civil rights which stresses the protection of clearly defined groups. Meshing essentialist identity with the claim of ethnic group status places lesbian and gay people within a series of frames acceptable to audiences: a history of victimage, benign difference, persecution versus celebration of diversity, bigotry versus the liberal rights paradigm. As Adam (1987) asserts, "like the Irish and Italians in the States in the first decades of this century, or the blacks of today, gay people have taken on many of the traits of ethnicity to assert their political will" (p. 122). This view is supported by Vaid (1995) who notes that the "minority group framework located gay and lesbian people within a long liberal democratic tradition of ethnic, racial, and cultural minorities" (p. 52). In fact, ethnicity has become a fundamental assumption in the gay/lesbian stance toward public policy issues. Weeks (1977) further points out that "at the heart of most gay activism was an assumption that homosexuals were a separate, minority group, participating in the general value system but simultaneously struggling for the right to a separate but equal existence" (p. 232).

The firmest link between an essentialized gay/lesbian identity and a particular minority group lies in the analogy of gay people to African Americans. This connection has been made throughout the history of gay/lesbian advocacy. In 1932, the now commonplace observation was made:

> Both race prejudice and the prejudice against homosexuals are bolstered and maintained by social taboo and law. Both prejudices make life in this world a living hell for men and women whose only crime is that of being DIFFERENT from the majority. (Prejudice, 1997, p. 229)

In the 1960s, the argument was advanced that the "drive to eliminate discrimination against homosexuals (sex fascism) is a direct parallel to the drive to eliminate discrimination against Negroes (race fascism)" (Ebreo, 1997/1965, p. 342). This tradition of linking sexuality to race has continued, becoming central to the liberal understanding of homosexuality. Sullivan (1995) perceptively suggests that "in the way that modern liberals construct the politics of homosexuality, they see it as virtually identical to the problem of racial discrimination" (p. 148).

The advantage of an essentialist identity hardened into self-representation as a biologically determined ethnic group became more obvious as public conflict increased over variant sexuality. This provides further proof that opposition strengthens essentialist identity. Militant progay social action came to public knowledge as a liberatory crusade to free people from a rigid sexual taboo against homosexuality, not to give equal civil rights protection to gays and lesbians. Freedom required the elimination of categorical boundaries of sexuality. Adam (1987), for example, notes that "gay liberation never thought of itself as a civil rights movement for a particular minority but as a revolutionary struggle to free the homosexuality in everyone, challenging the conventional arrangements that confined sexuality to heterosexual monogamous families" (p. 78).

Such liberatory rhetoric enjoyed a brief period in which organized opposition was not mobilized. When opposition developed, however, which not only stigmatized homosexuality and reinforced gender and sexual categorization, but also denounced gay/lesbian agencies of cultural and political change, the constructionist stress on the fluidity of sexual desire was displaced by discourse describing the nature of homosexual persons in an essentialist form more acceptable to most audiences. Certainly, over the past two decades of increasingly heightened confrontation, the "evolution from gay liberation to gay rights . . . places the political and social struggles of lesbians and gay men in a familiar, well-established equal rights framework, deeply rooted in American history" (D'Emilio, 1992, p. 181).

Adoption of essentialism is also reinforced by proximity to confrontation. Constructionism is the reigning position within lesbian and gay studies programs, and in the academy in general. Writer and editor Jeffrey Escoffier (1992) observes that the

> new generation of lesbian and gay scholars is explicitly building on the work of the social construction of identity paradigm and extending it to include the interpretation of all kinds of texts, cultural codes, signifying practices, and modes of discourse that shape underlying social attitudes towards homosexuality as well as the formation of sexual or gender identities. (p. 21)

Mohr (1992) confirms this observation, asserting that "within the emerging academic discipline of lesbian and gay studies, there is nearly universal agreement among scholars that social factors are in some sense determinant in homosexuality, that homosexuality is culturally constituted or produced" (pp. 221-222). Thus, in those places, most especially universities, where gay rights issues are least contested, a social constructionist view of homosexuality has become dominant. In contrast, essentialism has become the dominant assumption for gay activists, for progay organizations, and for gay and lesbian people as they seek to legitimate themselves in both public and private contexts. As Gross (1993) notes, "whatever the status of the theoretical and empirical debates waged by researchers and theoreticians, the public discourse concerning sexuality and sexual orientation is overwhelmingly essentialist" (p. 113). The result has been the production of a dominant interpretive package in which gays and lesbians are portrayed in essentialist terms and a challenge to that package produced largely by academics. Sociologist Steven Epstein (1990) describes the growing gap between those actively engaged in public policy debate and the theoreticians of sexuality by observing that "while constructionist theorists have been preaching the gospel that the hetero/homosexual distinction is a social fiction, gays and lesbians, in everyday life and in political action, have been busy hardening the categories" (p. 243). Thus, antigay depiction of homosexuality as a choice contributes to gay and lesbian representation of their identity as a fixed essence.

Traditionalist reduction of gay and lesbian identity to sexual behavior also exerts pressure toward a shift of gay and lesbian identity away from sex. Certainly, as historian Robert Padgug (1989) notes, the "existence of sexual institutions and identity encouraged the expansion of nonsexual institutions, including political and protest groups, self-help groups, and cultural institutions" (p. 304). In response to the characterization of gay culture as sex driven and homosexuals as sex obsessed, there is repeated insistence that lesbians and gay men cannot be defined by the sexual acts in which they engage. As Diane Helene Miller (1998) argues, the "love between two men or two women is no more reducible to sex (sodomite or otherwise) than is the love between a woman and a man" (p. 128). In addition, an obvious public progay response has been, in Bronski's (1984) characterization, to "play down the sexual identity of gay people" by presenting a "sanitized image of gay men and women to the general public" (p. 212). One element in this response, as many leading gay advocates have noted, is the "construction of a homosexuality without sex" (Bronski, 1995, p. 23). Blasius (1994) observes that while progay advocacy has done much to make sexuality a political and cultural issue, sexuality itself has been de-emphasized (p. 3). In extending this argument, Richard Herrell (1993) contends that "whereas in the 1960s and 1970s sex itself was foregrounded as the revolutionary act . . . sex and 'gendered' aspects of representing gay men are now 'automatized' (left in the background rhetorically)" (p. 233). He argues that "presenting the gay community as composed of families, of churches and sports leagues, of clubs and professional associations, of everything about normative society except simply sexual behavior, has become the new strategy" (p. 233).

Traditionalists are aware of and find implausible the gay/lesbian move toward essentialism and a nonsexual identity. In the 1980s, Rueda (1982) identified biological essentialism as a key issue in public policy debate over variant sexuality. He observed that the homosexual movement would be severely damaged if homosexuality were linked to seduction and recruitment. However, "if homosexuality is determined before the age of reason, and its establishment is not dependent on early sexual experience, the homosexual movement can count on the support of many heterosexuals who have come to believe that it is unavoidable" (p. 93).

Recently, Podhortez (1996) denounced biological determinism as an opportunistic and dangerous ploy. He asserts that "according to the new party line, homosexuality was in no degree a matter of choice; it was always and entirely an involuntary condition" (p. 36). This position was backed only by personal testimony: "novel after novel, play after play, and memoir after memoir poured from the presses, and with few exceptions the authors of these confessionals proclaimed that they had been attracted to other men as far back as they could remember" (p. 37). The effect of homosexual essentialism was to move "beyond the reach of moral judgment, for how could a person be judged for acting in accordance with his true nature or, as religiously inclined homosexuals would put it, in accordance with the way God created him?" (p. 36).

Such reasoning, according to Podhoretz (1996), is opportunistic. He argues that essentialism "served to get homosexuals included in the category of oppressed minority groups by defining their condition as no more a matter of choice than race or ethnicity" (p. 36). Evidence to establish biological determinism was used, he claims, only when it served political purposes. Consequently,

> no matter how much evidence might be amassed to demonstrate the heritability of intelligence, ways had to be found to discredit that evidence because it was considered bad for blacks. Conversely, however, the scantiest evidence for the existence of a 'gay gene' was enthusiastically seized upon because it was thought to be good for homosexuals. (Podhoretz, 1996, p. 37)

For Podhoretz, the implications of genetic determinism are significant because the "same logic would confer moral legitimation on pedophiles, who also could and did claim that they were made that way and were therefore unable to help themselves" (p. 36). Essentialism represents to him a considerable threat to young people who would be left unprotected because biological determinism "meant that children were not at risk of being seduced into homosexuality by homosexual teachers or encouraged into it by homosexual propaganda in the schools" (p. 36).

Traditionalists come into sharp disagreement with progay advocates over the sexuality/race analogy. One line of appeal is to deny flatly that race and homosexuality are equivalent. Burtoft (1995), for example, asserts that "there is no proof that certain people are homosexual 'by nature,' in the same way that some people are of a certain race or eye color" (p. 4). This distinction is taken further by Praeger (1993) who maintains that "sexual lifestyle is qualitatively different from skin color" (p. 76). This contention rests squarely on the assumption that homosexuality is defined solely as behavior: "Since blacks have been discriminated against for what they are and homosexuals have been discriminated against for what they do, a moral distinction between the two types of discrimination can be made in a handful of areas" (p. 76). In specific application, Praeger believes that "there is no moral basis to objecting to blacks marrying whites, but there is a moral basis for objecting to homosexual marriage" (p. 76). The threat which traditionalists claim to see in the homosexuality/ race analogy is that it will undermined protections for racial minorities. Dannemeyer (1989), for instance, claims that regarding homosexuality as a natural genetic variation diminishes "respect for civil rights legislation in general, with a consequent undermining of protections to those minorities who have been discriminated against because of accidents of birth" (p. 74).

The position of traditionalists on the fluidity of homosexual identity is regarded with considerable irony by gay/lesbian advocates. For instance, reporter Donna Minkowitz observed that such arguments "could have appeared in queercore rant" because they promoted a "remarkably Foucaultian view of queerness as a contingency category, whose members can slip in and out of its boundaries like subversive fish" (quoted in Gamson, 1995, p. 401). Similarly, emphasis on the authenticity of African American rights claims as opposed to counterfeit gay/lesbian claims is discounted as a ploy to drive a wedge between partners in an emerging coalition.

In the same vein, traditionalists are aware of the tendency of gay/ lesbian advocates to avoid discussion of sexual behavior. Magnuson (1994), for example, suggests that gay/lesbian advocates attempt to keep discussion at a high level of abstraction (p. 18). He denounces the strategy by which progay defenders "avoid being drawn into discussion of homosexual behavior" (p. 18). He asserts that when perverse sexual behavior is spotlighted, progay advocates charge their opponents with "being obsessed with sex, and the merely physical dimension of human relation-ships" (p. 18).

Progay Depiction and Antigay Response

A repugnant enemy is no less important for progay advocates than for their traditionalist counterparts. Rhetorical critic James Darsey (1991) points out that, for the gay movement, as for many other collective ef-forts, "what truly is common is the enemy. It is an old rhetorical dictum that it is easier to get people to agree on what they are against than on what they are for" (p. 52). The enemy depicted in the progay interpretive package is framed as opportunistic, irrational, duplicitous, subversive, and dangerous.

Progay discourse represents traditionalists as opportunists. Because traditionalists have lost their other enemies, or can no longer engage openly in racism and sexism, lesbians and gay men become convenient and often defenseless targets. A major influence on traditionalists was the disappearance of the threat of communism which caused the religious right to shift the "focus of their fund-raising appeals from the 'evil com-munist empire' to 'the homosexual agenda for the destruction of Amer-ica' " (White, 1994, p. 224). In the view of progay advocates, a "new scare tactic is needed, and that tactic is us. Radical right groups have found it fi-nancially rewarding to portray gay people as lecherous monsters with an evil agenda" (Trasandes, 1998, p. 12).

The motive for this shift is elaborated in a number of ways. For many years, gay advocates have found sinister reasons behind attacks on gays and lesbians. Using Cold War phrasing, Gerre Goodman and her fellow advocates (Goodman, Lakey, Lashof, & Thorne, 1983) asserted that the antigay movement is exploiting a "cultural appeal to build a stronger po-litical base for its own program . . . that includes an unprecedented mili-tary buildup, tax breaks for the rich and support for Third World dictator-ships" (p. 1). Journalist Randy Shilts (1993), referring to fundamental cultural anxieties, asserts that,

> Evangelical conservatives used the issue of gay rights to play upon fears over the confusing changes that had developed in the way women and men relate to one another. Politically, gays were a convenient target because so few would dare defend them. (pp. 370-371)

The appearance of AIDS made the gay community even more vulnerable. As Diamond (1989) notes, "in the age of AIDS, gay and lesbian people remain the most vulnerable targets of Christian Right venom, which is likely to spread along with the epidemic" (p. vi).

For many progay advocates, money is at the root of antigay activism. White (1994) stresses that antigay advocates use gay issues simply to raise funds for electronic and direct-mail ministries. With respect to the evangelical electronic ministry of James Kennedy, he asserts that

> he knew better than condemn us [gay people] with the avalanche of insinuations, innuendos, and lies that he was using to raise money, but he needed an easy target to raise quick cash, and gay and lesbian people seemed the easiest target in sight. (White, 1994, p. 227)

Such unmasking of traditionalists as greedy media entrepreneurs is a commonplace in progay discourse. With respect to traditionalists, Nava and Dawidoff (1994) assert that

> the image they project is of ordinary folks speaking from family homes and small churches. In fact the religious right is a group of mail-order wizards and lobbyists tied to religious "media personalities" who spend millions to raise millions with the twin object of advancing their own social and political agendas and enriching themselves and their organizations. (Mohr, 1988, p. 97)

Traditionalists are further depicted as arguing either in bad faith or irrationally.

> For the bigot, "arguments" are simply filler for the print media—he has to have something to say. . . . And on those occasions when connected ideas are called for, it turns out that the bigot's herd of stalking horses is large beyond counting and self-perpetuating. For the bigot, "reason" and "reasons" are pretexts. (Mohr, 1988, p. 3)

This view is confirmed by Bawer (1993) who observes of gay rights opponents that "if an argument they have advanced fails to stand up to scrutiny, they don't rethink their opposition; instead they invent another argument" (pp. 112-113). Progay advocates ascribe to their opponents a predilection for fantasy and fear of concerted efforts to achieve social change. "The proponents of these conspiracy theories characteristically suspect rationality as an instrument of politics and morality" (Nava & Dawidoff, 1994, p. 13).

Traditionalists are charged by their opponents with inciting violence. In this antagonistic depiction, antigay propaganda sanctions increasingly frequent verbal and physical assault on lesbians and gay men. For example, the videotape *Ballot Measure 9,* which presents a progay perspective on an Oregon initiative campaign, stresses how antigay agitation leads inevitably to violence (McDonald, 1994). The murder of Matthew Shepard in Wyoming in October, 1998, elicited a resurgence of progay denunciation of traditionalists for inspiring violence. Kerry Lobel, for instance, declared that antigays "foster an atmosphere of hostility that can lead to hate attacks such as the one against Matthew Shepard" (quoted in Kirby, 1998, p. 39). Although Gallagher and Bull (1996) concede that both traditionalists and progays denounce one another, they conclude that "gay activists do not go nearly as far as the religious right in defaming an entire group of people and creating an atmosphere that contributes to harassment or worse" (p. 269).

Central to the progay framing of antigay activists is the allegation that traditionalists subvert political order by injecting religion into politics. The charge is frequently made that attacks on gay people are being used to write evangelical views into public policy. Nava and Dawidoff (1994), for example, argue that "there is no doubt that evangelical attack on gay and lesbian rights is part of a broader strategy to impose specifically religious values on American politics" (p. 104). Progay advocates position themselves on the side of constitutional democracy, and place their opponents on the side of theocracy. Gallagher and Bull (1996) comment that the

> current debate casts into clear relief deep fissures in American culture and politics—between individual freedom, a classically liberal cornerstone of the nation's legal system, and absolute adherence to a strict Christian moral code, whose roots advocates claim date back to the country's founding. (p. 274)

A broad-based concern exists that " 'born-again' Christians have drifted away from the theological predilection for separation from mainstream society. Instead Christian Right preachers advocate 'taking dominion' over political parties, school boards, media outlets and military infrastructures" (Diamond, 1989, p. vii). Progay advocates see themselves as an important element in the discourse of the New Right, fearing that

> what is new about the antigay crusaders we face now is that they seek to collapse the relatively fragile boundary between church and state. They use the transformative culture of homosexuality . . . to argue for a fusion of the religious and the secular in order to preserve the status quo. (Vaid, 1995, p. 194)

The progay depiction of their opponents include elements both of an increasing trend toward theocracy and significantly augmented power. Herman (1997) notes that the more strongly the Christian Right "seeks to impose its orthodoxy on government, to take control of the state and to use state power to achieve religious ends, the more theocracy becomes the necessary culmination of these efforts—despite public disavowals" (p. 192). Traditionalists are, in this view, powerful enough to carry out their design for dominion over American politics and culture. Signorile (1993), for example, asserts that the Christian right in America, contrary to what many believe in light of recent evangelist sex scandals, amassed enormous power in the '80s rather than declining" (p. 242). Recently, this concern with the political power of antigay leaders has become a theme in both the gay and mainstream media (Berke, 1998; Brooke, 1998).

In response to their depiction in the progay interpretive package, antigays claim that they are not opportunistic, but citizens driven by the highest motives. They are a loving opposition which eschews violence. They do not threaten political order, but defend and fulfill it. They are not powerful, but an oppressed people responding to a usurpacious elite. Behind these claims lies a shift away from a religious persona toward a secular identity. For antigay advocates, the charges against them are wholly without merit. They resent being portrayed as "bigots, haters, discriminators, and deniers of basic human rights . . . because we were sincerely concerned for our children and our community" (Bryant, 1977, p. 22).

Traditionalists resist their portrayal in progay texts as opportunistic entrepreneurs. In rebuttal, they claim the highest motives. Bryant (1977) asserts that she was moved to political action "because of my love for Almighty God . . . because of my love for my country, because of my love for my children" (p. 13). In similar fashion, other antigays insist that they were compelled by duty to join a culture war initiated by subversive forces and that, given the profound threat to civilization, antigay response is unfortunately restrained.

> Social pressure caused by some educators, the media, and militant homosexuals has intimidated almost everyone into silence on the subject today. Even the most ardent moral activists are making almost no attempt to reverse the excessively lenient laws and practices that make homosexuality a very real threat to any family. (LaHaye, 1982, p. 199)

Traditionalists object to their characterization as homophobic or irrational. Burtoft (1995), for instance, concludes that "it is not even necessarily homophobic to support anti-sodomy laws, if such support is motivated by the belief that such behavior is harmful to both individuals and society" (p. 80). In their own self-representation, traditionalists engage in reasoned discussion, while their opponents do not. Magnuson (1994) asserts that in the course of debate on public policy, homosexual advocates "frequently resort to name-calling, while their opponents recite facts" (p. 17).

In response to charges that they are hate-filled bigots, many antigays strive to construct themselves as concerned and helpful. Key to this effort to appear civilized and responsible is adoption of what Hunter (1987) describes as an "ethic of civility" which stresses "gentility and studied moderation" (p. 152). One aspect of this self-representation is the antigay attempt to establish a benign public image by playing on the notion of loving the sinner but hating the sin.

This theme was a commonplace of antigay discourse as early as the 1960s (Herman, 1997, p. 46). It was prominently taken up by early traditionalist advocates. Falwell (1980), for instance, declared that "I believe that like other persons who have problems and need a change of lifestyle, homosexuals require love and help. . . . I love homosexuals as souls for whom Christ died; I love homosexuals, but I must hate their sin" (p. 186). This theme was subsequently explored by Jones (1993) who suggested that with respect to homosexuality, the "challenge here is to be the loving opposition, to imitate our Lord, who chases down his sinful creatures with aggressively open arms while all the while saying no to our sins" (p. 25). This position is extended by Magnuson (1985) to the conclusion that true love for homosexuals consists in *not* protecting them from discrimination. He argues that granting special protective rights is helpful neither to the homosexual person "who is not helped by social engagement of his lifestyle, nor to society at large, which in increasing measure is experiencing the costs—social, medical, and psychological—of disordered sexual behavior of all kinds" (p. x).

Therapy to heal homosexuals is a key expression of the "love the sinner" appeal. This theme is produced through emphasis on curing homosexuals and by allotting a prominent role for "ex-gays." Jones (1993), for example, believes that homosexuality can be cured, labeling as merely a myth

> that there is no hope for healing. Anyone who says there is no hope is either ignorant or a liar. Every secular study of change has shown some success rate, and persons who testify to substantial healing by God are legion. (p. 25)

Loving concern is such an important theme that publicizing therapy programs for homosexuals has become part of organized antigay political activity (Burress, 1994). Examples of healed homosexuals, in turn, reinforce the antigay mutability argument, supported by the assertion that "both the Scriptures and much secular literature provide evidence that homosexuality, though deeply ingrained and habitually practiced, can be overcome—both as a lifestyle and as an identity" (Davies & Rentzel, 1993, p. 20). As Burtoft (1995) argues, the "fact that there is *any* success in changing from homosexual to heterosexual orientation at least proves that some forms of homosexuality are not immutable" (p. 44). Consequently, the use of "ex-gays" demonstrates both love of homosexuals and the mutability of sexual deviance. Finally, the ex-gay fits neatly into a generic appeal with a lengthy history which includes use of converted Jews, ex-Catholics, and former Communists (Herman, 1997, p. 42).

The charge that traditionalists engage in denunciation which leads to violence is a sensitive issue for traditionalists. Several antigay advocates have emphasized the importance of avoiding "name-calling and ridicule" (Dannemeyer, 1989, p.18). With respect to violence, Burtoft (1995) asserts that "condemning gay-bashing is a red herring. No serious spokesman on either side of the controversy is in favor of such violence, and it is already against the law in every state" (p. 47). In an effort to turn the tables on progay advocates, traditionalists maintain that "while there are no organized attacks on homosexual by heterosexual groups with political aims, there are an increasing number of assaults by militant homosexuals on people who oppose their political aims" (Burtoft, 1995, p. 48). More specifically, antigay advocates accused progay activists of violence:

"Churches have been defaced and burned. Cars, homes, and businesses have been vandalized. Peaceful citizens going about their lawful business have been brutalized by goon squads of militant homosexual 'bigot busters' " (quoted in Watson, 1997, p. 139).

In defense against the charge that they are a powerful force bent on seizing control of the country, antigays articulate a sense of marginalization. They echo gay expression of oppression, claiming to be, at best, a beleaguered majority forced into invisibility by a secular progay elite. This self-representation grows out of a larger concern, expressed by Religious Right political leaders such as Ralph Reed (1994), who contends that "as a society, we have become biased against bigotry itself except when that bias is directed at religion. . . . In a country founded on the principle of basic freedoms guaranteed to all its citizens, people of faith find themselves marginalized and ridiculed" (p. 41). This position is consistent with a pervasive theme in Religious Right literature, the "victimization of evangelical Christians by a hostile secular culture" (Watson, 1997, p. 2). With respect to antigay advocacy, this sense of exclusion is expressed in several ways. First, traditionalists are intimidated. Magnuson (1994) complains that gay advocates are "not generally shouted down, disinvited, or threatened. But those who do not share their views often remain silent for fear of loss of academic status, personal intimidation, or physical safety" (p. 17). Second, the society as a whole is threatened by laws which could force religious organizations, including schools "to hire persons whose sexual practices contradict their religious doctrines; the laws could force these groups to hire people who practice behavior they consider sinful" (p. 111).

Taking the offensive against their detractors, antigays frame their political activity based on religious precept as consistent with American civic values. Against what they see as an unwarranted absolutist interpretation of church/state separation, advocates like LaHaye (1982) argue that "separation of church and state does not mean that Christian citizens are prohibited from taking an active part in the electoral process" (p. 211). The warrant for this position is the indictment of a

> trend in our political and legal cultures toward treating religious beliefs as arbitrary and unimportant, a trend supported by a rhetoric that implies that there is something wrong with religious devotion. . . . Too often, our rhetoric treats the religious impulse to public action as presumptively wicked—indeed, as necessarily oppressive. (Carter, 1993, pp. 6, 9)

An important traditionalist view, widely shared among antigay advocates, is that people of faith should not be denied legitimate voice in government simply because their political behavior is directed by strong religious belief (Conrad, 1983, p.163).

To the charge that they are extremists, antigay advocates project an image of moderation and political centrism. The effort toward self-representation as moderate partly occurs through a vigorous use of liberal language. Political scientist Matthew Moen (1992) notes that invocation of religious and moral terms make antigay leaders vulnerable to accusations of theocratic zealotry. Consequently, they "jettisoned much of the morality rhetoric. It was replaced with the rhetoric of liberalism, with its emphasis on freedom, liberty, rights, and choice . . ." (p. 91). Antigay activism, then, becomes a civilized effort to preserve majority rights—the freedom to say that homosexuality is wrong, the liberty to exclude homosexuals from employment or housing (Schacter, 1994, pp. 289-290).

The most fundamental effect of depicting antigays as religious zealots, however, is a shift toward an antigay rhetoric which substitutes secular for religious appeals. Theologian Richard Neuhaus (1984) observes that antigay advocacy faces a dilemma: "It wants to enter the political arena making public claims on the basis of private truths [but] . . . a public argument is transsubjective. It is not derived from sources of revelation or disposition that are essentially private and arbitrary" (p. 36). Although there are significant benefits to be derived by traditionalist advocates from associating religious belief with public issues, "this association runs directly counter to the largely privatized definitions of spirituality that otherwise dominate modern culture" (Wuthnow, 1994, p. 100). Former federal judge Robert Bork (1996) observes that "while most people claim to be religious, most are also not comfortable with those whose faith is strong enough to affect their public behavior" (p. 277). Consequently, an effort has been made by many antigay advocates to adopt a pattern of secular argument against positive government action on issues concerning homosexuals.

In secular argument, discouragement of homosexuality is advanced without religious reference as a secular civic good. Although this pattern is parallel to, consistent with, and implicitly grounded in religious antigay appeals, secular appeals do not directly rely on revealed authority or supernatural claims. Though religious claims about the sin of sodomy continue in wide circulation, secular discourse has become significant in antigay advocacy concerning public issues (R. Smith, 1997, p. 95).

Civic appeals are viable without support from beliefs rooted in religious culture. "Order" and "decency" remain central terms in such secular discourse. Order can be sanctioned by reference to community tradition as well as by biblical injunction, and decency can be justified by social function as well as by divine mandate. By featuring a secular pattern of argument, antigay advocates evade the imputation of religious zealotry, strive to create an image of rational civility, and reach beyond the evangelical community which forms the core support for antigay campaigns. The consequence of this effort is an increasing shift from homosexuality as sin to the alleged social consequences of homosexuality. Novelist and essayist Sarah Schulman (1994) observes that the "Christian right has replaced preachers with scientists in the propaganda videos" (p. 15).

The progay response to the general shift of antigay discourse toward secularism has been to launch charges of opportunism. Commentator John Judis (1994), for example, asserts that in order to move beyond their initial religious target audience, the "religious right's leaders have attempted to change its public face while retaining its private religious attraction" (p. 21). Another observer charges:

> Association of anti-homosexual organizing with religious (specifically Christian) principles is highlighted only when activists are targeting fellow Christians in order to recruit or educate them. When organizing in the wider political arena, anti-homosexual organizing is cast in secular terms. (Hardisty, 1993, p. 9)

More specifically, Gallagher and Bull (1996) assert that the "right could just as readily have turned solely to biblical interpretation to make its point, since that was the irreducible basis of its position. But science, even the brand practiced by antigay activists, had a genuine value in political arguments" (p. 116). However, antigay use of scientific proof, they claim, is fraudulent. "But the religious activists were using the trappings of science only, without adhering to a rigorous methodology. They knew what results they wanted, and they got them. It was science in the service of the Bible" (p. 116).

In brief, progay and antigay representations of identity are significantly influenced by their opponents' discourse. Beyond the fact that both represent themselves as victims of misrepresentation, each responds to oppositional discourse by modifying collective self-presentation. Progays adopt an essentialist identity and de-emphasize sexuality. Antigays adopt the language of liberalism and de-emphasize religious appeals.

Strategies in Antagonistic Encounter

Confrontation between progay and antigay advocates within an issue culture produces more than the evolution of identity just described. In creating their interpretive packages, each side defines the contest in which it is engaged by targeting certain areas in which clash is considered advantageous. Among these key sites for conflict are language and the definition of social reality. Further, both sides increasingly convert their contest into an effort to achieve dominance in the public sphere, specifically in law and politics.

Language is a crucial area of contention in social conflict, both in general and with specific reference to contests over public policy concerning variant sexuality. Hunter (1994) summarizes this line of thought by observing:

> Language both reflects and shapes social reality, for words themselves frame how we think about experience. Thus those who have the power to establish the language of public debate will have a tremendous advantage in determining the debate's outcome. Linguistic victories therefore translate into political victories. (p. 66)

Both progay and traditionalist advocates recognize that power over language provides significant advantage and that language change in a particular direction is an important outcome. Consequently, each side seeks terminological control. Progay advocates attempt to depathologize the language of gay identity, to defuse pejoratives like "queer" and to popularize terms such as "homophobic" and "heterocentric." For instance, English professor Ann Pellegrini (1992) asserts that "language is not immaterial to the experience of oppression. Far from it. Language too has its violence. Anyone who has ever been called a *faggot* or a *dyke* knows this" (p. 43). Clearly, an intent of gay/lesbian advocates is to change the vocabulary of oppression. Helms (1995), for instance, remarks that

> it still astounds me to think how many derogatory names the straight world has invented to designate gay men: fags, faggots, pansies, perverts, inverts, aunties, flits, queers, queens, cocksuckers, nellies, sickos, homos, sodom-

ites, pederasts, sissies, swishes, fairies, fruits, & the list goes on. The reverberations of that lexicon sounded even in our dreams. (p. 75)

A central concern of antigays is that they will lose terms of moral condemnation. Rueda (1982) believes that "should homosexual language and
ideology prevail, society would have no way of speaking—or thinking—
in traditional terms" (p. 71). Leading antigay advocates James Dobson
and Gary Bauer (1990), for example, believe that the "redefinition of
words to make it nearly impossible to define normal and abnormal has
been going on for some time" (p. 222). They are particularly concerned
that

> this redefinition of an old word—homosexuality—and the creation of a
> new word—homophobia—is not a minor event or a mere curiosity.
> Through these semantic changes, normalcy is put on the defensive. Parents
> who want to resist the demands of the homosexual movement are easily la-
> beled with a condemning word. (p. 223)

Magnuson (1994) attempts to establish that the "gay rights controversy
shows the mystifying power of language to forge a consensus" (p. 31). He
offers a catalog of expressions through which homosexuals attempt to
subvert the language:

> To be "compassionate" means to accept homosexual behavior. A "stable
> loving relationship" means that homosexual pairings are equivalent to mar-
> riage. "Stereotyping" means it is irrational to assume that all homosexual
> practices are wrong. "Sexual minority" suggests that homosexuals are a le-
> gitimate minority. All such expressions are designed to put nonhomo-
> sexuals on the defensive. (p. 33)

Traditionalists and progay advocates demonstrate a shared tendency to
frame variant sexuality in political terms by emphasizing electoral campaigns, legislative measures, and judicial decisions. Struggle is politicized
for several reasons. First, political action around specific questions reinforces consciousness of common identity. Alberto Melucchi (1985)
argues:

> Because of the fragmentation of collective action, social movements can't
> survive in complex societies without some forms of political representa-
> tion. The existence of channels of representation and of institutional actors

capable of translating in "policies" the message of collective action is the only condition preserving movements from atomization or from marginal violence. (p. 814)

Second, to gain news coverage, both sides thematize political issues as their central concern because the mass media report specific political competition but cannot cover more diffuse cultural conflict. As sociologist Tod Gitlin (1980) has shown, mass media reporters do not present complex material. Extending the news story would "entail hard and unaccustomed work, outside normal news-gathering routines, going beyond the given scene, the given press conference, and the given press release" (p. 35).

At the center of the effort to politicize the contest over variant sexuality, however, is a sense that recognition as a political agency is empowering for segments of the population which fear cultural marginalization. Political scientists Ellen Riggle and Alan Ellis (1994) have clearly described the conditions against which gay/lesbian persons struggle: "Homosexuals, having been defined in terms of their sexuality, are deemed to be out of the realm of politics. As such, political intolerance towards homosexuals is legitimized precisely because homosexuals are defined as not being a political group" (p. 143). Herman (1994) confirms this conclusion, noting that struggle for political goals, "whether or not they are achieved, is a politicizing process facilitating mobilization, identification, heightened public awareness, and the development of a lesbian and gay consciousness, practice, and theory" (p. 4). Consequently, a redefinition of the gay movement as a political cause is, in itself, a step toward legitimacy.

The progay interpretive package has increasingly come to emphasize politics and law as the sites where the most important battles must take place. D'Emilio (1992) confirms that the "gay and lesbian movement has evolved from one emphasizing gay liberation to one emphasizing gay rights. Within that shift in terminology lies a major alteration in social analysis, political strategy and ultimate goals" (p. 181). Gay liberationist efforts of the early 1970s centered on cultural change, whereas recent organizing pivots on referenda campaigns, legislation, and court decisions. Darsey (1991) observes that "gay rights activists have repeatedly waged our most important and visible battles in the legislative or judicial arenas, attempting to change our status through changes in the law and its interpretation" (p. 55). The reason for this shift lies, in part, in the emergence of strong antigay opposition. Historian Salvatore Licata (1981) argues that gay activism in the mid-70s

> faced a strong conservative reaction which had the ironic effect of confirm-
> ing the resolve of the highly politicized gay communities and fostering new
> coalitions between lesbians and gay men. The homosexual rights movement
> seemed to work best when meeting a specific target for which resources and
> personnel could be committed on a short-term basis. (p. 85)

In fact, the gay community continues to organize around specific issues involving discrimination, AIDS funding, and attainment of full citizenship (Cruikshank, 1992, pp. 8-9).

Evangelical Christians, who constitute an important cohort of antigay advocates, have also increasingly taken up political action in their struggle against homosexuality. Himmelstein (1983) observes that, beginning in the 1970s, evangelicals "reverted to the nineteenth century view that the church should infuse the political order with Christian values" (pp. 117-118). Opposition influenced this reversion. The emergence of feminist, proabortion and homophile movements provided action opportunities for evangelicals. Dependent as they are on the patriarchal-heterosexual model as normative, evangelicals could exploit body-oriented political issues as a rallying point.

Even though both antigay and progay discourses emphasize politics, they differ strikingly in their understanding of the link between politics and culture. Once the nature of conflict is defined as political by both sides, antigays gain advantage by further defining the struggle as cultural, a theme that is sounded by gay and lesbian civil rights advocates only in minor and negative ways. The question is not whether a culture war *really* exists, but whether and how agents in the debate over variant sexuality deploy this metaphor. Far more than their opponents, traditionalists find rhetorical advantage in the notion that the core struggle concerns foundational values. The concept of a deep culture war unifies traditionalists but divides progays.

Most progay advocates deny that they are engaged in deep cultural conflict. Some voices assert that fundamental cultural change is a necessary condition for acceptance of variant sexuality. Gay scholar Margaret Cruikshank (1992), for example, contends that, gay liberation demands a fundamental rethinking of sex:

> Since sexuality, sex roles, gender, the regulation of sex, and the constitu-
> tional guarantee of the right to "life, liberty, and the pursuit of happiness,"
> gay and lesbian liberation is a radical social movement, even though it may
> sometimes present itself as reformist. (p. 2)

However, as Darsey (1991) concludes, many gay advocates tend not to
emphasize culture clash, valorizing instead a multicultural tradition of
pluralistic tolerance. With respect to a specific antidiscrimination bill, he
observes that the progay appeals

> can be fairly characterized by the fact that they center on the legal arena,
> either the courts or the legislature, and rather than radically confronting
> society on its own god-terms, homosexuals and their supporters prefer to
> define the legal arena very narrowly, avoiding confrontation on fundamen-
> tals. (p. 59)

Through such a stance, gay/lesbian advocates avoid fundamental questions of moral value, natural law, and community belief. This interpretation is further strengthened by the fact that many individuals politically
active in the gay community are socially conservative and do not see
themselves undermining American society (Rees, 1992).

In contrast, antigays consistently emphasize their belief that homosexual advocacy is, by its very nature, an attack on American culture. They
habitually depict homosexual agitation as *"Kulturkampf"* (Scalia, 1996,
p. 1629), an aspect of a "Great Civil War of Values [which] rages today
throughout North America" (Dobson & Bauer, 1990, p. 19). In support
of this position, traditionalists take the cultural demands of certain gay
writers more seriously than do the progressive left and most gay intellec-
tuals (Blasius, 1994, p. 38). Even humor and parody are treated as deadly
serious statements. Moreover, there is a battle cry throughout new right
discourse with respect to homosexuality that can be sounded only in the
midst of a struggle understood to be cosmic. In one version of the call to
arms, LaHaye (1982) affirms that "there is yet time for us to defeat the humanists and reverse the moral decline in our country that has us on a collision course with Sodom and Gomorrah" (p. 10). Such depictions exploit
for persuasive purposes the perceived marginality of gays and lesbians.
They also fit the larger New Right frame of culture war. Buchanan (1997),
among many others, enunciates a view in which

America has ceased to be a moral community. We do not agree on whether God exists, whether there is a higher moral law than a show of hands can produce, whether abortion is killing a child, whether gay is good. . . . And a country that ceases to be a moral community will eventually cease to be a country. (p. B7)

For strategic reasons, then, culture is frequently defined as contested ground in the antigay interpretive package, but only infrequently in the progay package.

Both progay and antigay interaction not only converge at a political site, but at the same time they further narrow the struggle to limits on state power through the "rights" discourses discussed in the preceding chapter, leading ultimately to an invocation of totalitarianism. The conflict between recognition of the civil rights of lesbians and gay men and the concern with bestowing "special rights" on homosexuals has emerged as part of a larger social concern with a variety of "rights." Many social struggles in the United States are expressed using the ideograph "rights." Law professor Mary Ann Glendon (1991), for example, claims that "discourse about rights has become the principal language we use in public settings to discuss weighty questions of right and wrong" (p. x). She finds that the domination of popular culture by legal language is "both cause and consequence of our increasing tendency to look to law as an expression and carrier of the few values that are widely shared in our society: liberty, equality, and the ideal of justice under law" (p. 3).

With respect to public issues, progay advocates tend to employ a vocabulary in which the term "rights" is used ideographically. Law professor Carl Stychin (1998) has observed the "centrality of rights in political struggle and the particular way in which identity politics is frequently 'legalized' in the United States" (p. 22). Herman (1994) believes a number of benefits derived for progays from an emphasis on "rights" as a key term. In addition to achieving tangible benefits, winning rights for gay people sends a social signal that bigotry and discrimination are no longer acceptable attitudes and behaviors (p. 4). For traditionalists, rights discourse becomes an important way to respond to progay assertions of "rights." Rhetorician Martin Medhurst (1982), for instance, stresses the wisdom of adopting a First Amendment frame to insure that the "fight would be one of *rights vs. rights* (Constitutional vs. human) rather than *morals vs. rights* thus effectively preempting and neutralizing one of the gay activist's primary arguments—that the issue was one of human rights alone" (p. 4).

For him, an effective strategy lay in an appeal to the "freedoms guaranteed under the First Amendment of the Constitution and an unwillingness to see those freedoms eroded by granting additional rights to one minority group which could significantly infringe on the rights granted to all people, minority and otherwise" (p. 5).

Convergence on the contest over "rights" leads easily to framing the discussion over variant sexuality as a battle against totalitarianism. Both progays and antigays represent the opposition as totalitarian. According to Hunter (1991), they "accuse each other of supporting policies that engender the intrusion of the state into private life" (p. 128). "Nazi" is the condensation symbol that both sides use to dramatize this accusation. Such a condensation symbol evokes fear and anxiety without need to refer to objective information (Edelman, 1964, p. 6).

Progays frequently associate traditionalists with authoritarianism. According to Herman (1997), the Christian Right needs an active and expansionist state. She argues that "it is far more accurate to view the CR (but not all conservative Christians by any means) as hoping for, and indeed building (restoring) a *Christian* state—a Christian state that will actively promote Christian tenets through its lawmaking power" (p. 186). Similarly, David Cantor (1994) asserts that the traditionalist movement seeks "more closely to unite its version of Christianity with state power" (p. 1). An extension of this idea is the perception that traditionalists are authoritarians determined to impose the state on the private lives of citizens through "furious campaigns against individual liberty and individual freedom of choice about the most important and private matters" (Nava & Dawidoff, 1994, p. 138). In the end, progays frequently associate antigays with Nazis (McDonald, 1994; People, 1994).

Traditionalists also represent their homosexual opponents as authoritarians who try to intimidate their detractors into silence (Magnuson, 1994, pp. 14-17). The next step is to brand the swastika on their progay opposition. To a significant extent, this is simply a *tu quoque* argument. Lon Mabon, founder of the antigay Oregon Citizens Alliance (OCA) believes that the "gay Nazi" appeal began because the "homosexual community and many of those that support that position have called our proponents Nazis" (Notebook, 1994, p. 8). Scott Lively, the OCA public affairs director, confirms that "homosexuals were an integral part of the Nazi Party throughout history" (Notebook, 1994, p. 8). Elaborating this charge, Robertson declares that "many of those people involved in Adolf Hitler were Satanists, many of them were homosexuals—the two things seem to go together" (quoted in Cantor, 1994, p. 25). This line of reasoning ends in a holocaust against Christians. Robertson envisions that

> just like what Nazi Germany did to the Jews, so liberal America is now doing to evangelical Christians. . . . It is the Democratic Congress, the liberal biased media and the homosexuals who want to destroy all Christians. Wholesale abuse and discrimination and the worst bigotry directed toward any group in America today. More terrible than anything suffered by any minority in history. (quoted in Cantor, 1994, p. 14)

In reviewing the deployment of the "gay Nazi," Herman (1997) concludes that this "is a figure saturated with historical devil discourses: the anticommunist, anti-Semitic, and antigay genres are fused with potent imagery from the Second World War" (p. 90). Although such accusatory exchanges may seem to be mere name-calling, the label of Nazism points to convergence on limiting state control.

Relationships in Antagonistic Encounter

Both progay and antigay discourses construct their struggle with one another simultaneously as a battle against a repressive establishment and against revolutionaries bent on destroying the existing order. This double representation of each side means that all advocates project themselves as both aggressors and defenders.

A progay version of antiestablishment struggle focuses on modifying a society dominated by some combination of capitalism, patriarchy, heterosexism, homophobia, and religiosity. Gay activist Warren Blumenfeld (1992), for instance, claims that homophobia works through both institutions and the culture to oppress lesbians and gay men by formal laws and through exclusion and negative representation (pp. 5-6). Similarly, Mohr (1988) maintains that compulsory heterosexuality dominates society because it "is the lens and primary category through which society sees and structures social experience" (p. 335). In its most complete form, progay antiestablishment struggle is inclusive of all "male-supremacist, anti-homosexual institutions of our society: the legal system and the police, the church, the nuclear family, the mass media, and the psychiatric establishment" (Young, 1972, p. 7). Although most gay discourse does not call for such general social renovation, there is in the gay/lesbian community, as Adam (1987) asserts, a belief that the goals of gay movement "necessarily involve the fundamental restructuring of some of the basic institutions of society" (p. 164).

Antigays also cast themselves as warriors against an establishment which in some basic way has grown corrupt. Most broadly, they struggle against modernism. Religious antigays are part of a larger fundamentalist effort to oppose modernist trends which they find disruptive of an older order. As professors of religion John Hawley and Wayne Proudfoot (1994) suggest, "fundamentalists do not merely detach themselves from certain trends in modern culture; they commit themselves to battle against those trends. They are defined by that opposition and that battle" (p. 12). More specifically, "it was the perceived mistakes and failures of modernity in its guise as establishment America that provided the Protestant religious Right with the opportunity to go public once more" (Simpson, 1983, p. 202).

The key element of traditionalist antiestablishment appeals is a strong current of opposition to an elite that is alleged to suppress the religious majority. Distrust of an elite is a theme that has been sounded by many American movements which want to disrupt the "manipulation of the many by the few" (Lipset & Raab, 1970, p. 15). In its recent traditionalist manifestations, activists have been leading an attack "against cultural changes they identified with the stylish professionals of 'the new class' who allegedly controlled the mass media, the educational system, and the federal government" (Kazin, 1995, p. 256). In the traditionalist view, the American elite is imposing "secular humanism" on the nation, a doctrine which "had become entrenched in the government, schools, media, and other institutions that molded public perceptions" (Wald, 1992, p. 230). According to Francis Schaeffer (1982), a leading traditionalist theoretician, humanism has become "overwhelmingly dominant in about the last forty years. The shift has affected all parts of society and culture, but most importantly it has come largely to control government and law" (p. 135). LaHaye (1980) reiterates the same concept when he declares that a humanist elite has "almost virtual control of the national media, newspapers, magazines, book distribution, education, and to a large degree, government" (p. 182).

In its antigay variant, the attack on an establishment elite takes the form of claims that powerbrokers in American society are prohomosexual. LaHaye (1978) declares that the "propaganda barrage favoring homosexuality has increased relentlessly in newspapers, magazines, books, the schoolhouse, and even some churches. Television and films almost seem obsessed with making the American public accept homosexuality as 'an alternative life style' " (p. 20). Rueda (1982) provides an explanation for this attempt by elites to corrupt American attitudes by arguing that the "ostensibly widespread support for homosexuality is really the approval of this condition as a legitimate lifestyle by the nation's elites" (p. 11). Enforcement of this elite preference is then transformed into the ruthless exercise of government power against the average citizen (Kelly, 1975, p. 11).

Rueda (1982) and many other antigay advocates juxtapose the vast mass of religious people against the establishment controlled by an elite. He writes that "there is little question that the overwhelming majority of the American public rejects the practice of homosexuality" (p. 13). As a consequence, Brummett (1981) notes, antigay advocates "argue that majority rule creates properly moral standards for society. Therefore, society should be molded by decisions rendered through majority voting" (p. 299). The mobilization of a majority to attack a prohomosexual majority through the ballot box has thus become a basic traditionalist strategy, and one which raises fundamental questions about the locus of political and cultural authority in society (Kaplan, 1997, pp. 15-16).

Progay and antigay advocates also project the image that they are in some sense defenders of established values. This self-representation takes a number of different forms. Antigays project themselves as agents of the majority attempting to reverse the initial successes of the "homosexual agenda" which threaten to disrupt American tradition and society. Dannemeyer (1989), for instance, characterizes the progay movement as "essentially revolutionary, given its demands which call for no less than the complete restructuring of America" (p. 123). He declares that "in order to accommodate the homosexuals, we would have to discard those unquestioned values that have always undergirded the American social order" (p. 124). In contrast, progays project themselves as righteous defenders of American values against an emergent radical religious right which is determined to replace equality with intolerance. Bronski (1984) argues that gay movement "brought not only gay people, but also homophobia, out of the closet" (p. 4).

Each construction through which oppositional relationships are defined contains a persuasive strategy. When progay advocates present themselves as opponents of "the establishment," a progressivist narrative emerges which highlights oppression and invites coalition with other marginalized groups. In claiming an identity as opponents of right-wing extremists, progays argue that they are an aggrieved party responding to radical opponents of human progress. In contrast, when antigays present themselves as foes of a corrupt establishment, they employ a declension-redemption narrative long a part of our culture's persuasive repertoire (Lake, 1984, p. 426). In defining their effort as a defensive reaction to homosexual activism, antigays depict themselves as defenders of a just establishment, citizens wrongly aggrieved by marginal agitators.

In summary, progay and antigay advocates help shape one another's identities and reciprocally influence one another's understanding of the contest in which they are engaged. Antigay framing efforts push the progay interpretive package toward emphasis on immutable sexual orientation, essentialist identity, desexualization, concentration on law and politics as the disputed domain, and a construction of opponents as authoritarian theocrats. Progay framing efforts push the antigay interpretive frame toward self-representation as an idealistic "loving opposition" which is victimized by a powerful subversive opposition. To defend traditional culture, antigays must enter the civic arena with secular arguments to defend language against corruption and to prevent authoritarian government from destroying morality.

This description of how antagonistic enjoinment influences opposing interpretive packages depends upon generalization about dominant frames. Now, in turning to competition among interpretive frames within progay and antigay camps, we will qualify these generalizations by pointing out that the existence of opposition influences how rival advocates argue with one another over how best to represent themselves and their cause in a contentious environment.

5　Debate Within Communities

Despite generalizations made in the previous two chapters about the appeals and strategies of progay and antigay advocates, understanding the variant sexuality issue culture requires recognition that various factions within each camp sponsor different versions of their shared interpretive packages. Both progay and antigay interpretive packages are ambiguous in the sense that they imply a "range of positions, rather than any single one, allowing for a degree of controversy among those who share a common frame" (Gamson & Modigliani, 1989, p. 3). Neither side is monolithic in public debate about variant sexuality and each speaks with a multitude of voices (Gallagher & Bull, 1996, p. xii). In a variety of ways, antigay and progay advocates struggle not only against one another, but also within their own communities on behalf of particular ways to understand, articulate, and promote variations on their respective interpretive packages.

Antigay and progay discourses are not equally complex and elaborated. Tensions within the antigay position are less fully articulated than those in the progay stance, and they do not have a comparable effect on political action. Vaid (1995) correctly concedes that there is much uniting the antigay community, because the

> exclusionary politics of Christian identity—which pursues the realization of one Christian nation under one Christian God organized around one socially sanctioned definition of family, with clearly defined roles for men,

women, and children, all working in a free market economic order—serves
as glue to unify disparate people. (p. 294)

Supportive institutions plus an historical language which promotes cohesion are far more available to antigays than to progays. The gay community finds institutional support within some religious organizations and in
many universities, especially in humanities and gender studies programs,
and in a vocabulary of gay/lesbian advocacy developed in the last several
decades. This support and vocabulary, however, are not equivalent in extent, acceptance, or power to the help traditionally offered to antigays by
churches and other associations, or to the resonant language of religious
denunciation of sodomy forged through the years. Consequently, even
though we begin by examining disagreement over interpretive framing by
briefly discussing the divisions which exist among sponsors of antigay
public policy positions, significantly greater attention will be given to the
far more elaborated and complex divisions which exist among progay advocates.

Rival Antigay Interpretive Packages

The coalition of religious forces at the forefront of antigay activism is
composed of groups which are not entirely comfortable with one another.
Lienesch (1993) points out that "contrary to popular opinion, which saw
this movement as monolithic, it was in fact always deeply divided, both
religiously and politically" (p. 15). As a result internal strife is intense, extending to both short-term strategizing and longer-term goals. This is not
surprising because religious coalitions have usually been "messy affairs,
fraught with internal tensions, often incapable of any final resolution"
(Kellstedt, Green, Guth, & Smidt, 1996, p. 284). The Christian Right is
riven with a matrix of fissures, including "Protestant versus Catholic, diverse forms of Protestantism, elites versus grassroots, and challenges from
within by, among others, pragmatists and opportunists" (Herman, 1997,
p. 197).

The claim should not be accepted at face value, however, that all adherents to religious belief are antigay. To the contrary, many lesbians and gay
men are able to reconcile their sexuality to a Christian identity, even to a
strongly conservative evangelical commitment (Thumma, 1991, p. 333).
Members of mainline denominations have taken a variety of positions

with respect to same-sex relationships, ranging from a desire for silence on the subject through support of reform to radical demands for a revision of Christian concepts of sexuality (Bakelaar, 1997, pp. 39-40). Differences among believers have produced divisions in denominations. Despite such dissension, traditionalists have enjoyed a degree of success in projecting antigay consensus as definitive of Christian orthodoxy. The appearance of agreement is a rhetorical accomplishment of this effort. However, antigay advocates have not avoided either ideological or strategic division.

The most fundamental question which continues to face religious conservatives is whether to become involved in public policy questions. For much of the 20th century, conservative religious groups have withdrawn from politics:

> Premillennial dispensationalism had become the dominant eschatological belief of most fundamentalists and many evangelicals. . . . Such a view typically produces a mood of cultural and political pessimism in response to the strong expectation that life on earth will turn steadily worse until Christ returns. (Heinz, 1983, p. 136)

Thus, many conservatives who might morally condemn homosexuality keep themselves largely out of public debate on the grounds that rampant sexual sin is merely one of many "signs of the times." More pragmatically, a number of politically active religious leaders have recently taken the position that politics is too corrupt and distorted an arena for Christians to use to enact social change (Thomas & Dobson, 1999).

Choice of terminology is divisive among antigays. Herman (1997) notes that in their denunciation of homosexuality, some antigay advocates "are more vitriolic, others more tempered in their assessment" (p. 60). At times, disagreement over appropriate verbal style leads to publicized dissension. For example, Ralph Reed (1996), the founding leader of the Christian Coalition, has objected to the denunciatory style of many antigay advocates. Although he abandons neither his moral disapproval of homoerotic acts nor his opposition to government affirmation of homosexuality, he finds "some of the religious conservative movement's discourse on homosexuality disturbing. Calling gays 'perverts,' or announcing that AIDS is 'God's judgment' on the gay community, are just a few examples of rhetoric that is inconsistent with our Christian call to mercy" (p. 264). Other antigays have denounced such proposals for restraint as concessions to homosexuals (Watson, 1997, p. 80). For many on the Christian right, Herman observes, the "Christian Coalition is too compromising and pragmatic; its apparent downplaying of the antigay agenda is symbolic of this" (p. 16).

Fundamental attitudes toward homosexuality also govern the production of variation in the antigay interpretive package. Sullivan (1995) asserts that there are clear differences between those whom he labels "prohibitionists" who wish "to cure or punish people who practice homosexual acts, and deter all the others who might be tempted to stray into the homosexual milieu" (p. 22) and "conservatives" who combine a "private tolerance of homosexuals with public disapproval of homosexuality," and who "do not want to see legal persecution of homosexuals" (p. 97).

The most basic split among proponents of the antigay interpretive package occurs over the use of the older discourse of homosexuality as sin, sickness, and seduction and the newer discourse of "special rights." Herman (1997) writes that a "tension has arisen between 'old moralists' and 'new pragmatists'; the former insist on maintaining an antigay politics of disease and seduction, while the latter wish to bury this discourse under a veneer of liberalistic rights rhetoric" (p. 18). This tension develops out of the foundational ideology of New Right rhetoric which, as Himmelstein (1983) notes, "remains fraught with tensions and contradictions" (p. 17). The older rhetoric of moral conflict is supported by social traditionalists, whereas libertarians campaign on behalf of freedom which would be curtailed by antidiscrimination law. He believes that a key contradiction lies between economic libertarianism and social traditionalism.

> If economic libertarianism stresses the dangers of too much restraint on the individual, social traditionalism stresses the dangers of too little. Similarly, while economic utilitarianism is comfortable with self-oriented, materialist values, social traditionalism regards such values as dangerous and corrosive of the social bond. (Himmelstein, 1983, p. 17)

Tension between antigay appeals based on religion and morality and appeals based on "special rights" has long been a divisive element among traditionalists. Medhurst (1982), for example, argues that an important strategy for antigay advocates has been to recognize "the distinction between argument from religious doctrine and argument from constitutional rights," suppressing the former in favor of featuring the latter (p. 5).

Within the more recent "special rights" rhetoric lurk additional sources of division among traditionalists. For instance, in order to represent homosexuals as a "counterfeit" minority undeserving of "special rights," antigay discourse must construct other minorities as authentically deserving of special protection. Herman (1997) believes that the Christian Right's opposition to all except religious group rights "has proved problematic for CR politics—particularly for its race politics" (p. 112). For example, the antigay "special rights" position potentially contradicts opposition to affirmative action on the basis of race and ethnicity.

Rival Progay Interpretive Packages

A variety of demographic groups participate in the production of progay positions on public policy issues. These groups have not found themselves sharing the same interests or holding the same views. In fact, they often perceive themselves as enemies fighting for different causes. As gay/lesbian political activism became more prominent, D'Emilio (1989a) reports, "sexual orientation created a kind of unity, but other aspects of identity brought to the surface conflicting needs and interests" (p. 468). Gay advocate Eric Rofes (1996) recognizes that

> gay men were a new and fractured class with divisions reflecting not only racial and class distinctions but profound differences in political vision and principles. The formidable challenge facing gay organizing has been to take men whose values and original identities were formed in vastly different cultures and corral them into some semblance of a cohesive movement. (p. 30)

Difference surfaced in every aspect of life.

> For some gay men liberation meant freedom from harassment; for radicalesbians it meant overthrowing the patriarchy. . . . Gay male real-estate speculators displayed little concern for "brothers" who could not pay the skyrocketing rents. Gay men and women of color found themselves displaced by more privileged members of the community. (D'Emilio, 1989a, p. 468)

Differences within the gay/lesbian community which have surfaced to cause division occur along ideological, gender, and generational lines. Goodman and her collaborators (1983) note that throughout the history of gay/lesbian movement, participants have brought many different perspectives to the collective effort: "countercultural, personal growth, bourgeois reformist, Marxist, anarchist, pacifist, socialist, feminist, radical feminist, effeminist, and lesbian separatist" (p. 4). Such differences are a salient characteristic of gay/lesbian politics. Epstein (1999) observes that "one of the most noteworthy aspects of gay and lesbian movements in the United States is the *proliferation* of political beliefs, practices, and organizations that often *compete* with one another to be perceived as legitimate and preferred" (p. 30)

Strong division has often surfaced between lesbians and gay men (Adam, 1999, p. 14). Some believe that such division arises from differences in public policy objectives, with gay men more concerned with such issues as decriminalization and freedom from harassment, and lesbians with family issues such as child custody. Gay men have also been accused by lesbians and feminists of seeking to gain a place in a society dominated by sexism. Philosopher Marilyn Frye (1997/1981), for example, suggests:

> A look at some of the principles and values of male-supremacist society and culture suggests immediately that the male gay rights movement and gay male culture . . . [are] in many central points considerably more congruent than discrepant with this phallocracy, which in turn is so hostile to women and to the woman-loving to which lesbians are committed. (p. 500)

To many lesbians, gay male political activity seems profoundly self-serving and conservative, with the result that lesbians are alienated from their natural allies. For instance, Celia Kitzinger (1987) charges that

> gay men have produced relatively little in the way of political challenge, and such challenges as have emerged fail to command widespread support within the male gay movement, much of which . . . is modeled on the image of the swinging self-confident affluent homosexual male. (p. 62)

At the same time, gay men have expressed considerable irritation with the feminist views of lesbian activists (Miller, 1996/1994, pp. 24-37). Thus, Kitzinger (1987) concludes in a defiant note of separatism that "despite heterosexuals' assumptions of solidarity between lesbians and gay men, there is in fact . . . little reciprocal involvement between the male gay and lesbian communities" (p. 62).

Generational differences also cause division. Younger gays, especially those who style themselves as "queer," have frequently accused older gay leaders of timidity and ineffectuality. In response, older gays charge that the younger generation of militant queers has forgotten past achievements. English professor Arnie Kantrowitz (1997/1992), for example, concludes

> for all the accusations that have been heaped upon the "gaycrat" reformers of the 70s, it should be pointed out that all of the concrete signs of progress in our movement—repeal of sodomy statutes, changes in city and state anti-discrimination laws, bringing our faces out from behind potted palms that used to obscure them on television shows, fairer housing practices, the opening of public accommodations, the proliferation of a gay press, the advent of gay studies—can be attributed to gays. (p. 815)

The attempt to organize a progay movement has, in itself, caused or magnified differences among lesbians and gay men. For example, Gallagher and Bull (1996) suggest that gay leaders have remained out of sync with the more mainstream gay rank and file, from whose experiences a more pressing and resonant set of priorities might be derived (p. 240). As a result, a considerable gulf has developed as movement organizations become remote from everyday experience, "their members coming to see popular behavior as something to be educated, improved, disciplined." The constituents and beneficiaries of these organizations, the majority of gay people, "find the language and the mechanics of these movements remote and alienating" (Dirks, Ely, & Ortner, 1994, p. 5). Further, because of AIDS the gay and lesbian movement was forced "to institutionalize, nationalize, and aggressively pursue the mainstream" (Vaid, 1995, p. 78). Partly as a result, the "interests of a wealthy gay elite dominate the operations and politics of national organizations," with the result that "working class or middle-class queers lose national voice" (p. 78).

The effect of gay/lesbian ideological and objective differences as translated through organizations is to produce significant lines of division over how to frame the struggle on behalf of lesbians and gay men. Gallagher and Bull (1996) highlight the "growing diversity of the gay movement and the rambunctious, pluralistic nature of its politics" (p. 235). They assert that the continuing disagreements over strategy merely manifested "old

divisions that showed no signs of healing, much less of yielding construc-
tive, mutually conciliatory strategies for confronting the movement's
foes." Gays and lesbians lost the solidarity they needed, "complicating the
already difficult work of the national political groups by placing them in
the middle of a raging ideological battle within their own ranks" (p. 235).
Gay/lesbian advocates were placed in the position of needing to recognize
the truth of rhetorician Herbert Simons (1970) observation that

> actions that may succeed with one audience (e.g., solidification of the mem-
> bership) may alienate others (e.g., provocation of a backlash). For similar
> reasons, actions that may seem productive over the short run may fail over
> the long run (the reverse is also true). (p. 1)

Struggles over strategy within the gay/lesbian community can be understood using a number of different oppositions: conservative versus
subcultural radical, Left versus Right, "outer" versus assimilationist, cultural versus civil rights. The differences between conservatives and radicals have been established through mutual recrimination. Conservatives
attack radicals in terms nearly as vitriolic as those used by traditionalists.
Bawer (1993), for instance, has declared that for radicals

> gay activism doesn't mean self-sacrifice but self-indulgence; in addressing
> the general public, they seek not to illuminate but to inflame. Their goal is
> not to make it less problematic for homosexuals to live in stable homes and
> committed relationships but to liberate homosexuals—and as many hetero-
> sexuals as possible—from a world of stable homes and committed relation-
> ships into a world of sexual anarchy and political radicalism. (p. 176)

He argues that the result is embarrassment for the gay movement:

> While the great majority of homosexuals remained invisible . . . the world
> became increasingly familiar with the radical political ideas and sexual mo-
> res of those few gays who, in taking on the Establishment, had also begun to
> forge for their subculture a set of shared assumptions about politics, society,
> sex, and religion that were resolutely at odds with the received ideas of the
> mainstream culture. (p. 176)

Conversely, conservatives are taken to task for creating a gay white
male definition of the universal gay identity and experience, thereby

marginalizing all other potential participants in the struggle against defenders of traditionalist concepts of sexuality and gender. Vaid (1995), for
instance, observes:

> Conservative gay writers often assert that "most" gays are just like their
> straight counterparts but for their sexual desire. By doing so, these conser-
> vative writers, the majority of whom are white and male, universalize their
> own identities, their desire for upward mobility, and their pursuit of admis-
> sion into the status quo as the aspirations of "all" gay people. (p. 288)

Out of such differences arise important struggles over specific strategies.
For example, Schulman (1994) reports that, in reference to organizing
against an Oregon antigay measure, "there were enormous fights . . .
about how openly gay the campaign should be. Some elements of the national community argued that we should present ourselves exactly as we
are. Others wanted a more muted, assimilationist approach" (p. 87).

Implicated in this struggle over representation is a question of emphasis: Should the gay movement concentrate on public policy questions or
on attacking the cultural sites of opposition to gay/lesbian sexuality?
Some progay advocates contend that normal political action obscures
clear reflection about sexuality in the public sphere and mutes gay
self-presentation (Herman, 1994, p. 5). For instance, many members of
the gay/lesbian community objected to the fact that in the Oregon effort
against antigay Measure 9, the "campaign didn't have a *visible* presence of
lesbians and gay men" (Cagan, 1993, p. 68). In this view, conventional political activity makes homosexuality, not discrimination, the issue. As a result, the "official campaign left the Right's representation intact—the
fixed, essential predatory diseased homosexual identity . . . [and thus]
sparks flew . . . within the gay scene as struggles over representation and
self-representation grew" (Introduction, 1993, p. 12). In such struggles,
Vaid (1995) contends that "exclusive focus on legal, legislative, and ad-
ministrative policy reform helps end blatantly discriminatory practices,
but leaves unchallenged myths about variant sexuality which perpetuate
discrimination" (p. 25). Consequently, the "gay and lesbian movement
needs to concentrate far more on culture than on politics as we strive to
win deeper acceptance and genuine equality" (p. 25).

The choice of specific issues to be addressed also frequently causes considerable contention. For instance, although gay marriage has become an

important agenda item for established gay/lesbian civil rights organizations, articulate advocates have contended that

> Lesbians and gay men on the street are just as likely to be made slightly sick by the topic or to shrug it off as yet another example of that weird foreign language that people speak in the media world of politics, policy, and punditry. (Warner, 1999, p. 120)

In such a view, issues such as gay marriage have more significance for intramovement contests than for the battle against traditionalists. As Warner suggests, "since the campaign is not likely to result in same-sex marriage, despite the claims of its triumphal prophets, the most significant dimension of the marriage struggle may turn out to be these internal effects" (p. 158).

Identity and Progay Division

At the core of division among progay advocates are a number of interpretations of gay/lesbian identity. These interpretations are vigorously contested because they are understood as alternative frames for presenting gay/lesbian positions on public policy issues. In the previous chapter, we discussed essentialism as the dominant interpretation of lesbian/gay identity. In this understanding, gay identity is immutable, probably biologically determined, and transhistorical. We noted that an alternative understanding, particularly dominant among academics, describes gay identity as an historical construct, created in particular cultural circumstances, and definitely not genetically determined. Essentialism, we observed, is the primary mode for presenting the gay/lesbian subject in political contexts, but it is far from being uncontested as *the* gay/lesbian identity frame. To the contrary, struggle over the nature of gay/lesbian identity has emerged as the organizing figure for other divisions among gay/lesbian advocates.

Joshua Gamson (1995) provides a useful pattern for analyzing division over gay/lesbian identity. He directs attention to a central question of social movement action: Why and how do movements which struggle to construct boundaries around a unifying identity at the same time exhibit a "drive to blur and deconstruct group categories, and to keep them forever unstable?" (p. 393). The importance of this question is highlighted by the divisive debates over collective identity which frequently arise within the gay/lesbian community. In these debates, Gamson (1995) writes, "two different political impulses, and two different forms of organizing can be seen facing off. The logic and political utility of deconstructing collective categories vie with that of shoring them up" (p. 391).

For some advocates, measurable achievements in improving the lives of lesbians and gay men have been purchased at the price of accepting an exclusionary, rigid, and intellectually inelegant gay identity. For others, academic and radical disruption of a stable and positive gay identity impedes progress toward tangible political goals. In addition, there seems to be an inexorable process involved in creating and blurring identities. Law professor Daniel Ortiz (1993) observes that as a "group describes itself in thicker and thicker terms, disagreement within the group invariably appears over the content of the self-description" (p. 1856). Cultural analysts Caroline Evans and Lorraine Gamman (1995) define the paradox lucidly: "The necessary fiction of a cohesive identity must be spoken in order for political communities to maintain any sort of presence. But there are obviously problems with the articulation of any sort of fixed identity" (p. 38).

There is extensive agreement among lesbians and gay men on the need for an identity in order to be represented in the public sphere. The need for identity is often represented in conjunction with oppression. Cruikshank (1992) asserts:

> Sexual practices clearly are a private matter; they become politicized when groups or institutions try to stamp them out. If gay people claimed only the right to perform certain sexual acts, however, they would not have been able to create a movement. Their claim rests on sexual identity, which is a sufficient basis for a movement. (p. 2)

Thus, the appeal central to gay organizing is the premise that "lesbians and gay men constitute a minority because they are discriminated against on the basis of sexual orientation and because heterosexuality is promoted by the major institutions of society" (p. 60). Adam (1987) elaborates on this concept, pointing out:

> When homosexuality was a "vice," an "illness," or a "luxury," it could never resist the depredations of moral entrepreneurs, police, or kin, and Western history is the record of centuries of underground homosexual life. Only by

embracing it as an identity could homosexual desire be reorganized as a collectivity capable of defending itself from its enemies. (p. 107)

The significance of identity can best be appreciated if one conceives social movement as constructed through communication. From this perspective, movements do not exist in the phenomena of persons, organizations, or uninstitutionalized collectivities, but are constituted through communication in the "ideographs, culture types, characterizations, myths, metaphors, narratives, and topoi employed in public discourse to argue collective being into existence" (Condit & Lucaites, 1991, p. 1). Social scholar Alain Touraine (1985) summarizes this concept in his contention that the "notion of social movement, like most concepts in the social sciences, does not describe a part of 'reality' but is an element of a specific mode of constructing reality" (p. 749). One learns through communication about the identity of collective subjects, because, as Eder (1993) observes, "cultural change in modern society is produced by a collective learning process whose logic is defined by the logic of discursive communication" (p. 23). From this perspective, movement as symbolic production requires a "subject in whose name the movement acts and articulates its demands" (Scott, 1990, p. 29). The magic of movements is not to give voice to a preexisting class, but to "conjure up a symbolic 'people' from cultural commonplaces, cultivating a compelling dream of significance" (McGee & Martin, 1983, p. 47).

As discussed in Chapter 1, during the past half century, movements centered on variant sexuality have called up diverse gay spirits. In the now standard chronicle, the homophile movement of the 1950s and 1960s created gay/lesbian consciousness. Homophile activists "had not only to mobilize a constituency, first they had to create one" (D'Emilio, 1983, p. 4). The Mattachine Society's founders "pioneered in conceiving homosexuals as an oppressed minority" (p. 58). This position was opposed by a strong assimilationist faction which took the position that gay and straight people are identical to one another except for the minor difference of sexual object choice (p. 79). Struggles within the Mattachine Society produced issues about gay identity that would consistently divide gay people through the decades:

> Whether homosexuality was an unimportant characteristic or an aspect of a person's life so significant that it bound gay men and women together as a minority group, whether homosexuals and lesbians should accommodate

themselves to the mores of society or assert their difference; whether they were victims of prejudiced opinion or of a system of oppression inherent in the structure of American society. (D'Emilio, 1983, p. 90)

Subsequently, gay liberationists brought into this debate renewed emphasis on fundamental institutional and cultural change. Liberation "saw itself as one piece of a much larger political impulse that strove for a complete reorganization of institutions, values, and the structure of power in American life" (D'Emilio, 1992, p. 181). Of central importance to gay liberation was the obliteration of the established order which structured both gender and sexuality. Mario Mieli (1980/1970), an influential gay liberation theoretician, declared that the

> object of the revolutionary struggle of homosexuals is not that of winning social tolerance for gays, but rather the liberation of the homoerotic desire in every human being. If the only result were that so-called "normal" people should "accept" homosexuals, then the human race would not have recognized its own deep homosexual desire. (p. 82)

In the 1970s, with attenuation of all forms of radicalism in the United States, the themes of gay liberation were supplanted by increasing emphasis on civil rights. D'Emilio (1992) suggests that this change from liberation to rights encouraged the expression of gay/lesbian political demands through the well established civil rights frame (p. 181). However, in recent years, queer theorists and activists have rigorously and stridently challenged the strategy behind gay rights rhetoric, and in particular the essentialist identity central to that strategy. Rhetorical critic R. Anthony Slagle's (1995) analysis of Queer Nation neatly justifies the deconstruction of mainstream gay identity by problematizing binary oppositions such as gay/straight through developing a "celebration of difference rather than the imposition of a fixed identity" (p. 93). Indeed, he writes, "queer identity is the refusal to name what the identity means" (p. 97). By valorizing difference, queer theorists avoid the "essentialist nature of the dominant codes and the modes of classification (used both by the dominant group and earlier gay and lesbian liberation groups)" (p. 93). From this perspective, "acceptance, much less celebration, of externally imposed categories as authentic differences reinforces rather than undoes identity-based oppression" (Miller, 1998, p. 35).

Threading through the history of gay/lesbian movements is contention over concepts of identity which snarls and knots in the essentialism versus constructionism debate described in the previous chapter. This debate is situated in a complex social and intellectual context because conviction about the nature of gays or queers as collective subjects is inextricably bound up in ideological choices and social locations. As professor of English Alan Sinfield (1994) maintains, "our terms—'gay,' 'lesbian and gay,' 'lesbian, gay and bisexual,' 'dyke,' 'queer'—are markers of political allegiance, far more than ways of having or thinking about sex" (p. 72).

Conceptual differences between lesbians and gay men bring into focus contention over choice of identity construct and the political stance implied by that choice. We suggested earlier that exposure to opposition is key to identity choice, because those most directly involved in confrontation over gay issues are most likely to adopt an essentialist identity. Adoption of an identity construct, moreover, may be influenced by gender, race, and class. Sociologist Michael Kimmel (1993), on the basis of survey evidence, claims that "by far gay *men* believe that their homosexuality is natural, biological, and inborn, while lesbians are more likely to believe that their homosexuality is socially constructed" (p. 579). Further, many groups have developed a sense of marginality and exclusion which fuels deconstruction of the universalist claims of a privileged middle class, white gay male identity. A link between essentialist identity politics and white gay males is taken as axiomatic by many commentators. Feminist scholar Lisa Duggan (1995), for example, claims:

> *Any* gay politics based on the primacy of sexual identity defined as unitary and "essential," residing clearly, intelligibly and unalterably in the body or psyche, and fixing desire in a gendered direction, ultimately represents the view from the subject position "twentieth century, Western white, gay male." (p. 162)

Also implicated in division over identity is choice of theoretical position on gender. The extent to which one is influenced by poststructuralist feminist theory may effect selection of identity construct. The feminist version of poststructuralism is summarized by Stevi Jackson (1993) as a "current within feminism . . . which sought to 'deconstruct' gender categories, to reveal the ways in which they have been culturally constructed and to demonstrate that they are fictions rather than natural facts" (p. 4).

Psychologists John DeCecco and John Elia (1993) contend further that a dominant trend in the feminist movement is

> to "deconstruct" gender, to show that inequality of opportunity, status, achievement, and reward is *not* an inevitable product of women's biology. In this view, women are not biologically mandated to be only nurturers of men and the sole emotional guardians of human relationships. (p. 16)

Consequently, poststructuralist feminists oppose gay/lesbian activists who "have endorsed the biologization of homosexuality and the heterosexual-homosexual dichotomy" (p. 16).

Choice of mode for activism also operates to influence a selection of identity. A preference for cultural action as a means to undermine social concepts of gender and sexuality is involved with rejecting essentialist identity. Cultural politics which would release individuals from social regulation shares with constructionist arguments an "insistence that sexual typologies are social, rather than natural facts; that these categories are highly fluid; and that they need to be transcended" (Epstein, 1990, p. 253).

Selection of an identity construct has become a significant ground for disagreement among lesbians and gay men, functioning as a means of expressing conflict which arises out of disagreements produced by gender, social location, and ideology. The result is that a significant body of writing makes claims about the merits of essentialism as opposed to constructionism as ways of framing the larger debate about public issues centering on sexuality. What has evolved is an extensive and divisive struggle over the rhetoric of sexuality which explicitly recognizes that the "rhetorical strategies and the media to transmit these strategies are ideological in origin and use" (Chesebro, 1994, p. 78). Claims about the persuasive power of essentialist and constructionist identity accounts consist of assertions that one or the other is a better fit to the larger society's understanding of sexuality and a better response to cultural premises, legal theory, and appropriate social purpose.

Several arguments are presented in defense of an essentialist gay/lesbian identity frame. As discussed in Chapter 3, essentialism is consistent with gay male self-understanding, with the treatment accorded gay persons, and with the American civil rights tradition. Consequently, gay/lesbian discourse concerning public issues is overwhelmingly essentialist. Underlying this position is a pair of anxious questions: "If we [gay/lesbian

people] cannot make political claims based on an essential and shared nature, are we not left once again as individual deviants? Without an
essentialist foundation, do we have a viable politics?" (Whisman, 1996,
p. 122). Within the American political tradition, identity politics requires
the production of a stable self-representation. Simply put, "activists and
theorists suggest that collective identities with exclusive and secure
boundaries are politically effective" (Gamson, 1995, p. 400). This position is backed through experience because identity as a political strategy is
hardly novel. As legal scholars Davina Cooper and Didi Herman (1995)
assert, "identity politics have played a powerful part in political struggles,
in the past focusing on ethnicity, religion, and class, and in contemporary times focusing on race, gender, sexual orientation, and disability"
(p. 211).

The political, legal, dialectical, and movement forces which fix and
harden categorical identities will doubtless remain strong. Politics in its
many forms, political scientist William Connolly (1991) points out, "contains powerful pressures to become a closed circuit for the dogmatism of
identity through the translation of difference into threat and threat into
energy for the dogmatization of difference" (p. 210). Put another way, the
invocation of identity may be necessary in order to offer protection to
threatened individuals. The dominant paradigm of liberal pluralism obscures differences within groups in the effort to provide "legal protection
for identities through anti-discrimination statues, sexual harassment policies, constitutional rights, hate crime statutes and affirmative action policies" (Danielson & Engle, 1995, p. xiv).

In addition, the argument is put forward that discourse, in order to be
persuasive, must contain essentializing terms. Commentators have noted
that "even those constructionists among us for whom the word 'identity'
conjures up a pit of positivist snakes acknowledge the mobilizing power
implicit in the use of terms like 'lesbian,' 'gay,' 'bisexual,' 'transexual,'
and so on" (Chinn & Franklin, 1992, p. 18). In this view, the most dogmatic constructionists must use terms which imply an essentialist unity. As
Smith (1994) observes, "even the most radical critique of identity, and
even the most naive championing of absolute indeterminacy, reproduce
some degree of sameness and identity" (p. 90). Consequently, the most
dedicated efforts to destabilize gay/lesbian identity are threatened by the
necessity to create an essentialized vocabulary into which their adherents
are absorbed. Thus, Vaid (1995) observes, queer activists "quickly established a new and fairly orthodox vocabulary" (p. 296).

The defense of constructionism as a viable political position encompasses necessity, consistency, and empowerment. First, constructionism undermines discourses of power which oppress gay people. English professor Diane Fuss (1991) explains this concept: "What is called for is nothing less than an insistent and intrepid disorganization of the very structures which produced this inescapable logic" of inside/outside constructs which underlie the homosexuality/heterosexuality binary (p. 6). Second, given the diversity of the gay community, constructionism builds an open category which all people who are in some sense "different" can enter without fear of marginalization (Crain, 1993, p. 18). Third, constructionism is consistent with a variety of disciplinary trends, including "anthropology and contemporary literary theory and their intellectual forbears, structural linguistics and structuralism, which all emphasize the ultimate relativity and subjectivity of language and observation" (Boswell, 1990, p. 148). Fourth, professor of art and gay scholar Wayne Dynes (1990) argues that gay people gain a new sense of openness and flexibility by recognizing that "traditional cultural arrangements, previously taken to be 'natural' and unalterable, are only the imposition of ideological structures whose reign is doomed to pass away" (p. 232).

Advancing a position involves criticizing rival beliefs. Essentialist rhetoric has been condemned on a number of grounds. Progressive critics, especially those on the Old New Left, have challenged the concept of identity politics of which essentialism is the central principle. Editor and commentator David Brooks (1996) notes that many "liberal and left-wing writers argue that identity politics is a cul-de-sac which has ghettoized left-wing ideas and allowed the white middle class to drift to the right" (p. 116). Such criticism is, of course, not new. Political philosopher John Thompson, for instance, observed in 1984 that divisions along the lines of gender and race form barriers that obstruct the development of movements which could change the social order. He argued that "divisions are ramified along the lines of gender, race qualifications and so on, forming barriers which obstruct the development of moments which could threaten the *status quo*." And he concluded that an oppressive social order "may depend less upon a consensus with regard to dominant values or norms than upon a lack *of consensus* at the very point where oppositional attitudes could be translated into political action" (pp. 63-64). One observer writes that emphasis on identity prevents coalition among the oppressed, leading inevitably to the "balkanization and fragmentation of the left" (Kauffman, 1990, p. 76). Recently, this theme has been elaborated by commentator Michael Tomasky (1996) and by Tod Gitlin (1995).

Related to this objection is anxiety that identity politics has meandered into a "preoccupation with self and the politics of representation" (Seidman, 1993, p. 136). The result of obsession with identity is critique which ignores social and political contexts (Nicholson & Seidman, 1995, p. 9). The reason for such an unmooring of identities from material circumstances lies in the nature of language itself because "categorical identities can be invoked and given public definition by individuals or groups even where they are not embodied in concrete networks of direct interpersonal relationships" (Calhoun, 1994b, p. 26).

A more profound challenge to identity politics, however, comes from theorists who argue that any identity is regulative and that identity politics is exclusionary. In this view, all forms of identity politics perpetuate disabling myths of the social agent as transparent, natural, and homogeneous, prevent coalition and create disabling division, repress intragroup differences, and suppress multiple identities. Drawing primarily on the works of Foucault and secondarily on Judith Butler, anti-identity theorists "slide into viewing identity itself as the fulcrum of domination" (Seidman, 1993, p. 132). In this critique, identity inevitably limits understanding or produces hierarchies (Seidman, 1995, p. 117). Cooper and Herman (1995) observe that "categories of identity risk becoming fixed and essential; rigid lines are drawn. Men cannot be feminists; whites cannot be partners in antiracist efforts" (p. 211). As a consequence of rigid categorization, experiential privilege becomes the singular ground for authority. As professors of English Judith Roof and Robyn Wiegman (1995b) note, "women can only speak about/for women, lesbians about/for lesbians, and so on" (p. 94).

Categorical identities, it is charged, impose a fable of subjects fundamentally allied by nature who have only one meaning that is the inspiration of all their behavior. Social critic Chantal Mouffe (1995) writes that it is "impossible to speak of the social agent as if we were dealing with a unified, homogeneous entity. We have rather to approach it as a plurality, dependent on the various subject positions through which it is constituted within various discursive formations" (p. 187). In similar vein, social scientist Kwame Appiah (1995) argues that identities "flourish despite . . . our 'misrecognition' of their origins; despite, that is, their roots in myths and in lies" (p. 110). Further, such identities prevent coalition. They produce instead social fragmentation and a proliferation of divisions

(p. 111). Identity politics has also been denounced for suppressing difference within progressive communities (Warner, 1993, p. xvi). Such suppression is ultimately divisive. Despite universalist claims to community by various gay/lesbian factions, a clash within movements for progressive social change occurs between center and periphery. Individuals rebel against being forced to choose one identity from among the multiple social identities constituted in the categorizations derived from gender, sexual orientation, race, ethnicity, lifestyle, and locale (Seidman, 1993, p. 129).

With specific reference to gay/lesbian identity, essentialist rhetoric has been condemned on additional grounds. The argument has been advanced that essentialist appeals divide gay men from feminists who seek to deconstruct the naturalness of gender identities. Herman (1994) asserts that the essentialist concept of immutability is "fundamentally at odds with those theories of sexuality which deconstruct the naturalness of heterosexuality and gender identities. . . . A feminist sexual politics is largely marginalized by mainstream lesbian and gay rights discourse" (p. 5). In addition, essentialist identity prevents a normalizing recognition of the social presence of gays and lesbians: "To view gay identity as a species difference is to regard gay people as being so separate, so different in kind, that many heterosexuals believe they do not know and have never met a lesbian or gay man" (Weston, 1991, p. 203).

Essentialist identity also stands accused of reinforcing a binary understanding of sexual orientation in such a way as to simply confirm the heterosexual order. In English professor Lee Edelman's (1994) words, adoption of essentialism confirms the heterosexual symbolic order by naming a "condition that must be represented as determinate . . . metaphorized as an essential condition, a sexual orientation, in order to contain the disturbance it effects as a force of disorientation" (p. 14). In this view, the "institutionalization of difference" serves only as a method of isolating the gay category (p. 21). Such isolation is unnecessary because an essentialist sexual identity is only a language game. John Champagne (1995) suggests that progay advocates have become caught in a web of words, declaring that "because the category of the homosexual exists, we must have a politics around sexuality, and because we have a politics around sexuality, the category of homosexual must exist" (p. 66).

From another position, homosexuality becomes the term through which oppression is deployed. In an essentialist construction, homosexuality

becomes the excluded; it stands in for, paradoxically, that which stands
without. . . . The "homo" in relation to the "hetero," much like the feminine
in relation to the masculine, operates as an indispensable interior exclusion
. . . a transgression of the border which is necessary to constitute the border
as such. (Fuss, 1991, p. 5)

Mary Eaton (1995) expresses a similar idea when she writes that the "existence of an inside, privileged class and an outside, subordinate class depends on a clear differentiation between those on each side of the divide"
(p. 65). In short, only by producing a clearly defined homosexual can the
certainty of heterosexuality be assured. The editors of the *Harvard Law
Review* (Sexual Orientation, 1990) summarize this concept, reporting
that social constructionists hold that "basing legal protections for lesbians
and gay men on the fundamental difference of their sexual orientation reinforces the very repression sought to be removed" (p. 7)

   The contention is also advanced that an essentialist gay identity is an
inadequate defense against oppression. As Halperin (1990) puts this criticism, "no account is so positive as to be proof against hostile appropriation and transformation" (p. 52). Sinfield (1994) substantiates this claim,
arguing that if homosexuality is a matter of volition:

> Lesbians and gay men can boldly assert our choices; on the other hand, we
> may be judged to have perversely chosen a wrong or inferior lifestyle. If we
> are genetically determined, it might seem futile to harass people who are
> only manifesting a natural condition; on the other hand, our enemies might
> regard us as an inferior species. (p. 70)

He concludes that in balancing the liberationist position against minority
politics, "if everyone is potentially gay, anxiety about expressing that gayness and consequent hostility might be greater. If few of us really are, it
might be easier to scapegoat us" (p. 69). For example, essentialist identity
grounded in biology fails to prevent oppression since "from the Holocaust to the history of racial prejudice in America, one can see that being
born a certain way does not cushion anyone against persecution" (Vaid,
1995, p. 136). Similarly, professors of criminology Donald West and
Richard Green (1997) warn that while belief in biological causation can
lessen social condemnation, "biological determinants of unwanted traits
are increasingly being intercepted with prenatal and postnatal interventions" (p. 334). Implicit in this criticism is the idea that essentialism is simply out of date, a once useful tool which is now more limiting than liberat-

ing. D'Emilio (1992) writes that an essentialism which constitutes transhistorical gay persons was empowering "when we battled an ideology that either denied our existence or defined us as psychopathic . . . [but] has confined us as surely as the most homophobic medical theories, and locked our movement in place" (p. 5). Finally, the suggestion has been advanced that assimilationist appeals based on identity are contradictory. Miller (1998) asserts that "while civil rights arguments draw upon the assumption of an identity-based community . . . their guiding objective of assimilation undercuts the very principle of difference on which such a community is based" (p. 48).

Essentialists have also been accused of supporting an expression of the normalization and commodification of sexuality. Rofes (1996) notes that in the 1980s, a normalizing identity culture became powerful which emphasized a singular gay identity. "We formed choruses, baseball leagues, and community centers, joined the Democratic Party, and rapidly transformed the counter culture into an upscale, commercialized 'lifestyle' " (p. 111). Taking up a similar theme, Warner (1993) writes:

> In the lesbian and gay movement, to a much greater degree than in any comparable movement, the institutions of culture-building have been market-mediated: bars, discos, special services, newspapers, magazines, phone lines, resorts, urban commercial districts. Nonmarket forms of association that have been central to other movements—churches, kinship, traditional residence—have been less available for queers. (p. xvi-xvii)

As a result, he concludes, "this structural environment has meant that the institutions of queer culture have been dominated by those with capital: typically, middle-class white men" (p. xvi).

Finally, essentialism is arraigned for limiting individual choice. In general, as law professor Theo van der Meer (1993) claims, "identity limits us as much as it sets us free" because it reinforces general social belief that "homosexuality should not spill over into the rest of society" (p. 135). DeCecco and Elia (1993) elaborate this idea, arguing:

> Those people who make the heterosexual-homosexual dichotomy, conceived as an incontrovertible biological, individual, or social division of the human race, the central focus of their lives end up living in communities that endorse one preference to the exclusion of others. The price of community membership is the surrender of the freedom to change one's mind and behavior and to participate broadly in society. (p. 17)

Only by escaping an essentialist identity can individuals "form relationships with either gender that meet personal and social needs while retaining the fluidity of relationships necessary in a rapidly changing world"
(p. 18).

Essentialists are equally willing to attack constructionism on a number
of grounds. The constructionist frame has been criticized because it disor-
ganizes gay political action and erases the gay subject, undercuts moral
claims on equality, is intellectually vacuous, and offers a reductionist portrayal of gay people. Sullivan (1995) argues that constructionist appeals
impede gay/lesbian mobilization because

> its politics was inevitably a confused and seamless flux of competing con-
> structions; a recipe for political paralysis and chaos [which] stemmed from
> the core meaning of what such a movement should be about; and it made it
> impossible for the movement to move anywhere coherently or together.
> (p. 89)

More fundamentally, constructionism threatens to eliminate consciousness of gay identity necessary for political and cultural action. Literary
scholar Leo Bersani (1995), for example, argues that constructionism,
deconstructionism, and postidentarian politics in general threaten the
erasure of gay people. He maintains that "we have erased ourselves in the
process of denaturalizing the epistemic and political regimes that have
constructed us" (p. 4). The consequences of this erasure are unilateral disarmament, desexualization, and assimilation. In rejecting essentializing
identities, advocates must mount a "resistance to homophobia in which
the agent of resistance has been erased" (p. 56). Further, the current political expression of deconstructionism "puts all resisters in the same queer
bag—a universalizing move I appreciate but that fails to specify the sexual
distinctiveness of the resistance" (p. 71). Moreover, having de-gayed
themselves, "gays [will] melt into the culture they like to think of themselves as undermining" (p. 4).

The constructionist frame is also alleged to deny implicitly any warrant
to claims of gay/lesbian oppression. Mohr (1992) complains of the

> dissipating indeterminacy from the contemporary intellectual forces of
> deconstructionism, historicism, and relativism. If all norms are socially rel-
> ative, as most gay academics now hold, there can be no concept of oppres-
> sion, only more or less pervasive regimes of knowledge, discourse and
> power. (p. 4)

In addition, constructionism tends to emphasize the operation of language at the expense of analysis of the material world. As English professor Rosemary Hennessy (1995) suggests:

> Because it is the social order—the distribution of wealth, of resources, and power—that is at stake in the struggle over meanings, a politics that contests the prevailing constructions of sexual identity and that aims to disrupt the regimes they support will need to address more than discourse. (p. 152)

Finally, constructionism may also limit freedom. Dynes (1990) offers the proposition that "while [constructionism's] malleability offers a promise of openness, it does so at the cost of a reductive portrayal of the individual as a mere puppet jerked about by collective forces" (p. 233). In support of this concept, sociologist Craig Calhoun (1994b) contends that "social constructionist approaches could be just as determinist as naturalizing approaches, for example, when they denied or minimized personal or political agency by stressing seemingly omnipresent but diffuse social pressures as the alternative to biological causation" (p. 16). In this view, constructionism has not fulfilled its promise either to gain freedom from identity's constraints or to dissolve the boundaries of social categories. Thus, for some critics, the narratives of constructionism are not, as a practical matter, much different from essentialist narratives because each leads to a fixed identity. Seidman (1995) points out that "both essentialist and social constructionist versions of lesbian/gay theory in the 1970s and 1980s have related stories of the coming of age of a collective gay subject" (p. 125). In Calhoun's words, the "emphases on early socialization and on the power of social structure also lead many social constructionists to treat identities in terms nearly as 'essentialist' as those of biological determinists" (p. 16).

In the 1990s, disagreement between queer theorists/activists and mainstream political advocates has rearranged rather than merely repeated previous patterns of dispute over gay identity. Queer theory directs attention to the disruption of foundational constructs. Warner (1993) argues that the current sexual order pervades dominant institutions and narrations and that queer struggle must challenge these institutions and accounts rather than seeking accommodation within them (p. xiii). In general, queer theory "rejects a minoritizing logic of toleration or simple political interest-representation in favor of a more thorough resistance to regimes of the normal" (p. xxv).

As part of queer theory's attempt to deconstruct sexuality, there has been a strong effort to move beyond a dispute over collective identity. Adherents to this effort believe that the "arcane polemics between constructionists and essentialists has evolved into a sterile metaphysical debate void of moral and political import" (Seidman, 1993, p. 105). Present in queer theory is a move

> beyond an anti-identity politics to a politics against identity *per se*. Implicit in this subversion of identity is a celebration of liminality, of the spaces between or outside structure, a kind of anarchistic championing of 'pure' freedom from all constraints and limits. (p. 133)

In political form, queer theory seeks to unite "all those heterogeneous desires and interests that are marginalized and excluded in the straight and gay mainstream" (p. 133). At the same time, queer theory makes identity a continuing problem. Warner (1993) believes that blurring boundaries and recognition of the multiplicity of identity come together in queer theory in which a "lesbian and gay population . . . is defined by multiple boundaries that make the question of who is and is not 'one of them' not merely ambiguous but rather a perpetually and necessarily contested issue" (p. xxiv).

Queer advocacy, Seidman (1993) points out, is an articulation of the differences which once were ignored in the gay/lesbian community (p. 118). Thus, the "struggle over homosexuality has been grudgingly acknowledged to be a struggle among lesbian, gay, bisexual, and queer individuals and groups who hold to different, sometimes conflicting, social interests, values, and political agendas" (Seidman, 1995, p. 117). The aim of queer theory has been to subvert the sexual order and the sense of identity on which it is based. "Queer interventions aim to expose their unconscious complicity in reproducing a heteronormative order and an order that condenses sexual freedom to legitimating same-sex gender preference" (p. 139). Such critique can be regarded as a politics "in which struggles over meaning and social identities are struggles for cultural hegemony, that is, for the power to construct authoritative definitions of social situations and legitimate interpretations of social needs" (Fraser, 1989, p. 6).

Queer theory has, of course, produced its own chorus of critics. The principal line of criticism is summarized in Patton's (1993) assertion that "queer theory has been better at pointing out the essentialist moments and problems of identity than it has been in suggesting a postidentarian politics" (p. 164). This supports Seidman's (1993) more general observation that "to the extent that poststructuralism, like its political counterpart, Queer Nation, edges into a postidentity politic, its exquisite intellectual and political gesturing draws its power more from its critical force than any positive program of change" (pp. 110-111). Halperin (1995) provides an excellent summary of criticism which includes charges that queer theory and activism promote (a) "unproductive political conflict and generational division among lesbian and gay men," (b) "gives a false impression of inclusiveness," and (c) multiplies "opportunities for disidentification, denial, and discontent" (p. 64). Queer theorists have also been accused of distorting women's experience. Sociologist Suzanne Walters (1996) indicts queer theory because it "erases lesbian specificity and the enormous differences that gender makes, evacuates the importance of feminism, and rewrites the history of lesbian feminism and feminism generally" (p. 843). A final key question which has been debated is whether queer activism in its many forms is effective or merely an "empty politics of gesture or disruptive performance that forfeits an integrative, transformative politics" (Seidman, 1993, p. 134).

During the past half century of competition among progay advocates to identify the most effective among the available identity frames for variant sexuality, two impulses have run through the literature on gay/lesbian political appeals: the impulse to resist containment and the impulse to resist erasure. Resistance to containment by any particular identity can be understood as struggle against power in the Foucauldian sense which channels, regulates, and normalizes. This position is founded on the premise that "all signifying practices, that is, all practices that have meaning—involve relations of power" (Jordan & Weedon, 1995, p. 11). Such struggle against containment is continual because the "minoritized subject who has sought to speak from the specificity of its cultural position has been recontained through a new deafening 'authenticity,' one that disturbingly reduces the complexity of social subjectivity" (Roof & Wiegman, 1995a, p. x). The impulse against containment is based on the complex concept that the

> demand to *ethicize* or universalize the entrenched contingencies on the grounds that they flow from a true identity is a recipe for repression of difference. . . . This demand grounds your sexual ethic in the self-idealization of a contingent, relational identity that takes itself to be natural and independent. (Connolly, 1991, p. 177)

The impulse against containment, however, is consistently accompanied by the impulse against erasure. Indeed, a paradox of identity is generated by the contradictory desires inherent in the modern politics of the West to affirm both the idiosyncratic self and the defining group. As philosopher Bernard Williams observes (1995):

> Ever since the Enlightenment a recurrent aspiration of distinctively modern politics has been for a life that is indeed individual . . . yet at the same time expresses more than me, and shapes my life in terms that mean something because they lie beyond the will and are concretely given to me. (pp. 10-11)

Ironically, in political processes which create power "through categorization, identity is often built on the very categories it resists" (Gamson, 1989, p. 358). This produces an unresolved dilemma in which the "logic and political utility of deconstructing collective categories vie with that of shoring them up; each logic is true, and neither is fully tenable" (Gamson, 1995, p. 391).

Remaining a contentious issue for gay/lesbian self-representation is the question of how public perception of sexuality should be managed. Many progay advocates demand that the gay image be sanitized. Bawer (1993), for instance, has denounced gay publications because the "narrow sex-obsessed image of gay life that they presented bore little resemblance to my life or the lives of my friends" (p. 19). Because of this depiction

> many heterosexuals tended to equate homosexuality with the most irresponsible and sex-obsessed elements of the gay population. That image had provided ammunition to gay bashers [and] had helped to bolster the widely held view of gays as a mysteriously threatening Other. (p. 19)

Opponents of this position respond that to modify gay and lesbian self-presentation in order to secure immediate political gains is "to deny gay experience and culture, and to sacrifice it to and for the values of others—to be dignified without having dignity" (Mohr, 1988, p. 333). Bersani (1995) supports this argument by maintaining that "de-gaying gayness can only fortify homophobic oppression; it accomplishes in its own way the principal aim of homophobia: the elimination of gay" (p. 5). With respect to demands for self-censorship of public gay activity, a similar contention is advanced that the "rowdy, raucous, outrageous, or cross-dressing members of the gay population are as central to the movement as those who are outwardly more conventional" (Cruikshank, 1992, p. 172). The view that the gay culture should be desexualized has met with stern opposition from groups such as Sex Panic" which hold that promiscuous sex is important to the central meaning of gay culture (Stolberg, 1997).

These internal struggles have significance for the public representation of the lesbian and gay community. Joshua Gamson (1997) observes that "internal movement debate over inclusion and exclusion are best understood as *public communications*" (p. 180). At times, the externally directed nature of internal struggle is obvious, as in the battles over the inclusion of intergenerational sex advocates in the gay coalition. But even the more arcane disputations over the nature of identity and difference are performed with bystander publics as the audience.

The effect of these disputes may not necessarily be negative. Benford (1993) points out that intramural conflicts have positive effects. Disagreement may damage some organizations, deplete resources, and provoke factionalism. However, some groups benefit in growth of membership and support, resources are more easily concentrated, and cohesiveness within groups may be increased (p. 694). Although the effects of intramovement conflict may remain uncertain, there is little reason to doubt that, with respect to both antigay and progay movements, unceasing though evolving disputes will shape each movement and affect their degree of success.

Progay and antigay advocates use interpretive packages which invoke a united community, and both struggle over nuances and major differences in how to present a persuasive interpretive package which will achieve cultural dominance. There would appear to be less division among traditionalists than progays. Each, however, is challenged to hold together a cohesive block of followers sufficiently strong to manipulate and control certain public policy decisions. How to present gay/lesbian identity for maximum rhetorical effect remains the most widely deliberated of the many divisive questions which arise in public debates over sexuality. This is the inevitable question to which progay advocates continually return. The conundrum always allows disparate groups to express their varying and inconsistent visions as well as their mutual animosity. Antagonistic enjoinment makes choice of frame important in that a wrong selection can lead to political/legal disaster. Moreover, events in the actual world of confrontation among opponents often impose a logic of their own which compels the choice of one representation over another.

6 Same-Sex Marriage: A Case Study

Various versions of progay and antigay interpretive frames are highlighted in different public policy disputes about variant sexuality. Many policy questions continue to be important, including the repeal of sodomy laws, government funding for homoerotic art, custody and adoption of children by gay persons, and adding "sexual orientation" to hate crime laws. Consequently, no single instance of a public issue contest can serve as a master example of discourse or provides an occasion in which all voices are heard. In recent years, however, four public policy areas have been most important in the variant sexuality issue culture.

First, dozens of antigay initiatives have been placed on local and state ballots throughout the United States. The general thrust of these measures has been to forbid governments from protecting the civil rights of lesbians and gay men. In the interpretive packages which are advanced in the campaigns for these initiatives, the antigay position is framed through emphasis on the dangers of homosexual conduct and the right of the majority to determine the nature and scope of minority rights. The progay position is framed as a struggle against discrimination, the need for tolerance, and the inalienable rights of gay and lesbian citizens to equal protection under the law (Donovan & Bowler, 1997, p. 111; McCorkle & Most, 1997, p. 73; Witt & McCorkle, 1997, p. 5).

Second, the nation has continued to debate whether openly gay persons should serve in the military. This debate, which resulted in the 1993 "don't ask, don't tell" policy plus an ensuing string of court cases, was framed around questions of gender roles, the borders between homosociality and homosexuality, and full participation as citizens by lesbians and gay men (Clymer, 1993; Manegold, 1993; Schmitt, 1993; Shilts, 1993; Verhover, 1993).

Third, a significant effort has been made to pass laws protecting individuals from job discrimination on the basis of sexual orientation. This debate is framed largely in relation to job security rights as opposed to the right of institutions and individuals to discriminate on the basis of their moral beliefs (*Congressional Record,* 6 September 1996 S9986-10005; all citations hereafter preceded by "H" or "S" refer to the *Congressional Record*).

The fourth widely publicized and broadly disputed subject is the right of gay persons to be licensed to be married. We will use dispute over the question of same-sex marriage as our primary case study because the interpretive packages promoted to influence public policy on this subject effectively demonstrate how frames are articulated in actual debate. Although examination of this debate does not illustrate the evolution of themes through time, it does give a portrait of public deliberation which illustrates many of the fundamental themes articulated by progay and antigay advocates.

Importantly, the Congressional debate over the Defense of Marriage Act (DOMA) illustrates the influence of antagonistic enjoinment in the production of key elements in progay and antigay interpretive packages discussed in Chapters 3 and 4. Advocates consistently vilified their opponents and attempted to restore acceptable representations. Civil rights were invoked as a central justification of progay policy, and their relevance denied in antigay advocacy. Themes of morality and social decline were invoked in the antigay package, and rejected in progay discourse. Both sides engaged in the *tu quoque* imputation of authoritarianism. Through this case study analysis of persuasive efforts in an institutional setting, it is possible to observe and analyze the influence of environment on oppositional effects. Specifically, with respect to the rival progay interpretive packages discussed in Chapter 5, the marriage debate in Congress featured an essentialist civil rights frame, and at the same time filtered out the constructionist/queer theory version of progay advocacy.

The Development of Debate on Same-Sex Marriage

Same-sex unions are not a recent invention of gay/lesbian movements. To the contrary, as law professor William Eskridge (1996) argues, "historical, anthropological, and ethnographic evidence of same-sex marriages in other times and other cultures is overwhelming" (p. 6). Boswell (1994), for example, has speculated that the early Christian church blessed forms of same-sex union. Public debate on the question of legally recognizing same-sex unions is, however, relatively recent. Until the early-1990s, discussion largely occurred in the courts where suits advancing claims on behalf of same-sex couples met with consistent rejection. Decisions denying the legal validity of gay marriage were based on the concept that only male/female marriage is traditional, and that there is no fundamental right to marry (Eskridge, 1996, pp. 91, 98-99, 131). Opponents of judicial recognition of gay marriage were prepared to advance the argument that the state has a compelling interest in restricting marriage to male/female unions on the basis of fostering procreation and avoiding state approval of homosexuality (pp. 137-138).

Because of the possibility that the judiciary in one state, Hawaii, would rule in favor of same-sex marriage, a major change in the nature of the discussion took place in 1993. On May 5, the Hawaii Supreme Court found in the case of *Baehr v. Lewin* that the exclusion of same-sex couples was discriminatory under the Hawaii Constitution. The case was remanded for trial to determine if such discrimination is permissible because it is compelled by state interest (Eskridge, 1996, p. 5). The Hawaii Supreme Court relied on gender discrimination as the basis of its decision. The Court did not find a state constitutional right to marry, much less a right grounded in the federal Constitution. The decision did not incorporate the claims of progay advocates that exclusion of gay people from the right to marry violates the equal protection of the laws understood as either the right to privacy or unlawful discrimination on the basis of sexual orientation (p. 131).

To both traditionalists and progay advocates, gay marriage is a singularly important issue, a public policy question which both sides could advantageously target. Hunter (1991) points out that the family "is an important symbolic territory because the social arrangements and relationships found there are very much a microcosm of those in the larger social order" (p. 173). As discussed in Chapter 3, both traditionalists and progay advocates are concerned with the relationship between private and public life. More particularly, for traditionalists, marriage exclusively between male and female is a non-negotiable truth the rejection of which is a fundamental challenge to moral authority (p. 122). They believe that there must be continuity between the public and private spheres, so that status, hierarchy, and power are understood in the same way in both family and society.

On the other side, the gay/lesbian challenge provides an injustice frame which can be used to mobilize adherents. Bringing the possibility of gay marriage into the public arena forces the sponsors of the existing hegemonic frame to defend their assumptions (Gallagher, 1996, p. 24). William Gamson (1992a) observes that the "sheer existence of a symbolic contest is evidence of the breakdown of hegemony and a major accomplishment for a challenger" (p. 68). In Bourdieu's (1994) terms, debate over same-sex marriage converted a doxic understanding of marriage into a challenged orthodoxy. Further, aside from the tangible benefits which accompany marriage, the right to form same-sex unions has important symbolic value to many lesbians and gay men. As Sullivan (1995) argues, "marriage is not simply a private contract; it is a social and public recognition of a private commitment. . . . Denying it to homosexuals is the most public affront possible to their public equality" (p. 179).

In mid-1999, citizens of Hawaii still did not have the right to marry a person of the same sex. Though the trial court found no compelling state interest in denying state licensing of same-sex marriages, the Hawaii Supreme Court delayed announcing a decision consistent with its earlier ruling until after the voters of Hawaii approved an amendment to the state's constitution that gives the legislature the power to reserve marriage to opposite sex couples (Foley, 1998). The main effect of this series of events in Hawaii, however, was to excite throughout the United States a series of legislative proposals which in effect would ban same-sex marriage. The fear was abundantly clear. Under the "full faith and credit" clause of the U.S. Constitution, a same-sex marriage legal in Hawaii would be binding on another state to which the couple might move. Legal scholars suggested that such a fear was well grounded in constitutional law (Hovermill, 1994; Keane, 1995; Kramer, 1997). Antigay marriage bills were introduced in 49 states. A majority of states passed legislation which either declared same-sex marriages null and void or which declared that same-sex marriages from another state would not be recognized as legal in that state (American Civil Liberties Union, 1998). Where legislatures have not acted, antigay organizations availed themselves of the initiative process. In California, for example, after a petition campaign which gathered more than 675,000 signatures, an antigay marriage measure is to appear on the state ballot in the year 2000 (Ayres, 1998).

Antigay marriage advocates insisted that federal as well as state action was needed. The Defense of Marriage Act (HR3396), introduced on May 7, 1996, in the U.S. Congress, contained two provisions. The first stipulated that states did not have to recognize same-sex marriages which were legal in another state. The second provision defined for federal purposes the word "marriage" to mean "only a legal union between one man and one woman" and specified that the "word 'spouse' refers only to a person of the opposite sex who is a husband or a wife" (Defense, 1996). Following the House debate on July 11 and 12, the bill was approved by a vote of 342 in favor, 67 opposed, 2 present, and 22 not voting (H7506). The Senate took up the bill on September 10, approving the measure that day by a vote of 85 to 14 (S10129). On September 22, President Clinton signed the bill into law (Purden, 1996).

The Congressional debate on same-sex marriage, augmented by testimony in committee hearings, discussion of the Employment Non-Discrimination Act (ENDA) (which came to the Senate floor during the DOMA debate), and comment on issues in the debate, provides an excellent case study of the collision of two interpretive packages. Some of the floor debate was devoted to constitutional issues concerning whether, under the full faith and credit clause, federal legislation is necessary to prevent states from being compelled to recognize same-sex marriages legal in another state (Kassenbaum, S10119; Sensenbrenner, H7464; Hyde, H7500; Gramm, S10106; DeFazio, H7466; Canaday, H7488; Nickles, S10103). The issues in the gay marriage debate presented difficult legal questions (Simones, 1998, p. 18). Emphasizing constitutional questions in the DOMA debate, however, also provided Congress a means to discuss same-sex marriage without envisioning intimate relationships and allowed legislators to take a position on DOMA without expressing an attitude toward same-sex marriage. However, much of the debate did concentrate on substantive issues related to homosexuality and gay marriage.

Every issue in contention between traditionalists and progay advocates was not raised. However, the debate exposed a number of core frames which we earlier identified in variant sexuality interpretive packages. Issues explicitly raised included the motives of the opposition, struggle over civil rights, the moral status of homosexuality, the effect of state approval of same-sex marriage on individuals and society, and the relation of government to its citizens. Progay advocates maintained that those who sought to prevent same-sex marriage were motivated by partisan politics; they were working against the civil rights tradition, they wrongly understood the nature of homosexuality; they falsified and exaggerated the effects of same-sex marriage on society; and they favored government intrusion into intimate life. Traditionalists described their opponents as social radicals who failed to recognize the moral evil of homosexuality and the destructive force of gay marriage, and who promoted the imposition by government of an unacceptable set of fundamental beliefs.

The Nature of the Opposition and Restoration of Representation

Vilification of the opposition arising from mutual incomprehension was a salient feature of the DOMA debate. Opponents of DOMA described proponents as mean spirited bigots who "pursue the politics of division, of fear, and of hate" (Gunderson, H7497). In a prepared statement to the House subcommittee hearing testimony on DOMA, the National Gay and Lesbian Task Force declared that DOMA "is clearly one piece of a larger agenda of the Radical Right to attack and undermine millions of American families, including gay, lesbian, bisexual and transgender families, single parent households, families in which grandparents are raising children and couples without children" (Subcommittee 41). More specifically, Elizabeth Birch, Executive Director of the progay Human Rights Campaign, declared in House Subcommittee testimony that DOMA "is nothing more than a campaign ploy to rip apart this country, divide, and to scapegoat one group of Americans. The political climate is marked by demagoguery, hatred, ignorance, and upheaval—with the scapegoating of gay Americans on the rise" (Subcommittee 189). Representative Collins suggested on the floor that DOMA "is nothing more than blatant homophobic gay-bashing" (H7497). DOMA itself was repeatedly described as "little more than a half-baked effort by the Republicans to find yet another issue which they can use to divide the country in a desperate search for votes" (Conyers H7447). Representative McDermott added that DOMA is a political game to obscure the real issues behind the failure of marriages and to divide Americans in an election year (H7448).

In counterattack, supporters of DOMA used the condensation symbol "radical" in describing their opponents as "extremists who are bent on completely eradicating the concept of marriage as all civilizations not only know it but have known it" (Barr H7445). Throughout the debate, pro-DOMA advocates described gay people as "activists," "radicals," and the like. For Representative Largent, opposition to DOMA was limited to "a very radical element that is in the process of redefining what marriage is" (H7443). Only by enacting DOMA could the plans of a "lot of gay activists" be derailed (Nickles S10129).

In attempting to restore appropriate self-representation, both sides in the debate took exception to their opponents' denunciatory language. Speaking against the measure, Representative Studds objected to terms such as "promiscuity, perversion, hedonism, narcissism . . . depravity and sin" (H7491). DOMA supporters mirrored this objection. In testimony on DOMA to the Senate Judiciary Committee, Gary Bauer, President of the Family Research Council, objected that

> good men and women of varying beliefs have been subjected to a barrage of name-calling and abuse simply for saying that marriage ought to be the union of a man and a woman and that the law should protect this vital social norm. It is not hatred to prefer normalcy. It is not bigotry to resist radical redefinition of marriage. It is not intolerance to believe in traditional morality. (Committee 23)

In floor debate, Representative Canady expressed resentment at descriptions of "opposition to same-sex marriage and support for this bill as laughable, prejudiced, mean spirited, cruel, bigoted, despicable, hateful, disgusting, and ignorant" (H7491). He asserted that it "is a slander against the American people themselves to assert that opposition to same-sex marriage is immoral" (H7491).

The Nature of Homosexuality and Gay Identity

Issues of identity were central to debate on DOMA, with progays attempting to establish an immutable gay/lesbian identity and antigays attempting to maintain a behavioral definition of homosexuality. An essentialist gay identity which emphasized biological determinism was reinforced by opponents of DOMA. Anti-DOMA advocates maintained that gays and lesbians do not choose their sexual orientation and therefore constitute a kind of ethnic group. Edward Fallon, a member of the Iowa State House of Representatives, in testimony to the U.S. House of Representatives subcommittee charged with hearing witnesses on DOMA, said:

> For those who might argue that homosexuality is a choice, I ask you, do you really believe that anyone in their right mind would choose to be in a class of people who are constantly made fun of, despised, fired from their jobs, denied housing, prevented from marrying, beaten up, and even killed? (Subcommittee 58)

Senator Robb claimed that the

> clear weight of serious scholarship has concluded that people do not choose to be homosexual, any more than they choose their gender or their race. . . . It's hard to imagine why anyone would actually choose to bear such a heavy burden unnecessarily. (S10112)

In similar fashion, Senator Kerrey of Nebraska asserted that the "overwhelming number of people who have looked at this say that sexual orientation is a trait. You do not wake up one morning and say, 'I think I will be homosexual'—or heterosexual, for that matter" (S9995).

Adoption of a biological/early childhood determinism was, perhaps, not necessary to sustain the anti-DOMA position. For instance, Cicchiono, Deming and Nicholson, who examined the seventeen year struggle for passage of the Massachusetts Gay Civil Rights Bill, note that the central frame of the Massachusetts campaign was harm avoidance. The central premise of this theme was that "regardless of whether being gay or lesbian is natural or unnatural . . . it is not so great a harm as to justify discrimination" (p. 145). Perhaps, as Schacter suggests, anti-DOMA legislators could have used an alternative strategy which emphasized the fluidity of the kinds of subordination and stigmatization against which citizens ought to be protected (p. 312). However, legislative debate has a general tendency to confirm essentialist identities, and an essentialist identity has figured prominently in legislative debate over gay rights (Griffin, 1996; Herman, 1994, pp. 5-6; Smith, 1994, p. 94).

Traditionalist advocates reserved for the Employment Nondiscrimination debate an elaboration of the definition of homosexuality as a chosen behavior and not a genetic trait. In that debate, for example, Senator

Hatch flatly declared that "sexual orientation involves conduct, not immutable non-behavioral characteristics" (S10132). Senator Ashcroft supported this position by reporting that "I do know that there are thousands of former homosexuals, individuals who once were engaged in a homosexual lifestyle, who have changed that lifestyle" (S10000). As we discussed earlier, though there has been a recent tendency for some antigay advocates to choose not to emphasize immutability, the Congressional debate demonstrates that it remains an important card to be played against gay/lesbian civil rights (Herman, 1997, p. 122).

Gay Marriage and Civil Rights

The DOMA debate also illustrates the dynamics of a progay interpretive package which emphasizes civil rights. DOMA opponents maintained that extending the right to marry to lesbian/gay persons was an inevitable step in the civil rights tradition. Robb lucidly phrased this contention:

> A basic respect for human dignity—which gives us the strength to reject racial, gender and religious intolerance—dictates that in America we also eliminate discrimination against homosexuals. I believe that ending this discrimination is the last frontier in the ultimate fight for civil and human rights. (S10122)

This appeal was voiced in the House by Representative Studds who, in recognizing that DOMA was certain to pass, looked to future vindication: "We are going to prevail just as every other component of the civil rights movement in this country has prevailed" (H7491).

Analogy to the African American civil rights struggle was pivotal to the anti-DOMA civil rights argument. Senator Moseley-Braun declared that DOMA

> is a step in the absolute opposite direction of extending the equal protection of the laws to Americans without regard to their sexual orientation, just as we moved so fitfully in this country to extend those protections to Americans without regard to their race. (S10105)

Representative Lewis fully identified the impulse behind DOMA with racism, asserting that "I have known racism. I have known bigotry. This bill [DOMA] stinks of the same fear, hatred and intolerance" (H7444).

Parallels to miscegenation laws figured prominently in the anti-DOMA appeal, just as they do in general discussion of gay marriage (Trosino, 1993, p. 94). Robb, among others, pointed out that

> until 1967, 15 States, including my own State of Virginia, had laws banning couples from different races to marry. . . . Today, we know that the moral discomfort—even revulsion—that citizens felt about legalizing interracial marriage did not give them the right to discriminate 30 years ago. Just as discomfort over sexual orientation does not give us the right to discriminate against a class of Americans today. (S10123)

Representative Eshoo echoed in the House that the U.S. Supreme Court had established through its rulings against anti-miscegenation laws that the right to marry is absolute. He quoted from the statement from the majority opinion in *Loving v. Virginia* that the right to marry is "one of the vital rights essential to the orderly pursuit of happiness by free men" (H7497).

A variety of claims were used to rebut anti-DOMA civil rights appeals, principally by using variations of the "special rights" frame. The argument was mentioned by Representative Lipinski that no harm was done by not recognizing same-sex marriage. He asserted that

> gays can legally achieve the same legal ends as marriages through draft wills, medical powers of attorney, and contracted agreements in the event that the relationship should end. Therefore, asking the rest of the country to recognize such marriages does nothing that the law cannot currently do, it is simply asking for special privileges. (H7495)

This argument was advanced by distinguishing between race and sexual orientation in order to dispel the effect of the miscegenation analogy. Hatch bolstered this distinction by quoting Colin Powell's statement from the controversy over gays in the military that "skin color is a benign nonbehavioral characteristic. Sexual orientation is perhaps the most profound of human behavioral characteristics. Comparison of the two is a convenient but invalid argument" (S9994). Less coherently, Largent advanced the view that gay people do have equal rights with respect to marriage. He asserted that homosexuals have the same rights I do. They have the ability to marry right now, today. However, when they get married, they must marry a person of the opposite sex, the same as me. . . . Just like a homosexual, I do not have the right to marry somebody of the same sex. It is the same for them as it is for me. There is no disparate [*sic*] between this rights issue. (H7443)

Eskridge (1996) correctly points out that this is a variation on the defense of miscegenation laws through the argument that such laws affected equally both whites and African Americans (p. 161).

An additional argument against marriage as a civil right which should be guaranteed to gay men and lesbians is that homosexuality in itself is a form of moral degeneracy. Representative Hyde identified a trend toward extending civil rights to homosexuals as merely another sign of decay. He asserted that anti-DOMA advocates

said that the unfinished business of the civil rights movement is homosexual acceptability. There is no power on Earth to stop it. Maybe and maybe not. He has something when I look around and see the entertainment stars in our country as Michael Johnson [*sic*] and Madonna he could be right. (H7501)

Relying on the behavior/status distinction we earlier discussed, Representative Coburn claimed that DOMA discriminated against sinful homosexual acts, not homosexuals. Referring to his constituents in Oklahoma, Coburn asserted that

what they believe is, is that homosexuality is immoral, that it is based on perversion, that it is based on lust. It is not to say that the individual is any less valuable than anybody that might believe that, but it is discrimination toward the act, not towards the individual. (H7444)

Clearly implied in this argument is a connection between criminalization of acts of sodomy and same-sex marriage because the "general connection between marital status and sexual activity is difficult to separate" (Hovermill, 1994, p. 472).

Gay Marriage, Immorality, and Social Decline

Moral questions raised in the DOMA debate point toward the considerable distance between the opponents' worldviews and suggest that a clash is occurring between defenders of antagonistic interpretive communities. The pattern of argument followed the scheme of appeals outlined in Chapter 3. The assumption motivating the bill was that neither states nor the federal government want to recognize same-sex marriage because, as pro-DOMA advocates claim, homosexuality is a moral evil. Mandatory different sex marriage is rooted in the belief that homosexual behavior is wrong and should not be condoned in law (LeVay, 1996, p. 291). Further, recognition of same-sex marriage would damage the institution of marriage understood as a heterosexual relationship, and such damage is intolerable because heterosexual marriage is the foundation of civilization.

Licensing same-sex marriage was construed as approval of homosexuality. Canady asked "should we tell the children of America that we as a society believe there is no moral difference between homosexual relationships and heterosexual relationships?" and answered that such a choice should be rejected (H7447). The argument that any positive government action toward gay/lesbian people must signal approval was also articulated in the ENDA debate. Senator Nickles charged that the effort to pass laws favorable to homosexuals "is part of a larger campaign to validate or to approve conduct that remains illegal in many states" (S10137). Such approval should be denied because homosexuality is evil in itself. Although homosexuality was not extensively described in the DOMA debate in terms of "sin" and "sickness," there were references to homosexuals as promiscuous. Coburn, for example, alleged that "there are studies to say that over 43 percent of all people who profess homosexuality have greater than 500 partners" (H7444). Representative Funderburk added that "homosexuality has been discouraged in all cultures because it is inherently wrong and harmful to individuals, families, and society" (H7487). He attributed the present anomaly of widespread acceptance of homosexuality to a media conspiracy: "The only reason it has been able to gain such prominence in America today is the near blackout on information about homosexual behavior itself" (H7487). This was added to the often repeated traditionalist theme that the introduction of same-sex marriage would not in any significant way moderate promiscuous gay male behavior (Wilson, 1996, p. 36).

In advancing the idea that same-sex unions subvert other-sex marriage, Representative Smith claimed that " 'same-sex marriages' demean the fundamental institution of marriage" (H7494). This damage occurs because, in the words of Representative Talent, "marriage cannot be pushed and pulled around like silly putty without destroying its essential stability" (H7446). This position was reinforced by two related appeals, one based on lexical fundamentalism, (i.e., concern for stabilizing the social order through maintaining a fixed vocabulary), and the other on the figure of the slippery slope. Pro-DOMA advocates maintained that the referent for the word "marriage" had always and exclusively been the procreative heterosexual couple. This position flowed from the idea that "language is normative. Its meanings and connotations communicate values. Thus everyone knows what the word 'marriage' means. It means what it has always meant" (Hart, 1997, p. 30). Largent asserted that "for thousands of years and across many, many different cultures, a definition of marriage that transcends time has always been one man and one woman united for the purpose of forming a family" (H7443). This assertion was at times given a religious tone. Representative Buyer, for example, exhorted that "God laid down that one man and one woman is a legal union. That is marriage known for thousands of years" (H7486). In similar vein, Representative Barr proclaimed that "marriage does not mean two men or two women getting married. It just does not mean that. You can say that it does, but it does not. You are talking about something completely different" (H7445). In this view, marriage could mean only one kind of intimate association. Senator Coats, for example, stoutly concluded that the

> definition of marriage is not created by politicians and judges, and it cannot be changed by them. It is rooted in our history, in our laws and our deepest moral and religious conviction, and in our nature as human beings. It is the union of one man and one woman. This fact can be respected, or it can be resented, but it cannot be altered. (S10113)

Despite their claim that traditional marriage is eternally unalterable, pro-DOMA advocates also represented marriage as so fragile that a single expansion of its definition would launch the entire concept down a slippery slope into meaninglessness. This argument builds on lexical fundamentalism. Antigay advocate Robert Knight (1997a), for example claims that "to describe such [same-sex] relationships as 'marriage' destroys the definition of marriage altogether" (p. 114). Once the meaning of marriage has been eliminated, then an endless variety of relationships can be recognized as marriages. Largent elaborately traced this downward skid; once same-sex marriage is recognized,

What logical reason is there to keep us from stopping expansion of that definition to include three people or an adult and a child, or any other odd
combination that we want to have? There really is no logical reason why we
could not also include polygamy . . . as long as these are consenting human,
and it does not even have to be limited to human beings. . . . There is no reason why we cannot just completely erase whatever boundaries that currently exist on the definition of marriage and say it is a free-for-all, anything
goes. (H7443)

This position was backed by Hadley Arkes of Amherst College who asked
in a House hearing on DOMA "If marriage were detached from the natural teleology of the body, on what ground of principle could the law confine marriage to 'couples'? If the law permitted the marriage of people of
the same sex, what is the ground of principle then on which the law would
rule out as illegitimate the people who profess that their own love is not
confined to a coupling of two, but connected in a larger cluster of three or
four?" (Subcommittee 101)

In the DOMA debate, marriage was frequently connected to the procreative family. For example, Senator Ashcroft declared that "we have
set up our society on the basis of children who come into the world, and
we honor the institution that brings children into and gives them values,
by according special standing to marriage" (S10121). Jean Bethke
Elshtain (1997) has generalized the position taken in Congress when she
writes:

> Marriage is not, and never has been primarily about two people—it is and
> always has been about the possibility of generativity. Although in any given
> instance, a marriage might not have led to the raising of a family . . . the sym-
> bolism of marriage-family as social regenesis is fused in our centuries-old
> experience with marriage ritual, regulation, and persistence. (p. 59)

The next step was to claim that recognition of same-sex marriage
would damage the family as a child rearing institution. Much of this argument was based on the position that children should not be raised in
father-optional households (Zepezauer, 1997 p. 37). Representative
Weldon, for example, maintained that

> the marriage relationship provides children with the best environment in
> which to grow and learn. We need to work to restore marriage, and it is vital

that we protect marriage against attempts to redefine it in a way that causes the family to lose its special meaning. (H7493)

This argument led rapidly to the frequently voiced traditionalist theme that the "mom-and-dad family is the natural environment for child rearing and is the foundation of civilization" (Knight, 1997b, p. 88).

The argument that same-sex marriage would weaken the family broadened into the most frequently repeated appeal in the DOMA debate: Same-sex marriage destroys traditional marriage and marriage is the foundation of civilization; therefore, same-sex marriage will destroy society. Representative Hutchinson generalized that marriage "understood to be the social, legal and spiritual union of one man and one woman, has been the foundation of every human society" (H7442). Representative Ensign asserted that the "time honored and unique institution of marriage between one man and one woman is a fundamental pillar of our society and its values" (H7493). There were many other variations on the theme of marriage as the foundation of civilization. Canady declaimed that the "traditional family structure—centered on a lawful union between one man and one woman—comports with nature and with our Judeo- Christian moral tradition. It is one of the essential foundations on which our civilization is based" (H7441). Lipinski declared that "marriage has already been undermined by no-fault divorce, pregnancies out of wedlock, and sexual promiscuity. Allowing for gay marriages would be the final straw. It would devalue the love between a man and a woman and weaken us as a nation" (H7495).

Historical narrative buttressed the "destruction of civilization" appeal. Though examples of corrupt societies permitting same-sex marriage contradicted another pro-DOMA assertion that same-sex marriage is historically unknown, this did not deter legislators from plunging into the argument that societies were destroyed when they allowed same-sex marriage. Senator Byrd, for example, traced same-sex marriage in a number of cultures in order to conclude that "as history teaches us too often in the past, when cultures waxed casual about the uniqueness and sanctity of the marriage commitment between men and women, those cultures have been shown to be in decline" (S10109). After telling the biblical story of Belshazzar's feast, Byrd exhorted his colleagues to "defend the oldest institution, the institution of marriage between male and female, as set forth in the Holy Bible. Else we, too, shall be weighed in the balance and found wanting" (S10111).

Anti-DOMA advocates attacked elements of the moral case for DOMA. The state's action in granting marriage was described as morally neutral. Representative Frank, for instance, asked:

> What kind of an almost totalitarian notion is it to say that whatever the Government permits it sanctions and approves? . . . Does civil law, by allow-ing you to divorce and remarry, say, good, we approve of that, we sanction your walking out on that marriage and starting a new one? No, what civil law says is, in a free society that is a choice you can make. (H7483)

The comparison between marriage and divorce became a staple in anti-DOMA debate. Representative Gunderson articulated the compara-tive case with respect to religious condemnation, pointing out that "no where in the Bible does Jesus condemn homosexuality. There are many places where Jesus condemns divorce. How can people, who have been divorced, suggest that they can defend marriage by condemning those in-volved in single-sex relationships" (H7493). Divorce was frequently mentioned in the relationship between government and morality because many DOMA sponsors were divorced, several a number of times (Rich, 1996).

In addition, anti-DOMA legislators denied the significance of religious belief in different-sex marriage, attempting to apply the doctrine of the separation of church and state to this issue. Representative Mink pointed out that marriage is a civil rather than a religious institution: "Marriage is an instrument of the State. It may be ordained by the church, but it is a de-cree of the State, and it is dissolved by the State" (H7481). Consequently, according to Representative Jackson, it is also clear that the church can-not instruct the government to restrict the rights of the church, their fol-lowers, or their faith, nor can the church call upon Congress to contra-vene or undermine the Constitution" (H7496). Robb concluded that

> marriage, as a civil institution, recognizes the union of two individuals who are so committed to each other that they seek to have their civic rights and responsibilities merged into one. And . . . when that civil institution is sepa-rated from a religious ceremony, and that civil institution is recognized by a sovereign State, then denying Federal recognition of that union amounts to nothing short of indefensible discrimination. (S10123)

Anti-DOMA legislators also attacked the contention that same-sex marriage would create a slippery slope toward recognition of many different kinds of relationships as marriages. For instance, Frank asserted that a clear distinction could be drawn between same-sex marriage and polygamy. He chided pro-DOMA advocates for pretending "not to know the difference between a monogamous relationship between two human beings and polygamy" (H7500). In testimony to the House Subcommittee on DOMA, Sullivan said:

> You will be told that this is a slippery slope toward polygamy and other things—pedophilia or bestiality. But of course, same-sex marriage is the opposite of those things. The freedom to marry would mark the *end* of the slippery slope for lesbians and gay men, who right now have no institutions to guide our lives and loves, no social support for our relationships, no institution that can act as a harbor in the emotional storms of our lives. (Subcommittee 123)

The concept was implied that gay marriage would domesticate men, insure later-life caretakers, and strengthen all marriages (McNeil, 1988, p. 37; Rauch, 1996, pp. 22-23).

In addition, several legislators disputed the notion that marriage is an unchanging institution, reframing it as an evolving constellation of social commitments. For instance, Representative Jackson-Lee asserted that the "family as an institution has changed dramatically since the days when our own parents were children. Today, there is no single definition of family that applies to all individuals" (H7448). In its written statement to the Senate Judiciary Committee, the American Civil Liberties Union noted:

> While marriage has traditionally been defined as a union between people of different sexes, it was also traditionally defined as between people of the same race. . . . Marriage was also traditionally understood to involve a man owning a woman as property. We've recognized that these traditions had to be abandoned because they were unfair. (Committee 77)

Studds elaborated on this concept, noting that marriage has ceased to be a relationship in which the wife is property and different-race marriages are now legal (H7491).

The argument that same-sex marriage would damage traditional marriages was severely questioned by a number of anti-DOMA advocates. Frank found "it implausible that two men deciding to commit themselves to each other threatens the marriage of people a couple of blocks away" (H7482). He suggested that "I find it bizarre, even by the standards that my Republican colleagues are using for this political argument here, to tell me that two women falling in love in Hawaii, as far away as you can get and still be within the United States, threatens the marriage of people in other States" (H7482). Following a similar line of argument, Gunderson suggested that

> no gay man is after your wives, and no lesbian is after your husbands. If marriage is at risk in this country, and it may be—there are other more real factors at the heart of this problem. May I suggest that alcohol abuse, spousal abuse, and even Sunday football are more likely to destroy marriage. (H7493)

Representative Nadler joined the chorus, suggesting that "marriages in this country are threatened by a 50 percent divorce rate, by drugs, by alcoholism, by gambling, by immaturity, by lots of things, but not by allowing gay or lesbian couples to formalize their relationships and pursue their happiness" (H7446). Representative Maloney concluded that "despite the rhetoric of the religious right, one can honor the relationship between a man and a woman without attacking lesbian and gay people or their relationships" (H7497).

Pro-DOMA advocates were described as insincere in their "marriage as society's foundation" appeal because they were recommending no programs to address the real problems damaging marriages. Representative Gejdenson argued that "if we want to protect families, then we ought to give families health care . . . protect their pensions . . . [and] we ought not to be raiding Medicare to give tax breaks to billionaires" (H7487). In similar vein, Senator Boxer argued that Congress should defend marriage through positive action by passing legislation such as the Parental Leave Act rather than engaging in a "preemptive strike on a proposal that doesn't exist" (S10112). Representative DeFazio concluded:

> There is no question that we have real problems with family disintegration in this country, but this legislation is not intended to defend or improve the success of marriage, rather it is intended to further divide the country over the issue of gay rights. (H7498)

Finally, the affirmative view was advanced that the legal regularization of gay and lesbian relationships would be a positive social change, combined with the position that attacking same-sex marriage would do social damage. In testimony to a House subcommittee, the National Gay and Lesbian Task Force pointed out that gay/lesbian parents were

> only 25% less likely to be raising children than heterosexual adults. "The Defense of Marriage Act" proponents claim to have the best interests of children and their families in mind. Yet, their legislative solution will penalize and stigmatize the millions of children with lesbians, gay, bisexual and transgender parents. (Subcommittee 44)

In Senate Committee testimony, the American Civil Liberties Union pointed to the fundamental inequity of opposition to gay marriage:

> We live in a society which attaches enormous civil, legal consequences to marriage. It is fundamentally unfair to say on the one hand that you must marry to be treated as next of kin, and then tell an entire class of Americans who are next of kin in every real sense that they may not marry. (Committee 78)

As Skaggs argued:

> No one, I believe, would want, for example, to deny a claim of inheritance, or of participation in terminal health care decisions, for the life-long partner of a gay man or lesbian woman. Yet, by refusing as part of this legislation even to permit a formal study of disparate treatment of domestic partnerships in these areas, the proponents of this legislation may reveal their real motivation. (H7492)

Gay Marriage and Authoritarianism

Concerns we have earlier described over the proper relation of government to citizens were central to the DOMA debate. Although both sides claimed that the public good could best be served by limiting government power, they disagreed on the nature of the limitation. Anti-DOMA legislators depicted DOMA as invading states' rights and consigning some citizens to second-class status. With respect to states' rights, DOMA would prevent married Hawaiians from receiving the same benefits as married individuals in other states. Mink phrased the argument:

We hear constantly in this body the need for States to be left alone to determine the rights of their citizens and the programs that are to endure. Here
we have legislation before anything is done in my State, that will deliberately deny all of these rights that are characterized by Federal law by determining that what my courts have decided does not apply under Federal legislation, and that is an extreme travesty against the whole principle of equal
protection. (H7482)

More generally, the proposed federal definition of marriage, according to
Feinstein, "inject[s] the Federal government into an area that has, for 200
years, been the exclusive purview of the States" (S10118). As a result,
Nadler declared, "we are going to say those are second-class marriages because we overruled New York or Connecticut or Hawaii or whoever de-
cides to do that" (H7446).

Opponents of DOMA also suggested that it represented government
intrusion into the private sphere. Moseley-Braun asserted that "when two
people decide to come together, it seems to me it should be a matter for
them, their conscience, their God, and indeed that it . . . is inappropriate
for the U.S. Congress to intervene in that decisionmaking" (S10105). This
position was often expressed as the anti-DOMA version of the slippery
slope. DeFazio, for example, asked, "where would this type of legislation
lead us?" He answered:

We risk setting a dangerous precedent by crossing the threshold of preempting States. . . . What is to prevent the Federal government from setting a national age of majority and preempting all States as in China where the legal
marriage age has been set as high as 28 years old? (H7498)

Senator Kennedy suggested that DOMA "is a dangerous precedent. Today
it is marriage, tomorrow it may be divorce, the third day it may be custody. Where will it end?" (S10129). Kerrey amplified on these fears, suggesting that DOMA's language

could easily be amended to prevent States from recognizing divorce decrees
which occurred in the 1st year of marriage, 2nd year, or the 10th year. Beyond divorce, we could add custody language or other Federal requirements on married couples. Supporters of DOMA say they are not creating a

Federal certificate of marriage. True enough today. However, they are creating an easy way for us to reach that goal. (S10124)

The themes of government intrusion into States' rights and into private life were often interwoven in a depiction of DOMA proponents hypocritically limiting freedom. Moseley-Braun declaimed that

> it is almost curious that the very people who argue against the Federal Government as an activist government, the very people who argue in favor of smaller Government, have absolutely no compunction about encouraging the Federal Government to expand its activism, to expand its role, and expand its intrusiveness into our everyday lives when it comes to their own agenda. (S10105)

Pro-DOMA legislators denied that DOMA abridged states' rights or the right to privacy. With respect to states' rights, Ensign argued that DOMA "does not deny citizens the opportunity—either through their elected representatives or ballot referendum—to enact legislation recognizing same-sex marriages or domestic partnerships within their own borders" (H7494). Representative DeLay asserted that DOMA "does not tell people what they can or cannot do in the privacy of their own homes. It simply says it is not right to ask the American people to condone it" (H7487).

More important, pro-DOMA legislators offered their own version of the threat of state intrusion, a threat which we earlier described as significant in the antigay interpretive package. In general, by refusing to pass DOMA, the government would use its power to impose the acceptability of same-sex marriage and homosexuality on all citizens. Representative Funderburk, for example, argued:

> If you are a devout Christian or Jew, or merely someone who believes homosexuality is immoral and harmful, and the law declares homosexuality a protected status, then your personal beliefs are now outside civil law. . . . The entire power of the civil rights apparatus can be brought against you. Businessmen would have to subsidize homosexuality or face legal sanctions; school children will have to be taught that homosexuality is the equivalent of marital love, and religious people will be told their beliefs are no longer valid. (H7487)

Many other pro-DOMA legislators took similar positions which centered on a majoritarian understanding of the limits of government power. De-Lay asserted:

> We should not be forced to send a message to our children that undermines the definition of marriage as the union between one man and one woman. Such attacks on the institution of marriage will only take us further down the road of social deterioration. (H7487)

Senator Lott declared that "to force upon our communities the legal recognition of same-sex marriage would be social engineering beyond anything in the American experience" (S10101).

Fear of an authoritarian imposition of social acceptance of homosexuality was frequently expressed by antigay advocates. In committee testimony, Bauer declared that ratification of gay marriage "would be telling many, many people that their beliefs are no longer valid, and would turn the civil rights laws into a battering ram against them" (Committee 22). Another committee witness, Hadley Arkes, testified:

> It is hard to imagine a scheme of same-sex marriage voted in by the public in a referendum. These things must be imposed by the courts, if they are to be imposed at all, and that concert to impose them has been evident, on gay rights, over the last few years. (Subcommittee 106)

In floor debate, principal focus was on the threat of judicial tyranny. Sensenbrenner opposed "judges that are not elected and judges that are not responsible to the people bootstrap[ping] a decision in one State to national policy" (H7499). Byrd thought that "only after a majority of society comes to a consensus on the legality or illegality of one issue or another should that issue be written down in our legal institutions" (S10110). No such consensus had been reached. As Kassenbaum remarked, "same-sex marriage is a concept with which few Americans are comfortable, and I do not believe that the judgment of one court in a single state should hold sway over the rest of the Nation" (S10119). Because of their use of the judiciary, the "strategy of those who are advocating same-sex unions is profoundly undemocratic" (Nickles, S10103). Consequently, the judicial route to the ratification of same-sex marriage could be considered a "sneak attack on society by encoding this aberrant behavior in legal form before society itself has decided it should be legal" (Byrd, S10101).

Gay Marriage Debate and Queer Marginalization

A possible consequence of the advocacy in favor of same-sex marriage is that only monogamous, "mainstream" lesbians and gay men become visible. Gay/lesbian commentators have frequently expressed anxiety about the erasure of gay and lesbian people from public policy discussion. In the DOMA debate, there were significant attempts to make them visible. Three openly gay members of the House participated in the debate. Studds took the derogation of homosexuality as a personal insult (H7491). Gunderson placed the debate in the context of his domestic life, asking "why should my partner of 13 years not be entitled to the same health insurance and survivor benefits, the individuals around here, my colleagues with second and third wives, are able to give them?" (H7498). Other Representatives disclosed that family members were gay or celebrated committed constituents such as Phyllis Lyon and Del Martin (Woolsey, H7442; Pelosi, H7443). Gay/lesbian people committed to casual sex, bisexuals, queers of many descriptions, and sexual outlaws, however, remained invisible in anti-DOMA advocacy.

In addition, Congressional debate on same-sex marriage obscured important gay/lesbian ideological positions. The formal institutional setting functioned to filter out the queer perspective which we summarized in Chapter 5. Although many gay advocates as well as some nongay opinion leaders have long favored same sex marriage, there is widespread belief that marriage is an inherently dysfunctional institution whose imposition on gay people should be resisted ("Let them wed," 1996; Sullivan, 1995, pp. 178-185). Progay attorney Paula Ettlbrick (1992) articulates this position by arguing that "marriage runs contrary to two of the primary goals of the lesbian and gay movement: the affirmation of gay identity and culture and the affirmation of many forms of relationships" (p. 21). Similarly, legal scholar Nancy Polikoff's (1993) feminist analysis undercuts the notion that same-sex marriage will dismantle the current hegemonic understanding of marriage. Anthropologist Kath Weston (1991) brings to our attention that gay families have defined themselves as including several households or families that include friends (p. 208). Finally, the DOMA debate, as with all contests in which the civil rights frame is dominant, can be characterized as failing to "challenge the misleading notion of a single homogeneous gay and lesbian 'lifestyle' . . . [and] prohibiting the formulation of broader definitions and better understandings of the gay and lesbian movement" (Miller, 1998, p. 77).

At no time was the boundary of the DOMA debate expanded to include statements of the lesbian/gay antimarriage position. This silence was inherent in the situation because to admit that the gay/lesbian community did not accept monogamous marriage opens the possibility that those who engage in variant sexual practices might be the promiscuous predators so central to antigay rhetoric. Opponents did not need to be told that the gay male sexual regime tolerated a diversity which included marriage-like arrangements with other sexual liaisons on the side (Seidman, 1993, p. 124). Perhaps more important, featuring gay/lesbian dissent on the wisdom of promoting same-sex marriage might raise what Foucault identified as the "common fear that gays will develop relationships that are intense and satisfying even though they do not all conform to the ideas of relationship held by others" (quoted in Adam, 1987, p. 166).

A possible consequence of this silence is that an impression is created that the lesbian/gay community unanimously recognizes the positive value of legally sanctioned and monogamous marriage between two persons. The further result is that many individuals who do not want to embrace such marriages will be further alienated from the gay community and increasingly marginalized within it. Warner (1999) argues strongly that the dominant gay/lesbian civil rights organizations have induced through emphasis on marriage a collective amnesia about the original purposes of the gay movement, abandoning resistance to (a) state regulation of sexuality, (b) the denigration of diverse sexual and intimate relations, (c) the imposition of "straight" norms on queer life, and (d) coercion of individuals who remain outside the institution of marriage (pp. 123-124). He asserts that "if the campaign for marriage requires wholesale repudiation of queer culture's best insights on intimate relations, sex, and the politics of stigma, then it is doing more harm than marriage could ever be worth" (p. 122).

The 1996 debate in Congress over DOMA does provide a useful example of public discourse on variant sexuality. The debate shows the need to reconsider both what constitutes grounds for civil rights claims and how gay/lesbian identity ought to be represented in the public sphere. The debate brought into focus the struggle of interpretive communities to impose on others their understanding of public moral life and, at the same time, to resist government imposition on their beliefs and behaviors. Throughout the debate, advocates clearly adjusted their arguments to those of their adversaries, responding *tu quoque* to charges of immorality and government imposition, obscuring identity issues, and excluding moderate and dissenting views. The result was a debate to which rhetorical critics might well contribute both direction and advice. Most centrally for us, the debate demonstrated the reciprocal influence of antagonistic enjoinment on frames involving language, identity, and the nature of progay/antigay conflict.

7 Criticism of the Variant Sexuality Issue Culture

We have argued that antagonistic enjoinment influences the creation and content of the variant sexuality issue culture. Current conflict over homosexuality is a phenomenon caused by the convergence of two developments: (a) the recent intensification and extensive articulation of strong antihomosexual beliefs within Western societies, and (b) the invention and increasing visibility, especially in the media, of a gay/ lesbian identity, community, and culture. The result is the production of two distinct classes of antagonistic collective subjects—traditionalist antigay advocates and progay advocates.

The discourses produced by these collective subjects can be understood from three different perspectives. First, in the variant sexuality issue culture, language is used to achieve domination through the projection of arguments, condensation symbols, and narratives. Second, social entities— interpretive communities, social movements, and social movement organizations—become agencies voicing beliefs about variant sexuality which underlie public policy demands. Third, issue cultures develop in the process of policy contests in which sponsors of antagonistic interpretive packages engage in an evolving contest to gain hegemony for the ways in which they frame homosexuality, their own identities, and their mutual struggle.

In the analysis of the influence of oppositional interaction on this issue culture, an important first step is to examine persuasive appeals made by opponents. For traditionalists, the *desideratum* is homosexual invisibility in the public sphere. Discrimination against homosexuals is framed as reasonable and advisable, and government action to protect homosexuals is condemned as unnecessary and unconstitutional. Taken together, these two general lines of appeal create a traditionalist discourse which meshes antihomosexual appeals with attacks on the public policy objectives of homosexual movements. On the progay side, discrimination against lesbians and gay men is framed as unwarranted and impermissible. Government protection of a visible gay/lesbian minority is legitimate and mandatory. Combining these two lines of appeal, gay/lesbian interpretive packages consist of the refutation of antigay appeals and the justification of public policy favorable to the lesbian/gay community.

The overt appeals made by sponsors of interpretive packages are surface patterns of a deeper contest of representation in which participants in the variant issue culture strategically construct themselves, their relationships to antagonists, and their position in the public sphere. Key to this contest is a process of antagonistic depiction which exerts significant influence on collective self-representation. Traditionalists depict homosexuality as a chosen erotic style and gay advocates adopt an essentialist identity represented as immutable and nonerotic. In the same manner, because gay/lesbian advocates describe their opponents as homophobic religious bigots, traditionalists represent themselves as reasonable, caring proponents of a moderate belief system wholly consistent with American civic values. Because antagonists need to define in broadly acceptable ways the nature of their collective action, the battle between progays and antigays has increasingly concerned both politics and the law. Although public policy concerns are emphasized by each side, traditionalists for strategic reasons highlight the cultural basis of policy formation while many progay advocates avoid connections between gay/lesbian political action and demands for cultural change. Each side employs variations on the ideograph "rights" in order to claim legitimacy as well as a means to describe their adversarial "other" as totalitarian. Traditionalists and progay advocates opportunistically describe themselves both as defenders of the established order and as opponents of the establishment.

Briefly, the variant sexuality issue culture consists of opposed interpretive packages significantly influenced by adversarial interaction. The dominant progay packages contain a narration of liberation, the thematic development of a socially acceptable identity, and an extended argument to support civil rights for lesbians and gay men. The antigay package features condensation symbols and ideographs supporting government hostility to homosexuality, a narrative of social decline, and a structure of language within which rights claims for homosexuals are unthinkable. Lurking in both packages is a dangerous adversarial "other" against whom action must be taken. In the progay package, the dark figure of opposition is a religious, frightened, erotophobic bigot. In the antigay package, the dark figure is a sex-obsessed, child molesting wealthy libertine whose unbridled lusts will destroy all forms of social order.

These dominant interpretive packages are not without alternative versions or even outright rivals. For traditionalist advocates, the issue is how their interpretive package will be received. Choices among interpretation include whether and how to denounce homosexuals, and whether to emphasize moralism or libertarian rights concerns. Progay advocacy entails more divisive rivalry between interpretive packages. An alternative interpretation to the dominant progay package emphasizes a "queer" perspective in which liberatory struggle takes the form of deconstructing all essentialist identities, the celebration of difference as subversive of binary sexual boundaries, and the rejection of emphasis on civil rights in favor of creating a new cultural order which valorizes difference.

Variation within the sexuality issue culture is produced when specific public policy questions arise. Individual issues and institutional settings encourage particular emphasis within an interpretation, or favor one rival package over another. In some situations, one package excludes its rivals. In the debate over "gay marriage," civil rights and the denunciatory themes of both the antigay and progay packages were invoked, along with concerns over the nature of rights, the role of government, and social stability. Although antigay advocates were able to introduce into the marriage debate the full range of their positions against homosexuality, progay advocates seemed to be constrained not to depart from their dominant civil rights frame.

Limitations

Our emphasis on oppositional engagement should not obscure recognition that other forces operate to shape the variant sexuality issue culture, including the availability of models for imitation, the appearance of specific political opportunities, the operation of nonconfrontational motives, and the influence of different institutional settings. As we said at the outset, discourse is the outcome of the interaction among such forces.

To a significant extent, gay/lesbian movements have been based on the examples of other movements. Lesbians and gay men found precedent for their version of collective action in the race-based civil rights movement, Black Power, and feminist movements (Kauffman, 1990, p. 75; Richards, 1998, p. 337). More generally, the identity frame central to gay activism is precedented by many other postmodern collective efforts. Sociologist Jean Cohen (1985) believes that a wide variety of movements concentrate their efforts on constructing identities and creating social space within which to perform these identities (p. 690). That lesbians and gay men would be deeply involved in building and defending an identity may not require the special impetus of oppositional discourse. Further, dissent about how gay identity should be framed is also precedented, most notably in feminist divisions between essentialists and constructionists (Weston, 1996, p. 3). The processes of identity construction and deconstruction are, perhaps, endemic to a wide range of movements. The appearance of opposition, then, is one variable that influences the outcomes of these processes which are inherent in movements.

Desexualization is a key example of multiple causes for the current outcome in the evolution of gay/lesbian identity. We have previously argued that opposition is certainly an important element in the creation of a desexualized identity. An expected response to the depiction of homosexuals as sexually obsessed is to broaden gay identity to include not only sexual acts, affection, and fantasies, but an entire way of life. Desexualized identity has other origins as well. For instance, in lesbian feminism, desexualization was not a reaction to the problem of opposition, but to the opportunity for coalition building with other feminists. Phelan (1989) explains that in order to disarm the fears of heterosexual feminists, lesbianism was transformed into something safe by morphing itself into a "creature no longer of physical desire but of political desire—the desire for equal nonoppressive personal relationships" (p. 99). AIDS has also played an important role in desexualizing the gay identity. Chesebro (1994) writes that AIDS continues to operate "as a rationale for dramatic reversals for gay male and lesbian civil, legal, and social rights" (p. 80). Clearly, a way to disconnect the link between alleged gay male promiscuity and AIDS is to present the gay male as a nonsexual being.

In similar fashion, the shift among antigays from religious to secular appeals is motivated not only by progay representation of "right-wing zealotry," but also by a conscious effort to build coalitions that reach beyond core evangelical supporters to the larger community. Marty (1984) notes that traditionalist political messages have historically worked well largely within conservative Protestantism. To create a more powerful base, coalitions must be built (p. 67). Apart from the progay charge that antigays are religious bigots, the process of creating a broader movement demands that specific theological commitments must be downplayed in favor of more universal civic concerns.

Toward Improvement in the Variant Issue Culture

The public policy discussion of variant sexuality is hardly a model of responsible and productive debate. One might be unrealistic to expect that it is likely to be much improved. A review of the discourses produced in this debate suggests that several changes would make discussion of variant sexuality more probative and less unnecessarily divisive.

With respect to antigay advocates, discussion would be more useful if the question of the role of religious appeals in public debate were more carefully evaluated. To generalize, traditionalists have taken the position that policy should be debated in a "public square that does not restrict its access to citizens willing to speak in a purely secular language, but instead is equally open to religious and nonreligious argument" (Carter, 1993, p. 214). At the same time, they have not addressed several important implications of their position. Most notably, traditionalists have not taken into account that in a pluralistic society, a public policy issue cannot be rationally and fairly resolved when it is cast in supernatural terms. There is no ultimate resolution to the question of God's position on homosexuality and the expression of gay identity. In addition, appeals based on religious belief fail to take into account the fact that religious communities in the United States are deeply divided on many issues including homosexuality, that "most people who abhor homophobia are themselves Christian—and so, for that matter, are most gay Americans" (Rich, 1998). Clearly, a move away from claims based on supernatural appeals would drain the variant sexuality debate of some of the rancor which now obscures it.

The question of whether religious appeals embedded in traditionalist discourse disrupt public policy decision making leads to the generalization that public debate could be further improved if antigay advocates abandoned what appears to be a pattern of opportunism. There is substance to the charge that religion is used opportunistically by traditionalists to mobilize followers within a network of churches, but that, in contrast, in public campaigns and legislative debate support is built through secular appeals (R. Smith, 1997, p. 95). This strategy may directly damage traditionalist efforts because "movements that draw a distinction between their private and public discourse inevitably risk schism, on the one hand, and co-optation on the other" (Judis, 1994, p. 21). Equally important, this strategy emphasizes an issue—Are antigay advocates hypocritical bigots?—which serves to reduce discussion to name-calling.

Traditionalists also tend to lower the quality of debate by deploying indiscriminately any and every appeal discrediting to lesbians and gay men. For instance, gay people are depicted in antigay discourse as both diseased and rich. The first characterization is used to establish that homosexual behavior is a threat to public health because it transmits a wide variety of sexually transmitted diseases. The second is used to explain why gay men are not a "suspect class" in need of the protection of civil rights laws. However, the outcome of using both arguments is contradictory as well as confusing: People who are diseased most of their lives and who suffer premature mortality are simultaneously earning incomes significantly above the national average.

Similarly, traditionalists propound the logically contradictory conclusions that sexuality is chosen and that homosexuals form an unchanging and tiny proportion of the population (Herman, 1997, p. 75). They also describe homosexuality as unbridled masculine lust and then interestingly append lesbians to this characterization. As Herman points out, traditionalists more often than not "simply add the word 'lesbian' to a paragraph that has no application to women at all" (p. 92). Propounding such arguments can certainly be taken as a sign of arguing in bad faith. More important, however, any failure to think through the logical inconsistencies of the case for a public policy position suggests that one is engaged in an obfuscating polemic on behalf of a visceral impulse rather than in a search for a principled position.

The traditionalist introduction of unsupported or discredited scientific findings into the variant sex issue culture also tends to direct public discussion down blind alleys. In order to discredit gay people, traditional- ist advocate like Paul Cameron have made unreasonable and implausible claims that the average lifespan of a homosexual is 39 years, that 29% of all homosexuals urinate on their partners, and that homosexuals killed at least 68% of the victims of mass murders in the United States in the past 17 years. These studies have been widely recognized as employing clearly defective, if not thoroughly fraudulent, research procedures. Cameron himself has been expelled from the American Psychological Association. Still, a large group of antigay advocates, ranging from Pat Robertson and Pat Buchanan to Concerned Women for America and Accuracy in the Me- dia have all relied heavily on Cameron's work (Pietrzyk, 1994a, pp. 1, 3, 13). In the end, the introduction of specious evidence can only serve to undercut reasonable decision making.

Centrist calls for civility and reason may never have an important effect on antigay advocates. This will certainly be the case if it remains an article of faith in the traditionalist belief system that they are excluded from the dominant culture:

> Present normative pluralism, carefully defined, has seriously limited its cul-
> tural space and access to symbol production. It is not a symbolic universe in
> which the Right's story has been granted free access; hence it wills to seize
> access to symbol production and mount a counter mythology. (Heinz,
> 1983, p. 146)

Moreover, both sides will probably continue to avoid thoughtful and ra- tional encounters with one another, each afraid that their cherished be- liefs will become the object of ridicule and each unprepared to understand the terms and meanings central to the other's arguments (Pearce & Littlejohn, 1997, p. 70).

Progay participation in public discussion has also not been without de- fect. A principal problem has been that progressive forces, while claiming to present rational arguments, have too often relied on dogmatic sloganizing. Diamond (1995) asserts that "opponents' constant repetition of the 'radical right' slogan took the place of reasoned presentation and debate on what the Christian Right was really all about" (p. 306). That this should be the case is not surprising. Sullivan (1995) correctly main- tains that in the emotionally charged climate created by discussion of vari- ant sexuality, the usual arguments for equal rights are easily trumped by traditionalists' visceral appeals. Consequently, "liberals are forced to use their strongest emotional weapon. They accuse their opponents of being prejudiced. Almost before it has begun, the debate becomes one between 'perverts' and 'bigots' " (p. 160). In such a struggle, progay advocates tend to label too quickly their opponents' claims as mere ploys. As religious analyst Justin Watson (1997) argues, the ways Religious Right assertions of victimization and demands for recognition "have been and will continue to be used in contemporary American politics need to be understood, not simply dismissed" (p. 3).

Progay advocates have likewise been misled by the analogy of the black civil rights movement. Mohr (1988) observes that the legal successes of that collective effort "were achieved without anything remotely resembling an articulated, ramified pattern of reason and argument, let alone a political theory." This achievement was possible because "there was no articulated, substantive, argumentative opposition to that movement, and religious sentiment and appeal filled in where words failed or were lacking altogether." Such a pattern has not materialized, however, for the gay/lesbian movement (p. 2). Meeting opposition which relies on cleverly worded appeals, if not rigorous argument, the progay movement simply has not responded by generating a broad range of arguments which resonate with bystander audiences.

The postmodern tone of progay efforts also tends to drain its discourse of appeals which can be readily understood by the general public. Darsey (1994) maintains that gay and lesbian appeals reveal the "inherent weakness in a mode of argument so democratic that it refuses to impose a point of view on its audience" (p. 47). He asserts that gay/lesbian advocates rely on faith in the Constitution and the courts, but have abandoned the principles which lie at the foundation of rights rhetoric. As a result, the "rhetoric of gay rights establishes itself, not as a rhetoric of judgment, but as a rhetoric of nonjudgment. There is no potential for radical commitment in such a discourse" (Darsey, 1997, p. 184). This opens progay discourse to the charge that it is part of an overblown rights rhetoric which Glendon (1991) believes poorly serves the protection of individual rights:

> Our stark, simple rights dialect puts a damper on the processes of public justification, communication, and deliberation upon which the continuing vitality of a democratic regime depends. It contributes to the erosion of the habits, practices, and attitudes of respect for others that are the ultimate and surest guaranty of human rights. (p. 171)

From a very different perspective, critical legal scholars also reject reliance on contingent rights which reinforce domination (Gabel, 1992/ 1980, p. 18).

The progay movement is beginning to formulate appeals which move beyond the mere repetition of rights demands and thereby transcend the denunciation of "special rights." An excellent example of such an appeal is law professor David Richards's (1998) call for an understanding of legal and social protection for gay people which is based on the right of conscience. He argues that the fight to defend lesbian/gay identity "is our contemporary retelling of the oldest narrative of civil liberty, the struggle for the inalienable right of conscience against the manifold forms of subjugation" (p. 410). In his analysis, sexual preference is a claim to a personal and ethical identity as a particular kind of person. Assertion of sexual identity is "as central to self-authenticating claims to [gay/lesbian] personal and ethical identity . . . as race or gender or conventional religion, and the prejudice against such claims is politically unreasonable in the same way racism, sexism, and religious intolerance are unreasonable" (p. 356).

Making such claims on behalf of the marginalized may meet Darsey's (1997) call for a gay/lesbian rhetoric grounded in the past which speaks with prophetic voice to the future (p. 209). By establishing the connection between gay/lesbian identity and the American tradition of freedom of conscience, a powerful argument is established for ending discriminatory laws and providing civil rights protection. Through such appeals, gay people cease to be a special interest group lobbying for benefits and become instead the "insistent conscience and demanding prophet of American rights-based moral community" (Richards, 1998, p. 467). They move beyond victimage to morality (Jacobs, 1993, p. 747).

In addition, gay/lesbian advocates have begun to cope seriously with the rhetorical problems of identity in order to advance a rationale for public policy change which is both consistent with reality-as-understood and capable of being understood by policy decision makers. In the process, they have sought to mute division over identity in the gay community. A key example of efforts in this direction is an attempt to deploy what has been called "strategic essentialism." Even adamant constructionists recognize the need to use an essentialist identity in the effort to gain political access and power. Warner (1993) argues that "despite its language of postmodernism, multiculturalism tends to rely on very modern notions of authenticity, of culture as shared meaning and the source of identity"

(p. xvii). An extension of this recognition is to use multiple identities strategically, choosing to emphasize one identity over the other as the rhetorical situation demands, advancing what postmodern scholar Gayatri Spivak (1993) labels "operational essentialism." She concludes that the "strategic use of essentialism [is] something one cannot not use" (p. 5). Weston (1996) takes this position to mean that progressive advocates should "operate as though you are one thing through and through, a model of consistency and conviction . . . as though each identity you claim is natural and inescapable and quite simply 'who you are' " (p. 43). Such a position, Connolly (1991) believes, "accepts the indispensability of identity while refusing (while struggling to refuse) to live its own identity as intrinsic truth" (p. 46).

The attempt to establish a single way to frame gay/lesbian struggle on public issues has been challenged in recent years by less dogmatic views. In one approach, emphasis is placed on affirmation and erasure of identity as simply complementary functions of the nature of language. White (1992), for instance, draws a distinction between "language that coordinates action-in-the-world and language that is world-disclosing" (p. 25). He links the former with Habermas and the latter with Foucault, suggesting that Habermas "focuses primarily on language's capacity to coordinate action to solve a range of 'problems in the world,' " while poststructuralists are committed "to the world disclosing quality of language" (p. 25). Strategic claims to fixed identity have been used opportunistically in social justice discourses, while the deconstruction of identity has been employed in the project of undermining the cultural creation of oppressive identity models and social norms. Strong identity claims become no more than an emphasis on the coordinating function of language, and the paradox of the simultaneous tightening and loosening of identity is simply employment of two language functions at one time. Joshua Gamson (1995) argues that both resources should be used, given the "simultaneity of cultural sources of oppression (which make loosening categories a smart strategy) and institutional sources of oppression (which make tightening categories a smart strategy)" (p. 403).

Another approach to avoiding division over identity is both to localize and specify the representation of self in progay discourse. Legal scholar Dan Danielson (1995), for example, writes that there is no specific doctrine or strategy for performing the political representation of our core selves that "captures the 'reality' of our identities or that necessarily leads to social acceptance or fair legal treatment. Rather, we might take our cue from the apparently irreducible diversity, complexity and banality of the life strategies we see around us" (p. 58). In a similar vein, Duggan (1995) suggests that there is increasing recognition that "for people with multiple 'marked' identities, the political project begins at the level of the very problematic construction of identities and their relation to different communities and different political projects" (p. 162).

One approach to the implementation of a diversity of strategy is to recognize, as Phelan (1994) recommends, that progay efforts are "necessarily a local operation, one involving political action at particular locations in our lives independent of global or universal theories" (p. xvii). To escape universal theory in order to avoid division over how issues should be framed

> means that as we enter public discourse we do so, not as 'Lesbians' with a fixed eternal identity, but as lesbians, people occupying provisional subject positions in heterosexual society. As such, we must acknowledge that speaking and being heard does not mean simply drawing on our 'experience' in an unmediated way but means articulating our lives, interpreting and reinterpreting them in ways that link us to others. (p. 140)

The localization of the multiplicity of identities carried by each person leads Weston (1996) to favor an emphasis on narration. She concludes "that stories do a better job than geometric models of conveying how race, class, gender, sexuality, and the like come alive" (p. 126).

Strategic essentialism and the localization of identity narratives are attempts to cope with the reality that the gay/lesbian community, diverse as it is, will continue to produce multiple identities and carry on an oppositional politics under many different signs (Rofes, 1996, p. 260). Miller (1998) expresses this position when she writes that "we need to offer a multitude of different perspectives and different representations of lesbians and gays" (p. 155). Gay/lesbian advocates, however, should be aware that the polyvocality of variant sexuality carries a price in that divergent civil rights campaigns and cultural projects do create difficulties for one another. For example, there may be some political endeavors such as attempts to socialize gay/queer youth which cannot be sustained under the weight of particular versions of epistemological correctness. There is no doubt that socializing its young is an important task for the gay community (Martin & Hetrick, 1988). However, accepting the imperative to defend gay children and teens from heteronormativity may be impeded by calls for destabilization of the sexual regime, emphasizing choice and valorizing the fluidity of sexual identity. Such appeals raise the larger society's anxieties about intergenerational gay relations (Smith & Windes, 1999, p. 36). Or, to take an opposite view, the essentialization of the gay role may be conceptually unable to insulate the young from social interference (Sedgwick, 1993, p. 78). Such conundrums suggest that practical implications more than theoretical elegance are at stake as the gay/lesbian community ponders various interpretations of its identities.

Gay/lesbian advocates have been reflective enough to think seriously about their position in society and to probe the relationship among their politics of civil rights, the larger culture in which they operate, and the subculture which they have created. Whether to employ a civil rights strategy which de-emphasizes gay identity or a strategy which confronts cultural homophobia has long been an important question among gay/lesbian activists (Ehrensaft & Milkman, 1979). Antigay advocates have advanced the notion that political progress is being made by homosexuals because they have succeeded in subverting the culture. Podhoretz (1996), for instance, observes that the "approving attitude of the culture toward homosexuality is overcoming the resistance of majority sentiment as reflected in the polity" (p. 34). Progay advocates have, of course, taken a less sanguine view.

Critics of gay efforts which seek only to change public policy maintain that the underlying culture of antigay sentiment has not changed because of legal accomplishments and that achieving civil rights will not affect a cultural transformation. Vaid (1995) believes that a gay civil rights movement can coexist with homophobia, because the granting of civil rights does not necessarily displace the sexual and moral hierarchy that functions to stigmatize gays: "You do not have to recognize the fundamental humanity of gay people in order to agree that they should be treated equally and fairly under the law" (p. 179). In her conception, antigay feeling arises out of the present construction of sexual, family, racial, and economic systems. Refusal to address the transformation of these systems will only perpetuate cultural homophobia (p. 183). Consequently, Vaid argues for a gay/lesbian version of cultural politics, the merger of efforts to transform both the state and other institutions. She maintains that "being visible, challenging stereotypes, making queer family and community are all political acts. Conversely, passing laws, electing supportive politicians, and organizing ourselves into a voting bloc are power-oriented strategies, essential to cultural transformation" (p. 212).

Key to an emerging gay/lesbian cultural politics is the premise that the subordination of one group to another is "secured and reproduced through the practices and products of cultural institutions" (Jordan & Weedon, 1995, p. 4). Recognition has grown that it may be unwise to assume that lesbians and gay men should be protected only when they remain in the private sphere. They recognize the dangers of "building a political strategy on the narrow platform of the right to privacy" (Gross, 1993, pp. ix, 146). Instead, visible presence of gay/lesbian people is mandatory for advancing their cause. A renewed emphasis calls for a cultural politics which includes not only working within the political system for civil rights, but also striving for greater visibility in the media and entertainment industries (Signorile, 1993, p. xiv). Beyond this, embracing cultural politics means seeking complete gay visibility—in schools no less than in the media. Bronski (1998) contends that such visibility is a prerequisite for "organizing and struggling to become public—that is, to have the full responsibilities and privileges of public life and citizenship" (p. 212).

A number of rhetorical choices which damage public debate are shared by many advocates regardless of their position on variant sexuality. Perhaps the most salient is the strong tendency of advocates to pretend to reveal the secret "agenda" of the opposition. Rather than speaking to specific public policy issues, there is a tendency to portray the opposition as undermining society. For progay advocates, this often takes the form of depicting their opponents as theocrats desperate to achieve political power. The usual form of such declarations is to argue that the religious right is the inspiration for all forms of antigay agitation. On the other side, antigay advocates highlight the so-called "gay agenda," sedulously reading gay publications to cull exaggerated statements which disclose the subterranean motives behind homosexual agitation (Patton, 1993, pp. 143-144). As an extension of this strategy, both sides try to feature the opposition at its weakest. Progay advocates seek to make the vicious homophobe extremist Fred Phelps the poster child of the antigay forces. Antigay media feature videotaped segments of Gay Pride parades which are calculated to enflame middle class sensibilities (Gallagher & Bull, 1996, pp. 1-3). Each side tends to avoid intellectual encounter with the most reasonable, informed, and articulate champions of the opposition. As a result, disciplined, evidenced, and rigorous discussion drifts further out of reach.

The quality of debate in the variant sexuality issue culture also suffers from an often uninterested public which can rightly be characterized by its "uncritical majoritarian complacency" (Richards, 1998, p. 401). As early gay civil rights activists noted in the late 1970s, the public shows no interest in enhancing homosexual rights, but at the same time does not seem willing to deny gay people any of their civil rights (Ehrensaft & Milkman, 1979). Opinion polls reveal a public which is satisfied with limited protections of lesbians and gay men while seeking to defend children and religious organizations from potentially damaging or unwanted influence. Sinfield (1994) suggests that an ideology has become hegemonic which positions sexual deviance along a "spectrum extending from relatively 'good' types at one end (monogamous, same-age couples who keep their homes nice without drawing attention to themselves or aspiring to rear children) to 'bad' types at the other (childmolesters and the like)" (p. 56). This view is confirmed by Rubin (1993) who observes that "some forms of homosexuality are moving in the direction of respectability. . . . Promiscuous homosexuality, sadomasochism, fetishism, transsexuality, and cross-generational encounters are still viewed as unmodulated horrors incapable of involving affection, love, free choice, kindness, or transcendence" (p. 15).

Despite shifts toward greater acceptance of homosexuality in some measures of public opinion polling, the general audience for the discourses produced in the variant sexuality issue culture seems to be stalemated between conceptions of good versus bad homosexuals and the private/public distinction (LaCaye, 1998, p. 36). This can be taken by conservative analysts as a sign that public opinion is variegated and finely nuanced. Hunter (1994), for instance, believes that along with a stable moral rejection of homosexuality, there is a simultaneous and increasing acceptance of gay civil rights (p. 119). Smith (1994), writing from a progressive perspective, takes a darker view, concluding that the distinctions drawn between sex in the private and public spheres and between the good homosexual and the dangerous queer creates debate which favors hegemonic distinctions leading to complex figures of inclusion and exclusion based on differentiation between types of homosexuality (p. 17).

Perhaps the public debate is stalemated both in the sense that the same appeals are repeated over time in a wide variety of contexts and in the sense that a pattern of beliefs has solidified and become dominant with respect to sexuality. As Sinfield (1994) observes, the fundamental problem, at least from the gay/lesbian viewpoint, is that the issue culture has become stabilized. He asserts that the difficulty is "not so much that rights achieved so far by lesbians and gay men are contested, but that our societies seem well able to live with that contest" (p. 57). His explanation is that we have arrived at a juncture:

> From which it is going to be hard to advance very far. . . . The increased visibility of lesbians and gay men over the last 25 years has transformed our opportunities, at the same time, it has made us more accessible to hostile appropriations. (Sinfield, 1994, p. 57)

Our society has, perhaps, created from continuing opposition a drama which it is willing to enact repetitively.

At a deeper level, the opposition within the variant sexuality issue culture may be understood as a ritualized conflict which contributes to social stability. In Edelman's (1988) view of moral conflict

> well-established, thoroughly anticipated, and therefore ritualistic affirmation of the differences institutionalizes both rhetorics, minimizing the chance of major shifts and leaving the regime wide discretion, for there will be anticipated support and opposition no matter what forms of action or inaction occur. (pp. 18-19)

The continuation of a struggle provides stability in the sense that "opposing texts become bulwarks of one another while isolated texts, unsupported by opposition, are readily vulnerable to new language" (p. 19).

Variant Sexuality and the Constitution of Society

Public debate over variant sexuality, however, transcends ritualized conflict because it raises significant questions about the fundamental nature of society. Political scientist Patricia Boling (1996) suggests that the political discussion of divisive issues of sexuality raises important questions about the process of creating a just society and nurturing democratic citizens. As we have observed, this discussion is unfortunately obscured by "strategies engaged in by a variety of political groups—whether dismissing one's opponents as ideologues, expelling them from the community because their views are too divergent, or viewing any political compromise as conceding too much" (p. 36). She recognizes that a dismissive attitude toward others' views and an insistence on political purity undermines the possibility of democratic politics (p. 36). However, fundamental questions about the nature of politics and society are raised in cultural conflict which cannot be evaded when issues about intimate conduct are raised. Boling (1996) argues that out of such interaction emerges the norms of discourse which determine the kind of debate appropriate to public policy formation: "the degree of respect one owes one's opponents, as well as one's allies; the kinds of arguments and responses one needs to make to build agreement and consensus" (p. 36).

Within the variant sexuality issue culture, two general views have developed concerning the social foundations of disagreement and conflict. On the one hand, the progay interpretive package can be understood to feature human rights and individual autonomy. On the other, traditionalists advance a package which stresses social stability and moral/religious beliefs (Kaplan, 1997, p. 36). Such an understanding which divides political actors into pluralists and communitarians is fundamentally flawed in that communities can be understood to be more than conventional in the sense that they reflect dominant or majoritarian moral beliefs. The emergence of a distinct gay and lesbian community points to the existence of pluralism as a social fact as well as a goal. As Kaplan notes, "there are lesbian and gay communities as well as communities of fundamentalists, orthodox believers, and 'moral majoritarians' " (p. 37). Returning to the idea of interpretive communities discussed earlier, the gay/lesbian issue culture is not a struggle of the community against the individual, but a struggle of communities against each other.

Although the "culture war" approach to understanding the variant sexuality issue culture suggests that social division on fundamental beliefs may be an anomaly, an alternative view takes fundamental moral disagreement as a standard feature of modern democratic society. Political philosopher John Rawls (1993) points out that such a society is characterized "not simply by a pluralism of comprehensive religious, philosophical, and moral doctrines but by a pluralism of incomparable yet reasonable comprehensive doctrines" (p. xvi). In his view, the purpose of society is not to promote a single true doctrine, but to establish a society within which many incompatible though reasonable doctrines might circulate (p. 129). This would require that we accept two propositions: (a) that a permanent condition of a free society is a reasonable pluralism; (b) that the "idea of the reasonable is more suitable as part of the basis of public justification for a constitutional regime than the idea of moral truth" (p. 129). Such a position requires that citizens discipline themselves to avoid demands to employ state power in enforcing their own comprehensive doctrines while at the same time continuing to uncover the basis for a stable overlapping consensus (p. 152). In the progay/antigay issue culture, this would lead to the attenuation of claims to legitimate state action by both sides, recognizing that government should neither suppress gay/ lesbian identity nor simultaneously suppress all associational objections to it. In the case of gay marriage, for instance, this might mean government mandating domestic partnership in a form which guarantees a wide range of legal rights to persons in gay/lesbian relationships while, at the same time, reserving the term "marriage" to the civil sphere where religious organizations would be free to make their own judgments as to what sorts of moral sanction ought to be given to same-sex partnerships.

The creation of political pluralism in a society of moral division, however, is a daunting task. Moon (1993) urges us to recognize that

> there will be tragic moments in the political life of any society, moments in which its strategy for creating political community fails, in which conflicts can only be resolved through the imposition of the will of one party on another. (p. 12)

In his view, there are a number of prescriptions for preventing the development of tragic conflict out of moral disagreement. Emphasizing commonalities among groups can be presented as a basic strategy of social justice. Sharp distinctions can be drawn between public and private spheres (pp. 96, 149). Within the variant sexuality issue culture, some consensus is forming around the idea that rights are important. Less strongly, there is an increasing public acceptance of greater recognition of lesbians and gay men in the public sphere. Ultimately, however, as Moon believes, hope for resolution of moral conflict comes from the vision of a society committed to mutuality whose members

> have enough self-acceptance, enough self-confidence, that we can affirm the value of our ideals without demanding that others conform to them [since] ... to fully accept plurality, one must overcome the need to have others validate our aspirations and identities by adopting them for themselves. (p. 220)

Precisely at this point, however, questions about how to discuss public policy concerning homosexuality become exceedingly difficult. There is no doubt that strong efforts should be made at reconciliation between individuals with different political views on homosexuality. We should strive to recognize that an alternative exists "to denunciation and politically selective appropriation, namely, the development of different, and different *kinds* of, narratives and justifications, including less Manichaean accounts of Left and Right and more conceptually subtle and historically responsive analyses of political dynamics more generally" (B. Smith, 1997, p. 28). Such a development could begin with recognition that the dominant discourses of polarized public debate can be supplemented by dialogic communication (Becker, Chasin, Chasin, Herzig, & Roth, 1995). Such dialogue might arise from acceptance that the very grounds of controversy arise out of commonality. Employing the Gadamerian insight that every misunderstanding presupposes common accord, rhetorician Michael King (1998) suggests that "what we hold in common is what allows us to recognize difference in the first place" (p. 18). Consequently, there is a need to encourage dialogic search for commonality in which difference is translated through symbols of consubstantiality into a more civil and productive discourse.

Exploration of grounds for commonality and mutuality, however, runs into a fundamental problem arising out of a striking similarity between traditionalists and gay/lesbian persons. Both groups, as Gallagher and Bull (1996) observe, suffer from a sense of marginality produced by the fact that a majority of Americans tend to view each group with suspicion (p. xiv). Both groups are in some sense marginalized and, therefore, each seeks to use public policy as a way to emerge from the periphery of society. Kaplan (1997) asserts that the search for legitimation follows a pattern in which "demands of historically oppressed groups for democratic citizenship are framed in terms of affirmation and embrace of previously marginalized identities" (p. 153). In a real sense, the principal impediment to the formation of reasonable public policy about variant sexuality is the demand of both traditionalists and gay/lesbian advocates for affirmation through state action which necessarily marginalizes other identities.

We share Condit's (1987) hope that through public communication, society can "craft virtue." She believes that the struggle which produces shared commitments arises out of struggle against elites which increases "collective moral breadth and depth in some areas at some times" (1987, p. 84). For the moment, whether rhetorical struggle among the marginal can have the same effect remains speculative.

Avenues for Future Research

The core concept of oppositional effects in issue cultures suggests specific research topics for students and scholars concerned with discourses of sexuality, issue cultures, and identity formation and performance. Our analysis suggests a variety of directions for further needed research. Examples of such topics include the following:

- differences in progay and antigay language and presentational style in the varying contexts in which confrontation takes place
- argumentative deployment of scientific and social scientific evidence in debate over variant sexuality narratives of biological determinism and conversion in variant sexuality discourse
- diachronic and synchronic changes in ideographs used by progay and antigay advocates
- challenges presented to movement leaders who must mobilize and coordinate fractious movements under conditions of social conflict
- variation in the effects of confrontation revealed by case studies of confrontation in various institutional settings and media environments

Our purpose, however, is not to suggest specific investigative projects. We believe that through carefully focused study, we will learn how antagonistic enjoinment affects many aspects of communication about variant sexuality. Such study can illuminate symbolic action in discourses ranging from intimate memoir to movement exhortation and media coverage.

Understanding a particular issue culture can lead to a better sense of how other issue cultures function. An important additional way of elaborating this concept is to explore a wide variety of issue cultures (e.g., those concerned with labor relations, race, and gender). These cultures have produced opposing interpretive packages defining both identities and sites of contention, as well as the nature of adversarial relationships. It is important for the critic to remember that these definitions change over time and they are polyvocal. The discourses by which employees and owners antagonistically characterize one another may influence the way in which the collective subjects "worker" and "owner" are produced (Fantasia, 1988, p. 10). Feminist advocates and the proponents of "backlash" influence each other's choice of how to describe struggle over gender. Such speculation provides warrant, at least, to suspect that oppositional influence can be usefully identified in most issue cultures.

Assuming that this influence operates differently in each culture, only a careful investigation of each culture will produce a chart of oppositional influences which, in turn, can become the basis for statements of regularities and singularities in the antagonistic production of interpretive packages.

The frames central to the interpretive packages which we have analyzed concern identity. Identity is often the focus of political contests (Calhoun, 1994a, p. 4). As sociologist Ali Rattansi (1995) writes, "ethnicities, nationalisms, and other forms of collective identity are products of a process to be conceptualized as a cultural politics of representation in which narratives, images, musical forms, and popular culture more generally, have a significant role" (p. 274). Society's assumption of naturalized identities and the presumption of rhetorical theorists of the persuader's prediscursive identity, however, tend to impede exploring identity formation.

Examination of gay/lesbian identities begins with the concern that the construction and deployment of the "normal" self has been screened from view. Our usual way of talking, as Connolly (1991) points out, "does not support a problematization of established standards of normal individuality; the narrative and rhetorical designs of its texts do not pose disturbing questions about the dense construction of the normal individual and its abnormalities" (p. 75). But normal identities can be understood as unstable, paradoxical, and strategic. For example, the constructed nature of ethnic and racial identities has recently received considerable attention. Social scientist Joane Nagel (1994), for example, writes that "research has shown people's conception of themselves along ethnic lines, especially their ethnic identity, to be situational and changeable" (p. 154).

In like fashion, the naturalness of racial identities has been challenged. Social scientist F. James Davis (1991) argues that the "black population in the United States is a socially constructed category backed by law, not a grouping established by physical anthropologists or biologists" (p. 30). Similarly, English professor Elaine Ginsberg (1996) maintains that "racial categories have throughout history been created for the deliberate purpose of exploitation, domination, or persecution of one group by another" (p. 5). At the same time, the "naturalness" of other identities has been hardened by political tension. Discourses of masculinity and heterosexuality have yet to produce self-reflexive subjects, even though the growth of white studies, for example, serves as a beginning for dominant groups to acknowledge their positionality (Danielson & Engle,

1995, p. xiv). Instead, identity politics has caused the production of "retrospective, indeed nostalgic, constructions subject to a pathos of lost origins and demanding, on the part of the dominant culture, the violent disavowal and protection of its own contingent identity" (Rohy, 1996, p. 218). The analysis of subordinate identities (gay/lesbian, female, black) will result in more attention to the building of dominant identities.

Such analysis cannot be undertaken by rhetorical critics, however, as long as study of the discursive production of identity is impeded by the assumption that identity formation inevitably precedes rhetorical action. Habermas, for instance, assumes that the public sphere receives subjects from the private sphere whose identities are fully formed and settled (Calhoun, 1994b, p. 23). Many rhetorical critics are Habermasian in presuming that collective actors speak automatically from a transparent identity, and that the only rhetorical decisions which require analysis concern how a given identity is to be presented to a particular audience. This standard view of the persuader obscures questions about rhetorical action in the strategic construction of the subject. Butler addresses this problem, writing that "for the subject to be a pregiven point of departure for politics is to defer the question of the political construction and regulation of the subject itself" (quoted in Calhoun, 1994b, p. 23). Instead, recognition should be given to the premise proposed by Taylor and Whittier (1992) that "collective political actors do not exist *de facto* by virtue of individuals sharing a common structural location; they are created in the course of social movement activity" (p. 110). Only by recognizing that identity is a continuing project, not an assumption, can critics of public communication begin to respond to questions of how identity is constructed in the public sphere.

Once such recognition takes place, rhetorical critics are well prepared to extend the analysis of identity. As we suggested in the "Introduction," a good beginning point might be Burke's (1952) concepts of "identification" and "division." At the root of identity is the constitution of a group which necessarily entails rhetorical action to establish external and internal boundaries. Within a Burkeian framework, struggles over identity occur along a "wavering line between identification and division" (p. 45). Another entry point into the construction and strategies of identity is provided by McGee's (1975) thesis that " 'the people' are more *process* than *phenomenon*" (p. 242). Although McGee implicitly connects his argument to national identity, little effort is required to translate his terms into concepts appropriate to analysis of the dynamics of gender, sexuality, religion, race, and ethnicity. Narrative analysis also offers an excellent approach to the construction and defense of identity. The application of such analysis is important because stories may be superior to other discursive forms at conveying how race, class, gender, sexuality, and the like come alive (Weston, 1996, p. 126).

Finally, analyzing issue cultures through the concept of oppositional influence in the production of interpretive packages offers an additional frame for understanding the postmodern collapse of distinction between authority and advocacy. This collapse has been most often understood as "incredulity toward metanarratives," revision of relationships among author, text, and reader which radically diminishes authorial power, or as the recognition that discourses are composed of interpenetrating texts to which critics add yet other texts (Lyotard, 1984, p. xxiv; Rosenau, 1992, p. 24; Solomon, 1993). Throughout our text, individuals have appeared who make claim to authority in order to function as advocates. Further, progay and traditionalist interpretive packages assert their authority and construct confirming "authorities." Critics inevitably have preferences among and within interpretive packages. Following philosopher Richard Rorty's (1989) advice to treat ironically all final vocabularies, we have endeavored to distinguish between partisan statements and conclusions based on systematic observation. We have attempted judiciously to select and characterize texts with which we are in disagreement (pp. 89-90).

From the interpretive perspective, however, we must also recognize that criticism of rhetorical acts is a process of reading which provides, at best, another interpretive package. A continuing ethical obligation of rhetorical critics ought to be directed toward investigating how their interpretations mingle with the frames of their subject. Moreover, we should appreciate the social power generated by the abrasive meeting of incommensurable ideas. Public policy contests in which antagonistic enjoinment is important strongly reinforce the beliefs which give coherence to individual lives and help to determine the social and political conditions under which we live. Only the knowledge that the issues which we have discussed here are personally important to the lives of significant numbers of individuals keeps at bay the ironic perspective that, in the end, "when all the stories are told, and all the chips are in, counted, and compared, we will be unable not only to say who finally won but even to tell which was which" (B. Smith, 1997, p. 152).

References

Adam, B. D. (1985). Structural foundations of the gay world. *Comparative Studies in Society and History, 27,* 658-671.

Adam, B. D. (1987). *The rise of a gay and lesbian movement.* Boston: Twayne.

Adam, B. D. (1999). Moral regulation and the disintegrating Canadian state. In B. D Adam, J. W. Duyvendak, & A. Krouwel (Eds.), *The global emergence of gay and lesbian politics: National imprints of a worldwide movement* (pp. 12-29). Philadelphia: Temple University Press.

Adam, B. D, Duyvendak, J. W., & Krouwel, A. (1999). Introduction. In B. D Adam, J. W. Duyvendak, & A. Krouwel (Eds.), *The global emergence of gay and lesbian politics: National imprints of a worldwide movement* (pp. 1-9). Philadelphia: Temple University Press.

Aho, J. A. (1990). *The politics of righteousness: Idaho Christian patriotism.* Seattle, WA: University of Washington Press.

Altman, D. (1980). What changed in the seventies. In Gay Left Collective (Ed.), *Homosexuality: Power and politics* (pp. 52-63). London: Allison and Busby.

Alwood, E. (1996). *Straight news: Gays, lesbians, and the news media.* New York: Columbia University Press.

American Civil Liberties Union. (1998). Statewide anti-gay marriage laws. [On-line]. Retrieved in 1998 from http://www.aclu.org/issues/gay/gaymar.html

Appiah, K. A. (1995). African identities. In L. Nicholson & S. Seidman (Eds.), *Social postmodernism* (pp. 103-115). New York: Cambridge University Press.

Ayres, B. D. (1998, November 23). California to vote on gay marriages. *New York Times*, p. A12.

Bagemihl, B. (1999). *Biological exuberance: Animal homosexuality and natural diversity*. New York: St. Martin's Press.

We are everywhere: Historical sourcebook of gay and lesbian politics (pp. 234-236). New York: Routledge. (Original work published 1949)

Bailey, D. (1955). *Homosexuality and the western Christian tradition*. Boston: Beacon Press.

Bakelaar, P. J. (1997). *The issue culture of the gay and lesbian religious controversy in the age of AIDS: Moral argumentation in American mainline religious communities as a symbolic contest between competing interpretations*. Unpublished doctoral dissertation: Temple University, Philadelphia.

Baldwin, J. (1997). Preservation of innocence. In M. Blasius & S. Phelan (Eds.), Balmer, R. (1989). *Mine eyes have seen the glory: A journey into the evangelical subculture in America*. New York: Oxford University Press.

Balthrop, V. W. (1984). Culture, myth, and ideology as public argument: An interpretation of the ascent and demise of "southern culture." *Communication Monographs, 51*, 339-352.

Bass, J. D. (1991). "Levellers": The economic reduction of political equality in the Putney debates, 1647. *Quarterly Journal of Speech, 77*, 427-445.

Bawer, B. (1993). *A place at the table: The gay individual in American society*. New York: Simon & Schuster.

Bayer, R. (1981). *Homosexuality and American psychiatry: The politics of diagnosis*. New York: Basic Books.

Becker, C., Chasin, L., Chasin, R., Herzig, M., & Roth, S. (1995). From stuck debate to new conversation on controversial issues: A report from the Public Conversations Project. *Journal of Feminist Therapy, 7*(1/2), 143-163.

Benford, R. D. (1993). Frame disputes within the nuclear disarmament movement. *Social Forces, 71*, 677-701.

Benford, R. D., & Hunt, S. A. (1992). Dramaturgy and social movements: The social construction and communication of power. *Sociological Inquiry, 7*, 36-55.

Berger, P. L. (1966). Identity as a problem in the sociology of knowledge. *European Journal of Sociology, 7*, 105-115.

Berke, R. L. (1998, June 30). Flurry of anti-gay remarks has G.O.P. fearing backlash. *New York Times*, pp. A1, A19.

Bernstein, M. (1997). Celebration and suppression: The strategic uses of identity by the lesbian and gay movement. *American Journal of Sociology, 103*, 531-565.

Bersani, L. (1995). *Homos*. Cambridge, MA: Harvard University Press.

Birch, K. (1980). The politics of autonomy. In Gay Left Collective (Ed.), *Homosexuality: Power and politics* (pp.85-92). London: Allison & Busby.

Blanchard, D. A. (1994). *The anti-abortion movement and the rise of the religious right: From polite to fiery protest*. New York: Twayne.

Blasius, M. (1994). *Gay and lesbian politics: Sexuality and the emergence of a new ethic*. Philadelphia: Temple University Press.

Blasius, M., & Phelan, S. (1997). ONE. In M. Blasius & S. Phelan (Eds.), *We are everywhere: A historical sourcebook of gay and lesbian politics* (p. 309). New York: Routledge.

Blumenfeld, W. J. (1992). Introduction. In W. J. Blumenfeld (Ed.), *Homophobia: How we all pay the price* (pp. 1-19). Boston: Beacon Press.

Boggs, C. (1986). *Social movements and political power: Emerging forms of radicalism in the West.* Philadelphia: Temple University Press.

Boling, P. (1996). *Privacy and the politics of intimate life.* Ithaca, NY: Cornell University Press.

Bork, R. (1996). *Slouching toward Gomorrah: Modern liberalism and American decline.* New York: Regan Books.

Boswell, J. (1980). *Christianity, social tolerance, and homosexuality: Gay people in western Europe from the beginning of the Christian era to the fourteenth century.* Chicago: University of Chicago Press.

Boswell, J. (1990). Categories, experience and sexuality. In E. Stein (Ed.), *Forms of desire: Sexual orientation and the social constructionist controversy* (pp. 133-173). New York: Garland.

Boswell, J. (1994). *Same-sex unions in premodern Europe.* New York: Villard Books.

Bourdieu, P. (1991). *Language and symbolic power.* Oxford: Polity Press.

Bourdieu, P. (1994). Structures, habitus, power: Basis for a theory of symbolic power. In D. B. Dirks, G. Eley, & S. B. Ortner (Eds.), *Culture/power/history: A reader in contemporary social theory* (pp. 155-199). Princeton, NJ: Princeton University Press.

Bravman, S. (1996). Postmodernism and queer identity. In S. Seidman (Ed.), *Queer theory/sociology* (pp. 333-361). Cambridge: Blackwell.

Bronski, M. (1984). *Culture clash: Making of a gay sensibility.* Boston: South End.

Bronski, M. (1995). Sexual liberation versus identity politics. *Harvard Gay and Lesbian Review, 2*(1), 23-25.

Bronski, M. (1998). *The pleasure principle: Sex, backlash, and the struggle for gay freedom.* New York: St. Martin's Press.

Brooke, A. (1998, July 10). Moral majority: Lott ignites firestorm by mixing religion & politics. *Frontiers,* p. 17.

Brooks, D. (1996, Fall). Class politics versus identity politics. *The Public Interest,* pp. 116-124.

Brown, K. M. (1994). Fundamentalism and the control of women. In J. S. Hawley (Ed.), *Fundamentalism and gender* (pp.175-201). New York: Oxford University Press.

Browning, F. (1993). *The culture of desire: Paradox and perversity in gay lives today.* New York: Crown.

Brummett, B. (1981). Ideologies in two gay rights controversies. In J. W. Chesebro (Ed.), *Gayspeak: Gay male and lesbian communication* (pp. 291-302). New York: Pilgrim.

Bryant, A. (1977). *The Anita Bryant story: The survival of our nation's families and the threat of militant homosexuality.* Old Tappan, NJ: Revell.

Buchanan, P. J. (1997, June 10). Adultery issue is America's religious war. *Los Angeles Times,* p. B7.

Burg, B. R. (1981). Ho hum, another work of the devil: Buggery and sodomy in early Stuart England. In S. J. Licata & R. P. Peterson (Eds.), *Historical perspectives on homosexuality* (pp. 69-78). New York: Haworth Press.

Burgess, P. G. (1970). The rhetoric of moral conflict: Two critical dimensions. *Quarterly Journal of Speech, 56,* 120-130.

Burke, K. (1952). *A rhetoric of motives.* New York: Prentice Hall.

Burke, K. (1959). *Attitudes toward history.* Boston: Beacon Press. (Original work published 1937)

Burke, K. (1966). *Language as symbolic action: Essays on life, literature, and method.* Berkeley, CA: University of California Press.

Burke, K. (1968). Interaction: Dramatism. In D. L. Sills (Ed.), *International encyclopedia of the social sciences* (pp. 445-452). New York: Crowell Collier Macmillan.

Burress, P. (1994). Petition drives: Pros and cons. [Online]. Retrieved January 1995 from http://www.cyberzine.org/html/RRight/watch 129b

Burtoft, L. (1995). *Setting the record straight: What research really says about the social consequences of homosexuality.* Colorado Springs, CO: Focus on the Family.

Button, J. W., Rienzo, B. A., & Wald, K. D. (1997). *Private lives, public conflicts: Battles over gay rights in American communities.* Washington, DC: CQ Press.

Cagan, L. (1993). Community organizing and the religious right: Lessons from Oregon's Measure Nine campaign. *Radical America, 24*(4), 67-83.

Calhoun, C. (1994a). Preface. In C. Calhoun (Ed.), *Social theory and the politics of identity* (pp. 1-7). Oxford: Blackwell.

Calhoun, C. (1994b). Social theory and the politics of identity. In C. Calhoun (Ed.), *Social theory and the politics of identity* (pp. 9-36). Oxford: Blackwell.

Cantor, D. (1994). *The religious right: The assault on tolerance & pluralism in America.* New York: Anti-Defamation League.

Capps, W. H. (1992). *The new religious right: Piety, patriotism, and politics.* Chapel Hill, NC: University of South Carolina Press.

Carter, S L. (1993). *The culture of disbelief: How American law and politics trivialize religious devotion.* New York: Basic Books.

Cathcart, R. S. (1983). A confrontation perspective on the study of social movements. *Central States Speech Journal, 34,* 69-74.

Champagne, J. (1995). *The ethics of marginality: A new approach to gay studies.* Minneapolis, MN: University of Minnesota Press.

Charland, M. (1987). Constitutive rhetoric: The case of the *Peuple Quebecois. Quarterly Journal of Speech, 73,* 133-150.

Chauncey, G. (1994). *Gay New York: Gender, urban culture, and the making of the gay male world, 1890-1940.* New York: Basic Books.

Chesebro, J. W. (1994). Reflections on gay and lesbian rhetoric. In R. J. Ringer (Ed.), *Queer words, queer images: Communication and the construction of homosexuality* (pp. 77-88). New York: New York University Press.

Chinn, S., & Franklin, K. (1992). "I am what I am" (or am I?): The making and un-making of lesbian and gay identity in *High Tech Gays. Discourse, 15,*(1), 11-26.

Cicchino, P. M., Deming, B. R., & Nicholson, K. M. (1995). Sex, lies, and civil rights: A critical history of the Massachusetts gay civil rights bill. In D. Herman & C. Stychin (Eds.), *Legal inversions: Lesbians, gay men, and the politics of law* (pp. 141-161). Philadelphia: Temple University Press.

Clendinen, D., & Nagourney, A. (1999). *Out for good: The struggle to build a gay rights movement in America.* New York: Simon & Schuster.

Clymer, A. (1993, January 27). Lawmakers revolt over plan to lift ban on gay service. *New York Times,* pp. A1, A8.

Cohen, D, & Dyer, R. (1980). The politics of gay culture. In Gay Left Collective (Ed.), *Homosexuality: Power and politics* (pp. 172-186). London: Allison & Busby.

Cohen, J. L. (1985). Strategy or identity: New theoretical paradigms and contemporary social movements. *Social Research, 52,* 663-716.

Committee on the Judiciary, United States Senate. (1996, July 11). Hearing on S. 1740: A bill to define and protect the institution of marriage. Washington, DC: U.S. Government Printing Office.

Condit, C. M. (1987). Crafting virtue: The rhetorical construction of public morality. *Quarterly Journal of Speech, 73,* 79-97.

Condit, C. M. (1990). *Decoding abortion rhetoric: Communicating social change.* Urbana, IL: University of Illinois Press.

Condit, C. M., & Lucaites, J. L. (1991). The rhetoric of equality and the expatriation of African-Americans, 1776-1826. *Communication Studies, 42,* 1-21.

Condit, C. M., & Lucaites, J. L. (1993). *Crafting equality: America's Anglo-African word.* Chicago: University of Chicago Press.

Congressional Record. (1996). 11 July: H7441-H7449; 12 July: H7481-H7506; 6 September: S9986-S10005; 10 September: S10100-10139.

Connolly, W. E. (1991). *Identity/difference: Democratic negotiations of political paradox.* Ithaca, NY: Cornell University Press.

Conrad, C. (1983). The rhetoric of the moral majority: An analysis of romantic form. *Quarterly Journal of Speech, 69,* 159-170.

Cooper, D. & Herman, D. (1995). "Getting the family right": Legislating heterosexuality in Britain, 1986-91. In D. Herman & C. Stychin (Eds.), *Legal inversions: Lesbians, gay men, and the politics of law* (pp. 162-211). Philadelphia: Temple University Press.

Cover, R. M. (1983). *Nomos* and narrative. *Harvard Law Review, 97,* 4-68.

Crain, C. (1993, May 10). Gay glue. *New Republic,* p. 18.

Crompton, L. (1985). *Byron and Greek love: Homophobia in 19th-century England.* Berkeley, CA: University of California Press.

Cruikshank, M. (1992). *The gay and lesbian liberation movement.* New York: Routledge, Chapman & Hall.

Daniels, T. D., Jensen, R. F., & Lichtenstein, A. (1985). Resolving the paradox in politicized Christian fundamentalism. *Western Journal of Speech Communication, 49,* 248-266.

Danielson, D. (1995). Identity strategies: Representing pregnancy and homo-sexuality. In D. Danielson & K. Engle (Eds.), *After identity: A reader in law and culture* (pp. 39-60). New York: Routledge.

Danielson, D., & Engle, K. (1995). Introduction. In D. Danielson & K. Engle (Eds.), *After identity: A reader in law and culture* (pp. i-xviii). New York: Routledge.

Dannemeyer, W. (1989). *Shadow in the land: Homosexuality in America.* San Francisco: Ignatius Press.

Darsey, J. (1991). From "gay is good" to the scourge of AIDS: The evolution of gay liberation rhetoric. *Communication Studies, 42,* 43-66.

Darsey, J. (1994). *"Die non"*: Gay liberation and the rhetoric of pure tolerance. In R. J. Ringer (Ed.), *Queer words, queer images: Communication and the construction of homosexuality* (pp. 45-76). New York: New York University Press.

Darsey, J. (1997). *The prophetic tradition and radical rhetoric in America.* New York: New York University Press.

Davies, B., & Rentzel, L. (1993). *Coming out of homosexuality: New freedom for men and women.* Downers Grove, IL: InterVarsity Press.

Davis, F. J. (1991). *Who is black: One nation's definition.* University Park, PA: Pennsylvania State University Press.

DeCecco, J. P. (1981). Definition and meaning of sexual orientation. *Journal of Homosexuality, 6*(4), 51-67.

DeCecco, J. P., & Elia, J. P. (1993). A critique and synthesis of biological essentialism and social constructionist views of sexuality and gender. *Journal of Homosexuality, 24*(3/4), 1-26.

Defense of Marriage Act. (1996). [Online]. Retrieved February 1997 from http://www.hrcusa.org/issues/leg/doma/billtext.html

D'Emilio, J. (1983). *Sexual politics, sexual communities: The making of a homosexual minority in the United States, 1940-1970.* Chicago: University of Chicago Press.

D'Emilio, J. (1989a). Gay politics and community in San Francisco since World War II. In M. B. Duberman, M. Vicinus, & G. Chauncey (Eds.), *Hidden from history: Reclaiming the gay and lesbian past* (pp. 456-473). New York: New American Library.

D'Emilio, J. (1989b). The homosexual menace: The politics of sexuality in cold war America. In K. Peiss & C. Simmons (Eds.), *Passion and power: Sexuality in history* (pp. 226-240). Philadelphia: Temple University Press.

D'Emilio, J. (1992). *Making trouble: Essays on gay history, politics, and the university.* New York: Routledge.

Diamond, S. (1989). *Spiritual warfare: The politics of the Christian Right.* Boston: South End Press.

Diamond, S. (1995). *Roads to dominion: Right wing movements and political power in the United States.* New York: Guilford Press.

Dickstein, M. (1993). After the cold war: Culture as politics, politics as culture. *Social Research, 60,* 531-544.

Dirks, N. B., Eley, G., & Ortner, S. B. (1994). Introduction. In N. B. Dirks, G. Eley, & S. B. Ortner (Eds.), *Culture/power/history: A reader in contemporary social theory* (pp. 3-45). Princeton, NJ: Princeton University Press.

Dobson, J. C., & Bauer, G. L. (1990). *Children at risk: The battle for the hearts and minds of our kids.* Dallas, TX: Word Publishers.

Donovan, T., & Bowler, S. (1997). Direct democracy and minority rights: Opinions on antigay and lesbian ballot initiatives. In S. L. Witt & S. McCorkle (Eds.), *Anti-gay rights: Assessing voter initiatives* (pp. 107-125). Westport, CT: Praeger.

Douglas, M. (1978). *Purity and danger: An analysis of pollution and taboo.* London: Routledge & Kegan Paul. (Original work published 1966)

Douglass, D. (1997). Taking the initiative: Anti-homosexual propaganda of the Oregon Citizen's Alliance. In S. L. Witt & S. McCorkle (Eds.), *Anti-gay rights: Assessing voter initiatives* (pp. 17-32). Westport, CT: Praeger.

Doupe, G. E. (1992). True to our tradition. In W. J. Blumenfeld (Ed.), *Homophobia: How we all pay the price* (pp.187-204). Boston: Beacon Press.

Duberman, M. (1993). *Stonewall.* New York: Penguin.

Duberman, M. (1997). The Anita Bryant brigade. In M. Blasius & S. Phelan (Eds.), *We are everywhere: Historical sourcebook of gay and lesbian politics* (pp. 443-450). New York: Routledge. (Original work published 1977)

Duggan, L. (1995). Making it perfectly queer. In L. Duggan & N. D. Hunter (Eds.), *Sex wars: Sexual dissent and political culture* (pp. 155-172). New York: Routledge.

Dynes, W. (1990). Wrestling with the social boa constructor. In E. Stein (Ed.), *Forms of desire: Sexual orientation and the social constructionist controversy* (pp. 209-238). New York: Garland.

Eaton, M. (1995). Homosexual unmodified: Speculations on law's discourse, race, and the construction of sexual identity. In D. Herman & C. Stychin (Eds.), *Sexual inversions: Lesbians, gay men, and the politics of law* (pp. 46-73). Philadelphia: Temple University Press.

Ebreo, L. (1997). A homosexual ghetto? In M. Blasius & S. Phelan (Eds.), *We are everywhere: Historical sourcebook of gay and lesbian politics* (pp. 340-343). New York: Routledge. (Original work published 1965)

Edelman, L. (1994). *Homographesis: Essays in gay literary and cultural theory.* New York: Routledge.

Edelman, M. (1964). *The symbolic uses of politics.* Urbana, IL: University of Illinois Press.

Edelman, M. (1988). *Constructing the political spectacle.* Chicago: University of Chicago Press.

Eder, K. (1993). *The new politics of class: Social movements and cultural dynamics in advanced societies.* Newbury Park, CA: Sage.

Ehrensaft, D., & Milkman, R. (1979). Sexuality and the state: The Briggs initiative and beyond. *Socialist Review, 9*(3), 55-72.

Ellingson, S. (1997). Understanding the dialectic of discourse and social action: Public debate and rioting in antebellum Cincinnati. In D. McAdam & D. A.

Snow (Eds.), *Social movements: Readings on their emergence, mobilization, and dynamics* (pp. 268-280). Los Angeles: Roxbury Press.

Elshtain, J. B. (1997). Against gay marriage. In A. Sullivan (Ed.), *Same-sex marriage: Pro and con* (pp. 57-60). New York: Vintage Books. (Original work published 1991)

Entman, R. M. (1993). Framing: Toward clarification of a fractured paradigm. *Journal of Communication, 43,* 51-58.

Epstein, S. (1990). Gay politics, ethnic identity: The limits of social constructionism. In E. Stein (Ed.), *Forms of desire: Sexual orientation and the social constructionist controversy* (pp. 239-293). New York: Garland.

Epstein, S. (1999). Gay and lesbian movements in the United States: Dilemmas of identity, diversity, and political strategy. In B. D Adam, J. W. Duyvendak, & A. Krouwel (Eds.), *The global emergence of gay and lesbian politics: National imprints of a worldwide movement* (pp. 30-90). Philadelphia: Temple University Press.

Escoffier, J. (1992). Generations and paradigms: Mainstreams in lesbian and gay studies. *Journal of Homosexuality, 24,*(1-2), 7-26.

Eskridge, W. N., Jr. (1996). *The case for same-sex marriage: From sexual liberty to civilized commitment.* New York: Free Press.

Esterberg, K. G. (1997). *Lesbian and bisexual identities: Constructing communities, constructing selves.* Philadelphia: Temple University Press.

Ettlbrick, P. L. (1992). Since when is marriage a path to liberation? In S. Sherman (Ed.), *Lesbian and gay marriage* (pp. 20-26). Philadelphia: Temple University Press.

Evans, C., & Gamman, L. (1995). The gaze revisited, or reviewing queer viewing. In P. Burston & C. Richardson (Eds.), *A queer romance: Lesbians, gay men and popular culture* (pp. 13-56). New York: Routledge.

Fairclough, N. (1992). *Discourse and social change.* Cambridge: Polity.

Falwell, J. (1980). *Listen America.* New York: Bantam Books.

Falwell, J. (1981). *The fundamentalist phenomenon: The resurgence of conservative Christianity.* Garden City, NY: Doubleday.

Fantasia, R. (1988). *Cultures of solidarity: Consciousness, action, and contemporary American workers.* Berkeley, CA: University of California Press.

Finnis, J. M. (1994). Law, morality, and "sexual orientation." *Notre Dame Law Review, 69,* 1049-1076.

Fisher, W. R. (1987). *Human communication as narration: Toward a philosophy of reason, value, and action.* Columbia, SC: University of South Carolina Press.

Fiske, J. (1992). British cultural studies and television. In R. C. Allen (Ed.), *Channels of discourse, reassembled* (2nd ed., pp. 284-326). Chapel Hill, NC: University of North Carolina Press.

Flynn, L. (1995). The Irish Supreme Court and the constitution of male homosexuality. In D. Herman & C. Stychin (Eds.), *Legal inversions: Lesbians, gay men, and the politics of law* (pp. 29-45). Philadelphia: Temple University Press.

Foley, D. (1998). A loss that moves us forward, is in the end, a victory. Human Rights Campaign. [Online]. Retrieved September 1998 from http://www.hrcusa.org/issues/index.html

Foucault, M. (1990). *The history of sexuality: An introduction.* (R. Hurley, Trans.). New York: Vintage Books. (Original work published 1978)

Fraser, N. (1989). *Unruly practices: Power, discourse, and gender in contemporary social theory.* Minneapolis, MN: University of Minnesota Press.

Friedman, D., & McAdam, D. (1992). Collective identity and activism: Networks, choices, and the life of a social movement. In A. D. Morris & C. M. Mueller (Eds.), *Frontiers in social movement theory* (pp. 156-173). New Haven, CT: Yale University Press.

Frye, M. (1997). Lesbian feminism and the gay rights movement: Another view of male supremacy, another separatism. In M. Blasius & S. Phelan (Eds.), *We are everywhere: Historical sourcebook of gay and lesbian politics* (pp. 499-510). New York: Routledge. (Original work published 1981)

Fuss, D. (1991). Inside/out. In Diane Fuss (Ed.), *Inside/out: Lesbian theories, gay theories* (pp. 1-10). New York: Routledge.

Gabel, P. (1992). Reification in legal reasoning. In J. Boyle (Ed.), *Critical legal studies* (p. 18). New York: New York University Press. (Original work published 1980)

Gallagher, J. (1994). The rise of fascism in America. In M. Thompson (Ed.), *Long road to freedom: The* Advocate *history of the gay and lesbian movement* (p. 396). New York: St. Martin's Press.

Gallagher, J. (1996, July 23). Love & war. *Advocate,* pp. 22-28.

Gallagher, J., & Bull, C. (1996). *Perfect enemies: The religious right, the gay movement, and the politics of the 1990s.* New York: Crown.

Gamson, J. (1989). Silence, death, and the invisible enemy: AIDS activism and social movement "newness." *Social Problems, 36,* 351-367.

Gamson, J. (1995). Must identity movements self-destruct? A queer dilemma. *Social Problems, 42,* 390-406.

Gamson, J. (1997). Messages of exclusion: Gender, movements, and symbolic boundaries. *Gender & Society, 11,* 178-199.

Gamson, J. (1998). *Freaks talk back: Tabloid talk shows and sexual nonconformity.* Chicago: University of Chicago Press.

Gamson, W. A. (1992a). The social psychology of collective action. In A. D. Morris & C. M. Mueller (Eds.), *Frontiers in social movement theory* (pp. 53-76). New Haven, CT: Yale University Press.

Gamson, W. A. (1992b). *Talking politics.* New York: Cambridge University Press.

Gamson, W. A., & Meyer, D. S. (1996). Framing political opportunity. In D. McAdam, J. D. McCarthy, & M. N. Zald (Eds.), *Comparative perspectives on social movement: Political opportunities, mobilizing structures, and cultural framings* (pp. 275-290). New York: Cambridge University Press.

Gamson, W. A., & Modigliani, A. (1989). Media discourse and public opinion on nuclear power: A constructionist approach. *American Journal of Sociology, 95*(1), 1-37.

Gellner, E. (1992). *Postmodernism, reason and religion.* New York: Routledge.

Ghent, B. (1998, September 1). Truth in advertising. *Advocate,* pp. 25-29.

Gilbert, A. N. (1981). Conceptions of homosexuality and sodomy in western history. In S. J. Licata & R. P. Peterson (Eds.), *Historical perspectives on homosexuality* (pp. 57-68). New York: Haworth Press.

Ginsberg, E. K. (1996). Introduction: The politics of passing. In E. K. Ginsberg (Ed.), *Passing and the fictions of identity* (pp. 1-18). Durham, NC: Duke University Press.

Gitlin, T. (1980). *The whole world is watching: Mass media in the making & unmaking of the new left.* Berkeley, CA: University of California Press.

Gitlin, T. (1995). *The twilight of common dreams: Why America is wracked by culture wars.* New York: Metropolitan Books.

Glendon, M. A. (1991). *Rights talk: The impoverishment of political discourse.* New York: Free Press.

Golden, J. L., Berquist, G. F., & Coleman, W. E. (1997). *The rhetoric of western thought* (6th ed.). Dubuque, IA: Kendall/Hunt.

Gomes, P. J. (1996). *The good book: Reading the Bible with mind and heart.* New York: Morrow.

Goodman, G., Lakey, G., Lashof, J., & Thorne, E. (1983). *No turning back: Lesbian and gay liberation for the '80s.* Philadelphia: New Society.

Goss, R. (1993). *Jesus acted up: A gay and lesbian manifesto.* San Francisco: HarperSanFrancisco.

Greenberg, D. F. (1988). *The construction of homosexuality.* Chicago: University of Chicago Press.

Griffin, C. L. (1996). The essentialist roots of the public sphere: A feminist critique. *Western Journal of Communication, 60,* 21-39.

Griffin, L. M. (1952). The rhetoric of historical movements. *Quarterly Journal of Speech, 38,* 184-188.

Gross, L. (1993). *Contested closets: The politics and ethics of outing.* Minneapolis, MN: University of Minnesota Press.

Gusfield, J. R. (1989a). The bridge over separated lands: Kenneth Burke's significance for the study of social action. In H. W. Simons & T. Melia (Eds.), *The legacy of Kenneth Burke* (pp. 28-54). Madison, WI: University of Wisconsin Press.

Gusfield, J. R. (1989b). Introduction. In J. R. Gusfield (Ed.), *On symbols and society* (pp. 1-49). Chicago: University of Chicago Press.

Guth, J. L. (1996). The politics of the Christian Right. In J. C. Green, J. L. Guth, C. E. Smidt, & L. A. Kellstedt (Eds.), *Religion and the culture wars: Dispatches from the front* (pp. 7-30). New York: Rowman & Littlefield.

Hacking, I. (1999). Are you a social constructionist. *Linguafranca: The Review of Academic Life, 9*(4), 65-72.

Hall, S. (1993). Deviance, politics, and the media. In H. Abelove, M. A. Barale, & D. M. Halperin (Eds.), *The lesbian and gay studies reader* (pp. 62-90). New York: Routledge.

Halley, J. E. (1994). Reasoning about sodomy: Act and identity in and after *Bowers v. Hardwick.Virginia Law Review, 79,* 1721-1780.

Halperin, D. M. (1990). *One hundred years of homosexuality: And other essays on Greek love.* New York: Routledge.

Halperin, D. M. (1995). *Saint Foucault: Towards a gay hagiography.* New York: Oxford University Press.

Hannigan, J. A. (1991). Social movement theory and the sociology of religion: Toward a new synthesis. *Sociological Analysis, 52,* 311-331.

Hardacre, H. (1993). The impact of fundamentalism on women, the family, and interpersonal relations. In M. E. Marty & R. S. Appleby (Eds.), *Fundamentalisms and society: Reclaiming the sciences, the family and education* (pp. 129-150). Chicago: University of Chicago Press.

Hardisty, J. (1993, March). Constructing homophobia: Colorado's right-wing attack on homosexuals. *Public Eye,* pp. 1-10.

Hart, J. (1997). Adam and Eve, not Adam and Henry. In R. M. Baird & S. E. Rosenbaum (Eds.), *Same-sex marriage: The moral and legal debate* (pp. 30-31). New York: Prometheus.

Hawley, J. S., & Proudfoot, W. (1994). Introduction. In J. S. Hawley (Ed.), *Fundamentalism and gender* (pp. 3-44). New York: Oxford University Press.

Heinz, D. (1983). The struggle to define America. In R. C. Liebman & R. Wuthnow (Eds.), *The new Christian Right: Mobilization and legitimation* (pp. 133-148). New York: Aldine.

Helms, A. (1995). *Young man from the provinces: A gay life before Stonewall.* New York: Faber & Faber.

Hennessy, R. (1995). Queer visibility in commodity culture. In L. Nicholson & S. Seidman (Eds.), *Social postmodernism* (pp. 142-183). New York: Cambridge University Press.

Herdt, G., & Boxer, A. (1992). Introduction: Culture, history, and life course of gay men. In G. Herdt (Ed.), *Gay culture in America: Essays from the field* (pp. 1-28). Boston: Beacon Press.

Herek, G. M. (1984). Beyond "homophobia:" A social psychological perspective on attitudes toward lesbians and gay men. *Journal of Homosexuality, 10*(1-2), 1-21.

Herman, D. (1994). *Rights of passage: Struggles for lesbian and gay legal equality.* Toronto: University of Toronto Press.

Herman, D. (1997). *The antigay agenda: Orthodox vision and the Christian right.* Chicago: University of Chicago Press.

Herrell, R. K. (1993). The symbolic strategies of Chicago's gay and lesbian pride day parade. In G. Herdt (Ed.), *Gay culture in America: Essays from the field* (pp. 225-252). Boston: Beacon Press.

Highwater, J. (1997). *The mythology of transgression: Homosexuality as metaphor.* New York: Oxford University Press.

Himmelstein, J. L. (1983). The new right. In R. C. Liebman & R. Wuthnow (Ed.), *The new Christian Right: Mobilization and legitimation* (pp.13-30). New York: Aldine.

Himmelstein, J. L. (1990). *To the right: The transformation of American conservatism.* Berkeley, CA: University of California Press.

Hodge, R., & Kress, G. (1993). *Language as ideology* (2nd ed.). New York: Routledge.

Hoffman, R. J. (1984). Vices, gods, and virtues: Cosmology as a mediating factor in attitudes toward male homosexuality. *Journal of Homosexuality, 9*(2-3), 27-44.

Hooker, E. (1957). The adjustment of the male overt homosexual. *Journal of Projective Techniques, 21,* 18-31.

Hovermill, J. W. (1994). A conflict of laws and morals: The choice of law implications of Hawaii's recognition of same-sex marriage. *Maryland Law Review, 53,* 450-493.

Hunt, S. A., Benford, R. D., & Snow, D. A. (1994). Identity fields: Framing processes and the social construction of movement identities. In E. Larana, H. Johnston, & J. R. Gusfield (Eds.), *New social movements: From ideology to identity* (pp. 185-208). Philadelphia: Temple University Press.

Hunter, J. D. (1983a). *American evangelicalism: Conservative religion and the quandry of modernity.* New Brunswick, NJ: Rutgers University Press.

Hunter, J. D. (1983b). The liberal reaction. In R. C. Liebman & R. Wuthnow (Eds.), *The new Christian Right: Mobilization and legitimation* (pp. 149-163). New York: Aldine.

Hunter, J. D. (1987). *Evangelicalism: The coming generation.* Chicago: University of Chicago Press.

Hunter, J. D. (1991). *Culture wars: The struggle to define America.* New York: Basic Books.

Hunter, J. D. (1994). *Before the shooting begins: Searching for democracy in America's culture war.* New York: Free Press.

Iltis, R. S., & Browne, S. H. (1990). Tradition and resurgence in American public address studies. In G. M. Phillips & J. T. Wood (Eds.), *Speech communication: Essays to commemorate the 75th anniversary of the Speech Communication Association* (pp. 81-93). Carbondale, IL: Southern Illinois University Press.

Introduction. (1993). *Radical America, 24*(4), 1-13.

Jackson, S. (1993). Introduction—feminist social theory. In S. Jackson, K. Atkinson, D. Beddoe, & T. Brewer (Eds.), *Women's studies: Essential readings* (pp. 3-7). New York: New York University Press.

Jacobs, A. M. (1993). The rhetorical construction of rights: The case of the gay rights movement, 1969-1991. *Nebraska Law Review, 72,* 723-759.

Jeremiah Films. (1993). *Gay rights, special rights: Inside the homosexual agenda.* [Videocassette].

Johnston, H., Larana, E., & Gusfield, J. R. (1994). Identities, grievances, and new social movements. In E. Larana, H. Johnston, & J. R. Gusfield (Eds.), *New social movements: From ideology to identity* (pp. 3-35). Philadelphia: Temple University Press.

Jones, S. L. (1993, July 19). The loving opposition: Speaking the truth in a climate of hate. *Christianity Today,* pp. 18-25.

Jonsen, A. R., & Toulmin, S. (1988). *The abuse of casuistry: A history of moral reasoning.* Berkeley, CA: University of California Press.

Jordan, G., & Weedon, C. (1995). *Cultural politics: Class, gender, race and the postmodern world.* Cambridge: Blackwell.

Judis, J. B. (1994, September 12). Crosses to bear. *New Republic,* pp. 21-25.

Kaiser, C. (1997). *The gay metropolis: 1940-1996*. Boston: Houghton-Mifflin.

Kameny, F. (1997). Gay is good. In M. Blasius & S. Phelan (Eds.), *We are everywhere: Historical sourcebook of gay and lesbian politics* (pp. 367-376). New York: Routledge. (Original work published 1969)

Kantrowitz, A. (1997). Letter to the queer generation. In M. Blasius & S. Phelan (Eds.), *We are everywhere: Historical sourcebook of gay and lesbian politics* (pp. 812-817). New York: Routledge. (Original work published 1992)

Kaplan, M. B. (1997). *Sexual justice: Democratic citizenship and the politics of desire*. New York: Routledge.

Kauffman, L. A. (1990). The anti-politics of identity. *Socialist Review, 20,* 67-80.

Kazin, M. (1995). *The populist persuasion: An American history*. New York: Basic Books.

Keane, T. M. (1995). Aloha, Marriage? Constitutional and choice of law arguments for recognition of same-sex marriages. *Stanford Law Review, 47,* 499-532.

Keen, L., & Goldberg, S. B. (1998). *Strangers to the law: Gay people on trial*. Ann Arbor, MI: University of Michigan Press.

Kellstedt, L. A., Green, J. C., Guth, J. L., & Smidt, C. E. (1996). Religious voting blocs in the 1992 election: The year of the evangelical. In J. C. Green, J. L. Guth, C. E. Smidt, & L. A. Kellstedt (Eds.), *Religion and the culture wars: Dispatches from the front* (pp. 267-290). New York: Rowman & Littlefield.

Kelly, G. (1975). *The political struggle of active homosexuals to gain social acceptance*. Chicago: Franciscan Herald Press.

Kennedy, E. L., & Davis, M. D. (1993). *Boots of leather, slippers of gold: The history of a lesbian community*. New York: Routledge.

Kimmel, M. S. (1993). Sexual balkanization: Gender and sexuality as the new ethnicities. *Social Research, 60,* 571-587.

King, M. A. (1998). *Fractured dance: Steps and missteps in conversation and in application of Gadamer to a Mennonite debate on homosexuality*. Unpublished doctoral dissertation, Temple University, Philadelphia.

Kinsey, A. C., Pomeroy, W. B., & Martin, C. E. (1948). *Sexual behavior in the human male*. Philadelphia: W. B. Saunders.

Kirby, D. (1998, November 24). From soft words to hard fists. *Advocate,* pp. 39-41.

Kirk, M., & Madsen, H. (1989). *After the ball: How America will conquer its fear and hatred of gays in the '90s*. New York: Doubleday.

Kitzinger, C. (1987). *The social construction of lesbianism*. London: Sage.

Klandermans, B. (1992). The social construction of protest and multiorganizational fields. In A. D. Morris & C. M. Mueller (Eds.), *Frontiers in social movement theory* (pp. 77-103). New Haven, CT: Yale University Press.

Klatch, R. E. (1987). *Women of the new right*. Philadelphia: Temple University Press.

Klumpp, J. F., & Hollihan, T. A. (1989). Rhetorical criticism as moral action. *Quarterly Journal of Speech, 75,* 84-97.

Knight, R. H. (1997a). How domestic partnerships and "gay marriage" threaten the family. In R. M. Baird & S. E. Rosenbaum (Eds), *Same-sex marriage: The moral and legal debate* (pp. 108-121). New York: Prometheus.

Knight, R. H. (1997b). Mom-and-dad homes help mold healthy kids. In T. L. Roleff (Ed.), *Gay rights* (pp. 84-89). San Diego, CA: Greenhaven Press.

Kramer, L. (1997). Same-sex marriage, conflict of laws, and the unconstitutional policy exception. *Yale Law Journal, 106,* 1965-2008.

LaCaye, R. (1998, October 26). The new gay struggle. *Time,* pp. 33-36.

LaHaye, T. (1978). *The unhappy gays: What everyone should know about homosexuality.* Wheaton, IL: Tyndale.

LaHaye, T. (1980). *The battle for the mind.* Old Tappan, NY: Revelle.

LaHaye, T. (1982). *The battle for the family.* Old Tappan, NY: Revelle.

LaHaye, T., & LaHaye, B. (1994). *A nation without a conscience.* Wheaton, IL: Tyndale House.

Lake, R. A. (1984). Order and disorder in anti-abortion rhetoric: A logological view. *Quarterly Journal of Speech, 70,* 425-433.

Legg, D. (1997). I am glad I am a homosexual. In M. Blasius & S. Phelan (Eds.), *We are everywhere: Historical sourcebook of gay and lesbian politics* (pp. 323-326). New York: Routledge. (Original work published 1958)

Let them wed. (1996, January 6). *The Economist,* pp. 13-14.

LeVay, S. (1996). *Queer science: The use and abuse of research into homosexuality.* Cambridge, MA: MIT Press.

LeVay, S., & Nonas, E. (1995). *City of friends: A portrait of the gay and lesbian community in America.* Cambridge, MA: MIT Press.

Levin, D. (1997). The Constitution as rhetorical symbol in western anti-gay rights initiatives. In S. L. Witt and S. McCorkle (Eds.), *Anti-gay rights: Assessing voter initiatives* (pp. 33-49). Westport, CT: Praeger.

Levine, M. P. (1992). The life and death of gay clones. In G. Herdt (Ed.), *Gay culture in America: Essays from the field* (pp. 68-86). Boston: Beacon Press.

Lewes, K. (1988). *The psychoanalytic theory of male homosexuality.* New York: New American Library.

Licata, S. J. (1981). The homosexual rights movement in the United States: A traditionally overlooked area of American history. In S. J. Licata & R. P. Peterson (Eds.), *Historical perspectives on homosexuality* (pp. 161-189). New York: Haworth Press.

Lienesch, M. (1993). *Redeeming America: Piety and politics in the new Christian Right.* Chapel Hill, NC: University of North Carolina Press.

Lipset, S. M., & Raab, E. (1970). *The politics of unreason.* New York: Harper & Row.

Lo, C. U. H. (1982). Counter-movements and conservative movements in the contemporary U.S. *Annual Review of Sociology, 8,* 107-134.

Loughery, J. (1998). *The other side of silence: Men's lives and gay identities: A twentieth-century history.* New York: Henry Holt.

Luke, T. W. (1989). *Screens of power: Ideology, domination, and resistance in informational society.* Urbana, IL: University of Illinois Press.

Lyotard, J. F. (1984). *The postmodern condition: A report on knowledge.* Minneapolis, MN: University of Minnesota Press.

Magnuson, R. (1985). *Are "gay rights" right? A report on homosexuality and the law.* St. Paul, MN: Berean League Fund.

Magnuson, R. (1994). *Informed answers to gay rights questions.* Sisters, OR: Multnomah Press.

Manegold, C. S. (1993, April 18). The odd place of homosexuality in the military. *New York Times,* Section 4: pp. A1, A3.

Marcus, E. (1993). Coming of age. In E. Marcus (Ed.), *Making history: The struggle for gay and lesbian rights, 1945-1990* (pp. 257-259). New York: Harper Perennial.

Martin, A. D., & Hetrick, E. S. (1988). The stigmatization of the gay and lesbian adolescent. *Journal of Homosexuality, 15* (1-2), 163-183.

Marty, M. E. (1984). Fundamentalism as a social phenomenon. In G. Marsden (Ed.), *Evangelicalism and modern America* (pp. 56-68). Grand Rapids, MI: Eerdmans.

Marty, M. E., & Appleby, R. S. (1993). Introduction: A sacred cosmos, scandalous code, defiant society. In M. E. Marty & R. S. Appleby (Eds.), *Fundamentalism and society: Reclaiming the sciences, the family, and America* (pp. 1-19). Chicago: University of Chicago Press.

Mathews, D. G., & De Hart, J. S. (1990). *Sex, gender, and the politics of ERA: A state and the nation.* New York: Oxford University Press.

McAdam, D. (1994). Culture and social movements. In E. Larana, H. Johnston, & J. R. Gusfield (Eds.), *New social movements: From ideology to identity* (pp. 36-57). Philadelphia: Temple University Press.

McAdam, D. (1996). Conceptual origins, current problems, future directions. In D. McAdam, J. D. McCarthy, & M. N. Zald (Eds.), *Comparative perspectives on social movements: Political opportunities, mobilizing structures, and cultural framings* (pp. 23-40). New York: Cambridge University Press.

McAdam, D., & Snow, D. A. (1997). Introduction—social movements: Conceptual and theoretical issues. In D. McAdam & D. A. Snow (Eds.), *Social movements: Readings on their emergence, mobilization, and dynamics* (pp. xviii-xxvi). Los Angeles: Roxbury Press.

McCarthy, J. D., & Zald, M. N. (1987). The trend of social movements in America: Professionalization and resource mobilization. In M. N. Zald & J. D. McCarthy (Eds.), *Social movements in an organizational society: Collected essays* (pp. 337-391). New Brunswick, NJ: Transaction Books.

McCorkle, S., & Most, M. G. (1997). Fear and loathing on the editorial page: An analysis of Idaho's anti-gay initiative. In S. L. Witt & S. McCorkle (Eds.), *Anti-gay rights: Assessing voter initiatives* (pp. 63-76). Westport, CT: Praeger.

McDonald, H. (Producer). (1994). *Ballot Measure 9.* [Videocassette].

McGee, M. C. (1975). In search of "the people": A rhetorical alternative. *Quarterly Journal of Speech, 61,* 235-249.

McGee, M. C. (1980a). "Social movement": Phenomenon or meaning. *Central States Speech Journal, 31,* 233-244.

McGee, M.C. (1980b). The "ideograph": A link between rhetoric and ideology. *Quarterly Journal of Speech, 66,* 1-16.

McGee, M. C. (1990). The text, context, and the fragmentation of contemporary culture. *Western Journal of Speech Communication, 54,* 274-289.

McGee, M. C., & Martin, M. A. (1983). Public knowledge and ideological argumentation. *Communication Monographs, 50,* 47-65.

McIntosh, M. (1990). The homosexual role. In E. Stein (Ed.), *Forms of desire: Sexual orientation and the social constructionist controversy* (pp. 25-42). New York: Routledge.

McIntyre, A. (1981). *After virtue: A study in moral theory.* London: Duckworth.

McKerrow, R. E. (1989). Critical rhetoric: Theory and praxis. *Speech Monographs, 56,* 91-111.

McNeil, J. J. (1988). *The church and the homosexual* (3rd ed.). Boston: Beacon Press.

Medhurst, M. J. (1982). The First Amendment vs. human rights: A case study in community sentiment and argument from definition. *Western Journal of Speech Communication, 46,* 1-19.

Melucci, A. (1985). The symbolic challenge of contemporary movements. *Social Research, 52,* 781-816.

Meyer, D. S., & Staggenborg, S. (1996). Movements, countermovements, and the structure of political opportunity. *American Journal of Sociology, 101,* 1628-1660.

Mieli, M. (1980). *Homosexuality and liberation: Elements of a gay critique.* London: Gay Men's Press. (Original work published 1970)

Miller, D. H. (1998). *Freedom to differ: The shaping of the gay and lesbian struggle for civil rights.* New York: New York University Press.

Miller, S. H. (1996). Gay white males: PC's unseen target. In B. Bawer (Ed.), *Beyond queer: Challenging gay left orthodoxy* (pp. 24-37). New York: Free Press. (Original work published 1994)

Mitchell, A. (1998, June 16). Gay behavior is described as sin by Lott. *New York Times,* p. A24.

Moen, M. C. (1992). The Christian Right in the United States. In M. C. Moen & L. S. Gustafson (Eds.), *The religious challenge to the state* (pp. 75-101). Philadelphia: Temple University Press.

Mohr, R. D. (1988). *Gays/justice: A study of ethics, society, and law.* New York: Columbia University Press.

Mohr, R. D. (1992). *Gay ideas: Outing and other controversies.* Boston: Beacon Press.

Mohr, R. D. (1994). *A more perfect union: Why straight America must stand up for gay rights.* Boston: Beacon Press.

Moon, J. D. (1993). *Constructing community: Moral pluralism and tragic conflicts.* Princeton, NJ: Princeton University Press.

Mouffe, C. (1995). Feminism, citizenship, and radical democratic politics. In L. Nicholson & S. Seidman (Eds.), *Social postmodernism* (pp. 315-331). New York: Cambridge University Press.

Nagel, J. (1994). Constructing ethnicity: Creating and recreating ethnic identity and culture. *Social Problems, 41,* 152-176.

Nava, M., & Dawidoff, R. (1994). *Why gay rights matter to America.* New York: St. Martin's Press.

Neuhaus, R. J. (1984). *The naked public square: Religion and democracy in America*. Grand Rapids, MI: Eerdmans.

Nicholson, L., & Seidman, S. (1995). Introduction. In L. Nicholson & S. Seidman (Eds.), *Social postmodernism* (pp. 1-35). New York: Cambridge University Press.

Nicolosi, J. (1991). *Reparative therapy of male homosexuality: A new clinical approach*. Northvale, NJ: Jason Aronson.

Noel, L. (1994). *Intolerance: A general survey*. (A. Bennett, Trans). Montreal: McGill-Queens University Press.

Norton, R. (1992). *Mother Clap's molly house: The gay subculture in England 1700-1830*. London: GMP Publishers.

Notebook. (1994, November 14). *New Republic*, p. 8.

Oberschall, A. (1993). *Social movements: Ideologies, interests, and identities*. New Brunswick: Transaction.

Olson, K. M., & Goodnight, G. T. (1994). Entanglements of consumption, cruelty, privacy, and fashion: The social controversy over fur. *Quarterly Journal of Speech, 80*, 249-276.

Orlando on God's hit list, Robertson says. (1998, June 10). *Los Angeles Times*, p. A15.

Ortiz, D. R. (1993). Creating controversy: Essentialism and constructivism and the politics of gay identity. *Virginia Law Review, 79*, 1833-1857.

Padgug, R. A. (1989). Gay villain, gay hero: Homosexuality and the social construction of AIDS. In K. Peiss & C. Simmons (Eds.), *Passion and power: Sexuality in history* (pp. 293-313). Philadelphia: Temple University Press.

Padgug, R. A. (1990). Sexual matters: On conceptualizing sexuality in history. In E. Stein (Ed.), *Forms of desire: Sexual orientation and the social constructionist controversy* (pp. 43-67). New York: Garland.

Patton, C. (1993). Tremble, hetero swine. In M. Warner (Ed.), *Fear of a queer planet: Queer politics and social theory* (pp. 143-177). Minneapolis, MN: University of Minnesota Press.

Patullo, E. L. (1992, December). Straight talk about gays. *Commentary*, pp. 21-24.

Pearce, W. B. (1989). *Communication and the human condition*. Carbondale, IL: Southern Illinois University Press.

Pearce, W. B., & Littlejohn, S. W. (1997). *Moral conflict: When social worlds collide*. Thousand Oaks, CA: Sage.

Pearce, W. B., Littlejohn, S. W., & Alexander, A. (1987). The new Christian Right and the humanist response: Reciprocated diatribe. *Communication Quarterly, 35*, 171-192.

Pellegrini, A. 1992. S(h)ifting the terms of hetero/sexism: Gender, power, homophobia. In W. J. Blumenfeld (Ed.), *Homophobia: How we all pay the price* (pp. 39-56). Boston: Beacon Press.

People for the American Way (Producer). (1994). *Religious right: Then and now* [Videocassette].

Peters, P. J. (1996). Intolerance of, discrimination against, and the death penalty for homosexuals is prescribed in the Bible. [Online]. Retrieved March 1997 from http://www.kansas.net/ 7Esfa/files/homo.html

Phelan, S. (1989). *Identity politics: Lesbian feminism and the limits of community.* Philadelphia: Temple University Press.

Phelan, S. (1994). *Getting specific: Postmodern lesbian politics.* Minneapolis, MN: University of Minnesota Press.

Pietrzyk, M. E. (1994b, January 26). The man behind the myths: A report on the chief anti-gay researcher of the religious right. *LCR Briefing,* pp. 1-13.

Pietrzyk, M. E. (1994a, October 3). Queer science. *New Republic,* pp. 10-12.

Plummer, K. (1975). *Sexual stigma: An interactionist account.* London: Routledge & Kegan Paul.

Podhoretz, N. (1977, October). The culture of appeasement. *Harper's,* pp. 25-32.

Podhoretz, N. (1996, November). How the gay-rights movement won. *Commentary,* pp. 32-41.

Polikoff, N. D. (1993). We will get what we ask for: Why legalizing gay and lesbian marriage will not dismantle the legal structure of gender in every marriage. *Virginia Law Review, 79,* 1535-1550.

Posner, R. A. (1992). *Sex and reason.* Cambridge, MA: Harvard University Press.

Praeger, D. (1993, Summer). Homosexuality, the Bible, and us—a Jewish perspective. *Public Interest,* pp. 60-83.

Prejudice against homosexuals. (1997). In M. Blasius & S. Phelan (Eds.), *We are everywhere: Historical sourcebook of gay and lesbian politics* (pp. 229-330). New York: Routledge. (Original work published 1932)

Pronk, P. (1993). *Against nature?: Types of moral argumentation regarding homosexuality.* Grand Rapids, MI: Eerdmans.

Purden, T. S. (1996, September 22). Gay rights groups attack Clinton after midnight signing. *New York Times,* p. A22.

Quinn, D. M. (1996). *Same-sex dynamics among nineteenth-century Americans: A Mormon example.* Urbana, IL: University of Illinois Press.

Railsback, C. C. (1984). The contemporary American abortion controversy: Stages in the argument. *Quarterly Journal of Speech, 70,* 410-424.

Rattansi, A. (1995). Just framing: Ethnicities and racisms in a "postmodern" framework. In L. Nicholson & S. Seidman (Eds.), *Social postmodernism* (pp. 250-286). New York: Cambridge University Press.

Rauch, J. (1996, May 6). For better or worse? *New Republic,* 18-23.

Rawls, J. (1993). *Political liberalism.* New York: Columbia University Press.

Reed, R. (1994). *Politically incorrect: The emerging faith factor in American politics.* Dallas, TX: Word Publishing.

Reed, R. (1996). *Active faith: How Christians are changing the soul of American politics.* New York: Free Press.

Reed, T. V. (1992). *Fifteen jugglers, five believers: Literary politics and the poetics of American social movements.* Berkeley, CA: University of California Press.

Rees, M. (1992, January 8). Homocons: The march of the pink elephants. *New Republic,* pp. 30-31.

Rich, F. (1996, May 25). I got you, babe. *New York Times,* p. 15.

Rich, F. (1998, December 5). The family research charade. *New York Times,* p. A13.

Richards, D. A. J. (1998). *Women, gays, and the constitution: The grounds for feminism and gay rights in culture and law.* Chicago: University of Chicago Press.

Riggle, E. D., & Ellis, A. L. (1994). Political tolerance of homosexuals: The role of group attitudes and legal principles. *Journal of Homosexuality, 26,*(4), 135-147.

Rofes, E. (1996). *Reviving the tribe: Regenerating gay men's sexuality and culture in the ongoing epidemic.* New York: Harrington Park Press.

Rohy, V. (1996). Displacing desire: Passing, nostalgia, and *Giovanni's Room.* In E. K. Ginsberg (Ed.), *Passing and the fictions of identity* (pp. 218-233). Durham, NC: Duke University Press.

Roof, J., & Wiegman, R. (1995a). Introduction. In J. Roof & R. Wiegman (Eds.), *Who can speak: Authority and critical identity* (pp. ix-xi). Urbana, IL: University of Illinois Press.

Roof, J., & Wiegman, R. (1995b). Partially speaking. In J. Roof & R. Wiegman (Eds.), *Who can speak: Authority and critical identity* (pp. 93-95). Urbana, IL: University of Illinois Press.

Rorty, R. (1989). *Contingency, irony, and solidarity.* Cambridge: Cambridge University Press.

Rosenau, P. M. (1992). *Post-modernism and the social sciences: Insights, inroads, and intrusions.* Princeton, NJ: Princeton University Press.

Rubin, G. S. (1993). Thinking sex. Notes for a radical theory of the politics of sexuality. In H. Abelove, M. A. Barale, & D. M. Halperin (Eds.),*The lesbian and gay studies reader* (pp. 3-44). New York: Routledge. (Original work published 1982)

Rueda, E. (1982). *The homosexual network: Private lives and public policy.* Old Greenwich, CT: Devin Adair.

Ruse, M. (1988). *Homosexuality: A philosophical inquiry.* London: Blackwell.

Russo, V. (1987). *The celluloid closet: Homosexuality in the movies* (Rev. ed.). New York: Harper & Row.

Scalia, A. (1996). Dissent. *Supreme Court Register, 116,* 1629-1637.

Schacter, J. S. (1994). The gay civil rights debate in the states: Decoding the discourse of equivalents. *Harvard Civil Rights—Civil Liberties Law Review, 29,* 283-317.

Schaeffer, F. A. (1982). *A Christian manifesto.* (Rev. ed.). Westchester, IL: Crossways Books.

Schmitt, E. (1993, January 27). Military cites wide range of reasons for its gay ban. *New York Times,* pp. A1, A8.

Schulman, S. (1994). *My American history: Lesbian and gay life during the Reagan/ Bush years.* New York: Routledge.

Scott, A. (1990). *Ideology and the new social movements.* London: Unwin Hyman.

Sedgwick, E. K. (1993). How to bring your kids up gay. In M. Warner (Ed.), *Fear of a queer planet: Queer politics and social theory* (pp. 69-81). Minneapolis, MN: University of Minnesota Press.

Seidman, S. (1993). Identity and politics in a "postmodern" gay culture: Some historical and conceptual notes. In M. Warner (Ed.), *Fear of a queer planet: Queer politics and social theory* (pp. 105-142). Minneapolis, MN: University of Minnesota Press.

Seidman, S. (1995). Deconstructing queer theory or the under-theorization of the social and the ethical. In L. Nicholson & S. Seidman (Eds.), *Social postmodernism* (pp. 116-141). New York: Cambridge University Press.

Seidman, S. (1996). Introduction. In S. Seidman (Ed.), *Queer theory/sociology* (pp. 1-29). Cambridge: Blackwell.

Sexual orientation and the law. (1990). (Eds.), *Harvard Law Review.* Cambridge: Havard University Press.

Shaw, S. (1997). No longer a sleeping giant: The re-awakening of religious conservatives in American politics. In S. L. Witt & S. McCorkle (Eds.), *Anti-gay rights: Assessing voter initiatives* (pp. 7-16). Westport, CT: Praeger.

Shepherd, S., & Wallis, M. (1989). Introduction. In S. Shepherd & M. Wallis (Eds.), *Coming on strong: Gay politics and culture* (pp. 1-21). London: Unwin Hyman.

Shilts, R. (1993). *Conduct unbecoming: Gays & lesbians in the U.S. military.* New York: St. Martin's Press.

Short, B. (1991). Earth First! and the rhetoric of moral confrontation. *Communication Studies, 42,* 172-188.

Siegel, P. (1991). Lesbian and gay rights as a free speech issue: A review of relevant caselaw. *Journal of Homosexuality, 21*(1-2), 203-259.

Signorile, M. (1993). *Queer in America: Sex, sin, the media and the closets of power.* New York: Random House.

Silverstein, C. (1991). Psychotherapy and psychotherapists: A history. In C. Silverstein (Ed.), *Gays, lesbians, and their therapists: Studies in psychotherapy* (pp. 1-15). New York: Norton.

Simones, A. (1998, April). Do you take this person? The Constitution and same-sex marriage. Paper presented at the Western Political Science Association Conference, Denver, CO.

Simons, H. W. (1970). Requirements, problems, and strategies: A theory of persuasion for social movements. *Quarterly Journal of Speech, 56,* 1-11.

Simons, H. W. (1994). "Going meta": Definition and political applications. *Quarterly Journal of Speech, 80,* 468-481.

Simpson, J. H. (1983). Moral issues and status politics. In R. C. Liebman & R. Wuthnow (Eds.), *The new Christian Right: Mobilization and legitimation* (pp. 187-205). New York: Aldine.

Simpson, J. H. (1992). Fundamentalism in America revisited: The fading of modernity as a source of symbolic capital. In B. Misztal & A. Shupe (Eds.), *Religion and politics in comparative perspective: Revival of religious fundamentalism in East and West* (pp. 10-27). Westport, CT: Praeger.

Sinfield, A. (1994). *Cultural politics—Queer reading.* Philadelphia: University of Pennsylvania Press.

Slagle, R. A. (1995). In defense of Queer Nation: From *identity politics* to a *politics of difference.Western Journal of Communication, 59,* 85-102.

Smith, A. M. (1994). *New right discourse on race & sexuality: Britain, 1968-1990.* New York: Cambridge University Press.

Smith, B. H. (1997). *Belief and resistance: Dynamics of contemporary intellectual controversy.* Cambridge, MA: Harvard University Press.

Smith, R. R. (1997). Secular anti-gay advocacy in the Springfield, Missouri, bias crime ordinance debate. In S. L. Witt & S. McCorkle (Eds.), *Anti-gay rights: Assessing voter initiatives* (pp. 95-106). Westport, CT: Praeger.

Smith, R. R., & Windes, R. R. (1975). The innovational movement: A rhetorical theory. *Quarterly Journal of Speech, 61,* 140-153.

Smith, R. R., & Windes, R. R. (1993). Symbolic convergence and abolitionism: A terministic reinterpretation. *Southern Communication Quarterly, 59,* 45-59.

Smith, R. R., & Windes, R. R. (1997). The progay and antigay issue culture: Interpretation, influence and dissent. *Quarterly Journal of Speech, 63,* 28-48.

Smith, R. R., & Windes, R. R. (1999). Identity in political context: Lesbian/gay representation in the public sphere. *Journal of Homosexuality, 37*(2), 25-45.

Snow, D. A., & Anderson, L. (1987). Identity work among the homeless: The verbal construction and avowal of personal identities. *American Journal of Sociology, 92,* 1336-1371.

Snow, D. A., & Benford, R. D. (1992). Master frames and cycles of protest. In A. D. Morris & C. McClurg Mueller (Eds.), *Frontiers in social movement theory* (pp. 133-155). New Haven, CT: Yale University Press.

Snow, D. A., Rockford, E., B., Worden, S. K., & Benford, R. D. (1986). Frame alignment processes, micro-mobilization and movement participation. *American Sociological Review, 51,* 464-481.

Socarides, C. W. (1968). *The overt homosexual.* New York: Greene & Stratton.

Socarides, C. W. (1978). *Homosexuality.* New York: Jason Aronson.

Socarides, C. W. (1995). *Homosexuality: A freedom too far.* Phoenix, AZ: Adam Margrave.

Solomon, M. (1993). The things we study: Texts and their interaction. *Communication Monographs,60,* 62-68.

Somers, M. R., & Gibson, G. D. (1994). Reclaiming the epistemological "other": Narrative and the social constitution of identity. In C. Calhoun (Ed.), *Social theory and the politics of identity* (pp. 37-99). Oxford: Blackwell.

Spivak, G. C. (1993). *Outside the teaching machine.* New York: Routledge.

Stein, A., & Plummer, K. (1996). "I can't even think straight:" "Queer" theory and the missing sexual revolution in sociology. In S. Seidman (Ed.), *Queer theory/sociology* (pp. 129-144). Cambridge: Blackwell.

Stein, E. (1990). Conclusion. In E. Stein (Ed.), *Forms of desire: Sexual orientation and the social constructionist controversy* (pp. 325-353). New York: Garland.

Stewart, C. J. (1991). The internal rhetoric of the Knights of Labor. *Communication Studies, 42,* 67-82.

Stewart, C. J., Smith, C. A., & Denton, R. E., Jr. (1994). *Persuasion and social movements* (3rd ed.). Prospect Heights, IL: Waveland Press.

Stolberg, S. G. (1997, November 23). Gay culture weighs sense and sexuality. *New York Times,* Section 4, pp. 1, 8.

Streitmatter, R. (1993). *Unspeakable: The rise of the gay and lesbian press in America.* Boston: Faber & Faber.

Strozier, C. B. (1994). *Apocalypse: On the psychology of fundamentalism in America*. Boston: Beacon Press.

Stychin, C. F. (1998). *A nation by rights: National identities, sexual identity politics, and the discourse of rights*. New York: Temple University Press.

Subcommittee on the Constitution, Committee on the Judiciary, House of Representatives. (1990, May 15). Defense of Marriage Act. Washington, DC: U.S. Government Printing Office.

Sullivan, A. (1995). *Virtually normal: An argument about homosexuality*. New York: Knopf.

Swan, W. (1997). Foreword. In W. Swan (Ed.), *Gay/lesbian/bisexual/transgender public policy issues: A citizen's and administrator's guide to the new cultural struggle* (pp. xvii-xxii). New York: Harrington Park Press.

Tajfel, H. (1981). *Human groups and social categories: Studies in social categories*. Cambridge: Cambridge University Press.

Tarrow, S. (1994). *Power in movement: Social movements, collective action and politics*. New York: Cambridge University Press.

Taylor, C. A. (1992). Of audience, expertise and authority: The evolving creationism debate. *Quarterly Journal of Speech, 78,* 277-295.

Taylor, V., & Whittier, N. E. (1992). Collective identity in social movement communities: Lesbian feminist mobilization. In A. D. Morris & C. M. Mueller (Eds.), *Frontiers of social movement theory* (pp. 104-130). New Haven, CT: Yale University Press.

The other minority. (1992, March 30). *New Republic,* p. 7.

Therborn, G. (1980). *The ideology of power and the power of ideology*. London: Verso.

Thomas, C., & Dobson, E. (1999). *Blinded by might: Can the religious right save America*. Grand Rapids: Zondervan.

Thompson, J. B. (1984). *Studies in the theory of ideologies*. Berkeley, CA: University of California Press.

Thompson, J. B. (1991). Editor's introduction. In J. B. Thompson (Ed.), *Language and symbolic power* (pp.1-31). Oxford: Polity Press.

Thumma, S. (1991). Negotiating a religious identity: The case of the gay evangelical. *Sociological Analysis, 52,* 333-347.

Tilly, C. (1978). *From mobilization to revolution*. Reading, PA: Addison-Wesley.

Tomasky, M. (1996). *Left for dead: The life, death and possible resurrection of progressive politics in America*. New York: Free Press.

Touraine, A. (1985). The symbolic challenge to the study of social movements. *Social Research, 52,* 781-787.

Trasandes, M. (1998, July 12). Hate the sinner. *Frontiers,* p. 12.

Trosino, J. (1993). American wedding: Same-sex marriage and the miscegenation analogy. *Boston University Law Review, 73,* 93-120.

Vaid, U. (1995). *Virtual equality: The mainstreaming of gay & lesbian liberation*. New York: Anchor Books.

van der Meer, T. (1993). Review of J. Weeks, *Against Nature. Journal of Homosexuality, 25*(4), 131-135.

Vanderford, M. L. (1989). Vilification and social movements: A case study of pro-life and pro-choice rhetoric. *Quarterly Journal of Speech, 75,* 166-182.

Verhover, S. H. (1993, August 21). Gay groups denounce the Pentagon's new policy. *New York Times,* p. A16.

Wald, K. D. (1992). *Religion and politics in the United States* (2nd ed.). Washington, DC: Congressional Quarterly.

Walters, S. D. (1996). From here to queer: Radical feminism, postmodernism, and the lesbian menace (or why can't a woman be more like a fag?). *Signs, 21,* 830-868.

Warner, M. (1993). Introduction. In M. Warner (Ed.), *Fear of a queer planet: Queer politics and social theory* (pp. i-xxviii). Minneapolis, MN: University of Minnesota Press.

Warner, M. (1999). Normal and normaller: Beyond gay marriage. *GLQ: A Journal of Lesbian and Gay Studies, 5,* 119-171.

Warnick, B. (1977). The rhetoric of conservative resistance. *Southern Speech Communication Journal, 42,* 256-273.

Watson, J. (1997). *The Christian Coalition: Dreams of restoration, demands for recognition.* New York: St. Martin's Press.

Weeks, J. (1977). *Coming out: Homosexual politics in Britain, from the nineteenth century to the present.* London: Quartet Books.

Weeks, J. (1980). Capitalism and the organisation of sex. In Gay Left Collective (Eds.), *Homosexuality: Power and politics* (pp. 11-12). London: Allison & Busby.

Weeks, J. (1981). *Sex, politics and society: The regulation of sexuality since 1800.* New York: Longman.

West, D. J., & Green, R. (1997). Conclusion. In D. J. West & R. Green (Eds.), *Sociological control of homosexuality* (pp. 329-336). New York: Plenum Press.

Weston, K. (1991). *Families we choose: Lesbians, gays, and kinship.* New York: Columbia University Press.

Weston, K. (1996). *Render me, gender me: Lesbians talk sex, class, color, nation, studmuffins.* New York: Columbia University Press.

Whisman, V. (1996). *Queer by choice: Lesbians, gay men, and the politics of identity.* New York: Routledge.

White, H. C. (1992). *Identity and control: A structural theory of social action.* Princeton, NJ: Princeton University Press.

White, M. (1994). *Stranger at the gate: To be gay and Christian in America.* New York: Simon & Schuster.

White, M. (1999, June 10). An open letter to Jerry Falwell. *San Francisco Bay Times,* p. 26.

Wills, G. (1990). *Religion and American politics.* New York: Simon & Schuster.

Williams, B. (1995). Identity and identities. In H. Harris (Ed.), *Identity: Essays based on Herbert Spencer lectures given in the University of Oxford* (pp. 1-11). Oxford: Clarendon Press.

Williams, R. H. (1995). Constructing the public good: Social movements and cultural resources. *Social Problems, 42,* 124-144.

Wilson, J. Q. (1996, March). Against homosexual marriage. *Commentary,* 34-39.

Winters, J. (1997). A frank look at the Mattachine: Can homosexuals organize. In M. Blasius & S. Phelan (Eds), *We are everywhere: A historical sourcebook of gay and lesbian politics* (pp. 316-319). New York: Routledge Press. (Original work published 1954)

Witt, S. L., & McCorkle, S. (1997). Introduction. In S. L. Witt & S. McCorkle (Eds.), *Anti-gay rights: Assessing voter initiatives* (pp. 1-6). Westport, CT: Praeger.

Wittig, M. (1992). *The straight mind and other essays.* Boston: Beacon Press.

Wolfe, A. (1992). Democracy versus sociology: Boundaries and their political consequences. In M. Lamont & M. Fournier (Eds.), *Cultivating symbolic boundaries: Differences and the making of inequality* (pp. 309-325). Chicago: University of Chicago Press.

Wuthnow, R. (1994). *Producing the sacred: An essay on public religion.* Chicago: University of Illinois Press.

Yang, A. S. (1997). The polls-trends: Attitudes toward homosexuality. *Public Opinion Quarterly, 61,* 477-507.

Young, A. (1972). Out of the closets, into the streets. In K. Jay & A. Young (Eds.), *Out of the closets: Voices of gay liberation* (pp. 6-31). New York: Douglas.

Young-Bruehl, E. (1996). *The anatomy of prejudice.* Cambridge, MA: Harvard University Press.

Zald, M. N. (1996). Culture, ideology, and strategic framing. In D. McAdam, J. D. McCarthy, & M. N. Mayer (Eds.), *Comparative perspectives on social movements: Political opportunities, mobilizing structures, and cultural framings* (pp. 262-74). New York: Cambridge University Press.

Zald, M. N., & Useem, B. (1987). Movement and countermovement interaction: Mobilization, tactics, and state involvement. In M. N. Zald & J. D. McCarthy (Eds.), *Social movements in an organizational society: Collected essays* (pp. 247-272). New Brunswick, NJ: Transaction Books.

Zepezauer, F. S. (1997). Stopping the gay family: Now or never. In T. L. Roleff (Ed.), *Gay rights* (pp. 35-38). San Diego, CA: Greenhaven Press.

Zizek, S. (1989). *The sublime object of ideology.* London: Verso.

Index

About the Authors

Ralph R. Smith is Professor of Communication and Mass Media at Southwest Missouri State University. He received his doctorate from the University of Southern California and also holds degrees from the University of California, Los Angeles and Columbia University. He teaches courses in social movement communication, public relations, and rhetorical criticism. He has taught at The City University of New York and Dartmouth College. He has coauthored texts in nonverbal communication and in organizational communication. His scholarly works have appeared in the *Quarterly Journal of Speech,* the *Southern Communication Journal,* the *Central States Speech Journal,* and the *Journal of Homosexuality.* He is chair (1999-2000) of the Gay/Lesbian/Bisexual/Transgendered Communication Studies Division of the National Communication Association.

Russel R. Windes is Emeritus Professor of Communications at The City University of New York. He holds his doctorate from Northwestern University. He teaches courses in argumentation, persuasion, political communication, and conflict management. He is the author of books in argumentation, persuasion, and debate, as well as numerous articles in the

Quarterly Journal of Speech, Communication Monographs, the *Western Journal of Communication,* the *Southern Communication Journal,* and the *Journal of Homosexuality.* He has served as Chair of the Publications Board of the National Communication Association. As consulting editor for the Bobbs-Merrill Series, he edited 56 books in the field of communication. As consulting editor for Random House, he edited 14 books. He has also taught at Northwestern University and San Francisco State University. At Northwestern, he was Director of University Debating. His debaters twice won the National Championship.